My window opens up a world
Unknown. A source of ineffable,
Perfumed memories is offered me;
Wings beat at my window—

— C. P. Cavafy, from
    "By the Open Window"

Readings
in
World
Literature

HOLT, RINEHART AND WINSTON

A Harcourt Classroom Education Company

Austin • New York • Orlando • Atlanta • San Francisco
Boston • Dallas • Toronto • London

Requests for permission to make copies of any part of the work should be mailed to the following address: Permissions Department, Holt, Rinehart and Winston, 1120 South Capital of Texas Highway, Austin, Texas 78746-6487.

Acknowledgments appear on pages 290–292, which are an extension of the copyright page.

Cover illustration by Dave Stevenson.

Cover illustration patterns were inspired by the following (from top to bottom): Ancient Greek vase; African kinte cloth; Anglo-Saxon gold buckle; Native American rug; Japanese cloisonné sword case; Moroccan tile.

Printed in the United States of America

ISBN 0-03-056464-6

9 10 043 07 06 05

Contents

The World of Irony

The Power of Love

THE
MYTH MAKERS

Anansi Owns All Tales That Are Told

ASHANTI MYTH

Anansi, the spider, is a famous trickster figure from the mythology of the Ashanti people of Ghana in Africa. Anansi, the subject of many myths, can spin a tale as well as he can spin a web. His central position in Ashanti lore indicates how important storytelling is to the Ashanti culture—as it is to people everywhere. A good storyteller—like Anansi—provides imaginative ways for generations of people to connect with one another and to preserve their history and traditions. Here Anansi proves his worthiness to "own" all tales.

In the beginning, all tales and stories belonged to Nyame, the Sky God. But Kwaku Anansi, the spider, yearned to be the owner of all the stories known in the world, and he went to Nyame and offered to buy them.

The Sky God said: "I am willing to sell the stories, but the price is high. Many people have come to me offering to buy, but the price was too high for them. Rich and powerful families have not been able to pay. Do you think you can do it?"

Anansi replied to the Sky God: "I can do it. What is the price?"

"My price is three things," the Sky God said. "I must first have Mmoboro, the hornets. I must then have Onini, the great python. I must then have Osebo, the leopard. For these things I will sell you the right to tell all stories."

Anansi said, "I will bring them."

He went home and made his plans. He first cut a gourd from a vine and made a small hole in it. He took a large calabash and filled it with water. He went to the tree where the hornets lived. He poured some of the water over himself, so that he was dripping. He threw some water over the hornets, so that they too were dripping. Then he put the calabash on his head, as though to protect himself from a storm, and called out to the hornets: "Are you foolish people? Why do you stay in the rain that is falling?"

The hornets answered, "Where shall we go?"

"Go here, in this dry gourd," Anansi told them.

The hornets thanked him and flew into the gourd through the small hole. When the last of them had entered, Anansi plugged the hole with a ball of grass, saying, "Oh, yes, but you are really foolish people!"

He took his gourd full of hornets to Nyame, the Sky God. The Sky God accepted them. He said, "There are two more things."

Anansi returned to the forest and cut a long bamboo pole and some strong vines. Then he walked toward the house of Onini, the python, talking to himself. He said: "My wife is stupid. I say he is longer and stronger. My wife says he is shorter and weaker. I give him more respect. She gives him less respect. Is she right or am I right? I am right, he is longer. I am right, he is stronger."

When Onini, the python, heard Anansi talking to himself, he said, "Why are you arguing this way with yourself?"

The spider replied: "Ah, I have had a dispute with my wife. She says you are shorter and weaker than this bamboo pole. I say you are longer and stronger."

Onini said: "It's useless and silly to argue when you can find out the truth. Bring the pole and we will measure."

So Anansi laid the pole on the ground, and the python came and stretched himself out beside it.

"You seem a little short," Anansi said.

The python stretched farther.

"A little more," Anansi said.

"I can stretch no more," Onini said.

"When you stretch at one end, you get shorter at the other end," Anansi said. "Let me tie you at the front so you don't slip."

He tied Onini's head to the pole. Then he went to the other end and tied the tail to the pole. He wrapped the vine all around Onini, until the python couldn't move.

"Onini," Anansi said, "it turns out that my wife was right and I was wrong. You are shorter than the pole and weaker. My opinion wasn't as good as my wife's. But you were even more foolish than I, and you are now my prisoner."

Anansi carried the python to Nyame, the Sky God, who said, "There is one thing more."

Osebo, the leopard, was next. Anansi went into the forest and dug a deep pit where the leopard was accustomed to walk. He covered it with small branches and leaves and put dust on it, so that it was impossible to tell where the pit was. Anansi went away and hid. When Osebo came prowling in the black of night, he stepped into the trap Anansi had prepared and fell to the bottom. Anansi heard the sound of the leopard falling, and he said, "Ah, Osebo, you are half-foolish!"

When morning came, Anansi went to the pit and saw the leopard there.

"Osebo," he asked, "what are you doing in this hole?"

"I have fallen into a trap," Osebo said. "Help me out."

"I would gladly help you," Anansi said. "But I'm sure that if I bring you out, I will have no thanks for it. You will get hungry, and later on you will be wanting to eat me and my children."

"I swear it won't happen!" Osebo said.

"Very well. Since you swear it, I will take you out," Anansi said.

He bent a tall green tree toward the ground, so that its top was over the pit, and he tied it that way. Then he tied a rope to the top of the tree and dropped the other end of it into the pit.

"Tie this to your tail," he said.

Osebo tied the rope to his tail.

"Is it well tied?" Anansi asked.

"Yes, it is well tied," the leopard said.

"In that case," Anansi said, "you are not merely half-foolish, you are all-foolish."

And he took his knife and cut the other rope, the one that held the tree bowed to the ground. The tree straightened up with a snap, pulling Osebo out of the hole. He hung in the air head downward, twisting and turning. And while he hung this way, Anansi killed him with his weapons.

Then he took the body of the leopard and carried it to Nyame, the Sky God, saying: "Here is the third thing. Now I have paid the price."

Nyame said to him: "Kwaku Anansi, great warriors and chiefs have tried, but they have been unable to do it. You have done it. Therefore, I will give you the stories. From this day onward, all stories belong to you. Whenever a man tells a story, he must acknowledge that it is Anansi's tale."

In this way Anansi, the spider, became the owner of all stories that are told. To Anansi all tales belong.

Retold by Harold Courlander

The Great Flood

GREEK MYTH

"The Great Flood" is Olivia Coolidge's retelling of a story from the Metamorphoses, *a compilation of Greek and Roman myths made by the Roman poet Ovid (43 B.C.– A.D. 18). Many societies tell a similar story of immoral humans, angry divinities, and a worldwide flood.*

When evil first came among mankind, people became very wicked. War, robbery, treachery, and murder prevailed throughout the world. Even the worship of the gods, the laws of truth and honor, reverence for parents and brotherly love were neglected.

Finally, Zeus determined to destroy the race of men altogether, and the other gods agreed. All the winds were therefore shut up in a cave except the South Wind, the wet one. He raced over the earth with water streaming from his beard and long, white hair. Clouds gathered around his head, and dew dripped from his wings and the ends of his garments. With him went Iris, the rainbow goddess, while below Poseidon smote the earth with his trident until it shook and gaped open, so that the waters of the sea rushed up over the land.

Fields and farmhouses were buried. Fish swam in the tops of the trees. Sea beasts were quietly feeding where flocks and herds had grazed before. On the surface of the water, boars, stags, lions, and tigers struggled desperately to keep afloat. Wolves swam in the midst of flocks of sheep, but the sheep were not frightened by them, and the wolves never thought of their natural prey. Each fought for his own life and forgot the others. Over them wheeled countless birds, winging far and wide in the hope of finding something to rest upon. Eventually they too fell into the water and were drowned.

All over the water were men in small boats or makeshift rafts. Some even had oars which they tried to use, but the waters were fierce and stormy, and there was nowhere to go. In time all were drowned, until at last there was no one left but an old man and his wife, Deucalion and Pyrrha. These two people had lived in truth and justice, unlike the rest of mankind. They had been warned of the coming of the flood and had built a boat and stocked it. For nine days and nights they floated until Zeus took pity on them and they came to the top of Mount Parnassus, the sacred home of the Muses. There they found land and disembarked to wait while the gods recalled the water they had unloosed.

When the waters fell, Deucalion and Pyrrha looked over the land, despairing. Mud and sea slime covered the earth; all living things had been swept away. Slowly and sadly they made their way down the mountain until they came to a temple where there had been an oracle. Black seaweed dripped from the pillars now, and the mud was over all. Nevertheless the two knelt down and kissed the temple steps while Deucalion prayed to the goddess to tell them what they should do. All men were dead but themselves, and they were old. It was impossible that they should have children to people the earth again. Out of the temple a great voice was heard speaking strange words.

"Depart," it said, "with veiled heads and loosened robes, and throw behind you as you go the bones of your mother."

Pyrrha was in despair when she heard this saying. "The bones of our mother!" she cried. "How can we tell now where they lie? Even if we knew, we could never do such a dreadful thing as to disturb their resting place and scatter them over the earth like an armful of stones."

"Stones!" said Deucalion quickly. "That must be what the goddess means. After all Earth is our mother, and the other thing is too horrible for us to suppose that a goddess would ever command it."

Accordingly both picked up armfuls of stones, and as they went away from the temple with faces veiled, they cast the stones behind them. From each of those Deucalion cast sprang up a man, and from Pyrrha's stones sprang women. Thus the earth was repeopled, and in the course of time it brought forth again animals from itself, and all was as before. Only from that time men have been less sensitive and have found it easier to endure toil, and sorrow, and pain, since now they are descended from stones.

Retold by Olivia Coolidge

The Quest of the Golden Fleece

GREEK MYTH

Jason, a young man, exuberant and daring, sets forth to gain the throne that is his birthright—by bringing back the Golden Fleece of a ram, guarded by a fearful dragon. His travels take him through strange and distant lands, from ancient Greece to the shore of the Black Sea. On this quest he has help from Hera, the queen of the gods and the wife of Zeus, and Aphrodite, the goddess of love.

Unlike many other quests, Jason's story does not end happily. Jason performs heroically on his quest, but he does not, in the end, behave wisely or honorably. In the fifth century B.C., the great Greek dramatist Euripides took the last chapter of the story—Jason's final dealings with Medea—and created one of the world's great tragedies, Medea. *Edith Hamilton quotes Medea's anguished speeches from Euripides' play in the concluding portions of her retelling of Jason's story.*

The first hero in Europe who undertook a great journey was the leader of the Quest of the Golden Fleece. He was supposed to have lived a generation earlier than the most famous Greek traveler, the hero of the *Odyssey*. It was of course a journey by water. Rivers, lakes, and seas were the only highways; there were no roads. All the same, a voyager had to face perils not only on the deep, but on the land as well. Ships did not sail by night, and any place where sailors put in might harbor a monster or a magician who could work more deadly harm than storm and shipwreck. High courage was necessary to travel, especially outside of Greece.

No story proved this fact better than the account of what the heroes suffered who sailed in the ship *Argo* to find the Golden Fleece. It may be doubted, indeed, if there ever was a voyage on which sailors had to face so many and such varied dangers. However, they were all heroes of renown, some of them the greatest in Greece, and they were quite equal to their adventures.

A Rescue by the Golden Ram

The tale of the Golden Fleece begins with a Greek king named Athamas, who got tired of his wife, put her away, and married another, the Princess Ino. Nephele, the first wife, was afraid for her two children, especially the boy, Phrixus. She thought the second wife would try to kill him so that her own son could inherit the kingdom, and she was right. This second wife came from a great family. Her father was Cadmus, the excellent King of Thebes; her mother and her three sisters were women of blameless lives. But she herself, Ino, determined to bring about the little boy's death, and she made an elaborate plan how this was to be done. Somehow she got possession of all the seedcorn and parched it before the men went out for the sowing, so that, of course, there was no harvest at all. When the King sent a man to ask the oracle what he should do in this fearful distress, she persuaded or, more probably, bribed the messenger to say that the oracle had declared the corn would not grow again unless they offered up the young Prince as a sacrifice.

The people, threatened with starvation, forced the King to yield and permit the boy's death. To the later Greeks the idea of such a sacrifice was as horrible as it is to us, and when it played a part in a story, they almost always changed it into something less shocking. As this tale has come down to us, when the boy had been taken to the altar, a wondrous ram, with a fleece of pure gold, snatched him and his sister up and bore them away through the air. Hermes had sent him in answer to their mother's prayer.

While they were crossing the strait which separates Europe and Asia, the girl, whose name was Helle, slipped and fell into the water. She was drowned, and the strait was named for her: the Sea of Helle, the Hellespont. The boy came safely to land, to the country of Colchis on the Unfriendly Sea (the Black Sea, which had not yet become friendly). The Colchians were a fierce people. Nevertheless, they were kind to Phrixus, and their King, Æetes, let him marry one of his daughters. It seems odd that Phrixus sacrificed to Zeus the ram that had saved him, in gratitude for having been saved; but he did so, and he gave the precious Golden Fleece to King Æetes.

The Man with One Sandal

Phrixus had an uncle who was by rights a king in Greece but had had his kingdom taken away from him by his nephew, a man named Pelias. The King's young son, Jason, the rightful heir to the kingdom, had been sent secretly away to a place of safety, and when he was grown, he came boldly back to claim the kingdom from his wicked cousin.

The usurper Pelias had been told by an oracle that he would die at the hands of kinsmen and that he should beware of anyone whom he saw shod with only a single sandal. In due time such a man came to the town. One foot was bare, although in all other ways he was well-clad—a garment fitting close to his splendid limbs, and around his shoulders a leopard's skin to turn the showers. He had not shorn the bright locks of his hair; they ran rippling down his back. He went straight into the town and entered the marketplace fearlessly, at the time when the multitude filled it.

None knew him, but one and another wondered at him and said, "Can he be Apollo? Or Aphrodite's lord? Not one of Poseidon's bold sons, for they are dead." So they questioned each other. But Pelias came in hot haste at the tidings, and when he saw the single sandal, he was afraid. He hid his terror in his heart, however, and addressed the stranger: "What country is your fatherland? No hateful and defiling lies, I beg you. Tell me the truth." With gentle words the other answered: "I have come to my home to recover the ancient honor of my house, this land no longer ruled aright, which Zeus gave to my father. I am your cousin, and they call me by the name of Jason. You and I must rule ourselves by the law of right—not appeal to brazen swords or spears. Keep all the wealth you have taken, the flocks and the tawny herds of cattle and the fields, but the sovereign scepter and the throne release to me, so that no evil quarrel will arise from them."

Pelias gave him a soft answer. "So shall it be. But one thing must first be done. The dead Phrixus bids us bring back the Golden Fleece and thus bring back his spirit to his home. The oracle has spoken. But for me, already old age is my companion, while the flower of your youth is only now coming into full bloom. Do you go upon this quest, and I swear with Zeus as witness that I will give up the kingdom and the sovereign rule to you." So he spoke, believing in his heart that no one could make the attempt and come back alive.

The Adventure Begins

The idea of the great adventure was delightful to Jason. He agreed and let it be known everywhere that this would be a voyage indeed. The young men of Greece joyfully met the challenge. They came, all the best and noblest, to join the company. Hercules, the greatest of all heroes, was there; Orpheus, the master musician; Castor with his brother, Pollux; Achilles' father, Peleus; and many another. Hera was helping Jason, and it was she who kindled in each one the desire not to be left behind nursing a life without peril by his mother's side, but even at the price of death to drink with his comrades the peerless elixir of valor. They set sail in the ship *Argo*. Jason took in his hands a golden goblet and, pouring a libation of wine into the sea, called upon Zeus whose lance is the lightning to speed them on their way.

Great perils lay before them, and some of them paid with their lives for drinking that peerless elixir. They put in first at

Lemnos, a strange island where only women lived. The women had risen up against the men and had killed them all, except one, the old king. His daughter, Hypsipyle, a leader among the women, had spared her father and set him afloat on the sea in a hollow chest, which finally carried him to safety. These fierce creatures, however, welcomed the Argonauts and helped them with good gifts of food and wine and garments before they sailed away.

Soon after they left Lemnos, the Argonauts lost Hercules from the company. A lad named Hylas, his armor-bearer, very dear to him, was drawn under the water as he dipped his pitcher in a spring by a water nymph who saw the rosy flush of his beauty and wished to kiss him. She threw her arms around his neck and drew him down into the depths, and he was seen no more. Hercules sought him madly everywhere, shouting his name and plunging deeper and deeper into the forest away from the sea. He had forgotten the Fleece and the *Argo* and his comrades: everything except Hylas. He did not come back, and finally the ship had to sail without him.

The Foul Harpies

Their next adventure was with the Harpies, frightful flying creatures with hooked beaks and claws who always left behind them a loathsome stench, sickening to all living creatures. Where the Argonauts had beached their boat for the night lived a lonely and wretched old man, to whom Apollo, the truth-teller, had given the gift of prophecy. He foretold unerringly what would happen, and this had displeased Zeus, who always liked to wrap in mystery what he would do—and very sensibly, too, in the opinion of all who knew Hera. So he inflicted a terrible punishment upon the old man. Whenever he was about to dine, the Harpies, who were called "the hounds of Zeus," swooped down and defiled the food, leaving it so foul that no one could bear to be near it, much less eat it. When the Argonauts saw the poor old creature—his name was Phineus—he was like a lifeless dream, creeping on withered feet, trembling for weakness, and only the skin on his body held his bones together. He welcomed them gladly and begged them to help him. He knew through his gift of prophecy that he could be defended from the Harpies by two men alone, who were among the company on the *Argo*—the sons of Boreas, the great North Wind. All listened to him with pity, and the two gave him eagerly their promise to help.

While the others set forth food for him, Boreas' sons took their stand beside him with drawn swords. He had hardly put a morsel to his lips when the hateful monsters darted down from the sky and in a moment had devoured everything and were flying off, leaving the intolerable odor behind them. But the wind-swift sons of the North Wind followed them; they caught up with them and struck at them with their swords. They would assuredly have cut them to pieces if Iris, the rainbow messenger of the gods, gliding down from heaven, had not checked them. They must forbear to kill the hounds of Zeus, she said, but she swore by the waters of the Styx, the oath that none can break, that they would never again trouble Phineus. So the two returned gladly and comforted the old man, who in his joy sat feasting with the heroes all through the night.

The Clashing Rocks

He gave them wise advice, too, about the dangers before them, in especial about the Clashing Rocks, the Symplegades, that rolled perpetually against one another while the sea boiled up around them. The way to pass between them, he said, was first to make trial with a dove. If she passed through safely, then the chances were that they too would get through. But if the dove were crushed, they must turn back and give up all hope of the Golden Fleece.

The next morning they started, with a dove, of course, and were soon in sight of the great rolling rocks. It seemed impossible that there could be a way between them, but they freed the dove and watched her. She flew through and came out safe.

Only the tips of her tail-feathers were caught between the rocks as they rolled back together, and those were torn away. The heroes went after her as swiftly as they could. The rocks parted, the rowers put forth all their strength, and they too came through safely. Just in time, however, for as the rocks clashed together again, the extreme end of the stern ornament was shorn off. By so little they escaped destruction. But ever since they passed them, the rocks have been rooted fast to each other and have never any more brought disaster to sailors.

The Amazons

Not far from there was the country of the warrior women, the Amazons—the daughters, strangely enough, of that most peace-loving nymph, sweet Harmony. But their father was Ares, the terrible god of war, whose ways they followed and not their mother's. The heroes would gladly have halted and closed in battle with them, and it would not have been a battle without bloodshed, for the Amazons were not gentle foes. But the wind was favorable and they hurried on. They caught a glimpse of the Caucasus as they sped past and of Prometheus on his rock high above them, and they heard the fanning of the eagle's huge wings as it darted down to its bloody feast. They stopped for nothing, and that same day at sunset they reached Colchis, the country of the Golden Fleece.

The Heroes Arrive at Colchis

They spent the night facing they knew not what and feeling that there was no help for them anywhere except in their own valor. Up in Olympus, however, a consultation was being held about them. Hera, troubled at the danger they were in, went to ask Aphrodite's help. The Goddess of Love was surprised at the visit, for Hera was no friend of hers. Still, when the great Queen of Olympus begged for her aid, she was awed and promised to do all she could. Together they planned that Aphrodite's son Cupid should make the daughter of the

Colchian King fall in love with Jason. That was an excellent plan—for Jason. The maiden, who was named Medea, knew how to work very powerful magic and could undoubtedly save the Argonauts if she would use her dark knowledge for them. So Aphrodite went to Cupid and told him she would give him a lovely plaything, a ball of shining gold and deep blue enamel, if he would do what she wanted. He was delighted, seized his bow and quiver, and swept down from Olympus through the vast expanse of air to Colchis.

Meantime the heroes had started for the city to ask the King for the Golden Fleece. They were safe from any trouble on the way, for Hera wrapped them in a thick mist, so that they reached the palace unseen. It dissolved when they approached the entrance, and the warders, quick to notice the band of splendid young strangers, led them courteously within and sent word to the King of their arrival.

Medea Pierced with Love

He came at once and bade them welcome. His servants hastened to make all ready, build fires and heat water for the baths and prepare food. Into this busy scene stole the Princess Medea, curious to see the visitors. As her eyes fell upon Jason, Cupid swiftly drew his bow and shot a shaft deep into the maiden's heart. It burned there like a flame, and her soul melted with sweet pain, and her face went now white, now red. Amazed and abashed, she stole back to her chamber.

Only after the heroes had bathed and refreshed themselves with meat and drink could King Æetes ask them who they were and why they had come. It was accounted great discourtesy to put any question to a guest before his wants had been satisfied. Jason answered that they were all men of noblest birth, sons or grandsons of the gods, who had sailed from Greece in the hope that he would give them the Golden Fleece in return for whatever service he would ask of them. They would conquer his enemies for him or do anything he wished.

A great anger filled King Æetes' heart as he listened. He did not like foreigners any more than the Greeks did; he wanted them to keep away from his country, and he said to himself, "If these strangers had not eaten at my table, I would kill them." In silence he pondered what he should do, and a plan came to him.

The Test of the Dragon's Teeth

He told Jason that he bore no grudge against brave men and that if they proved themselves such, he would give the Fleece to them. "And the trial of your courage," he said, "shall be only what I myself have done." This was to yoke two bulls he had, whose feet were of bronze and whose breath was flaming fire, and with them to plow a field. Then the teeth of a dragon must be cast into the furrows, like seed-corn—which would spring up at once into a crop of armed men. These must be cut down as they advanced to the attack—a fearful harvesting. "I have done all this myself," he said; "and I will give the Fleece to no man less brave than I." For a time Jason sat speechless. The contest seemed impossible, beyond the strength of anyone. Finally he answered, "I will make the trial, monstrous though it is, even if it is my doom to die." With that he rose up and led his comrades back to the ship for the night, but Medea's thoughts followed after him. All through the long night, when he had left the palace, she seemed to see him, his beauty and his grace, and to hear the words he had uttered. Her heart was tormented with fear for him. She guessed what her father was planning.

Returned to the ship, the heroes held a council, and one and another urged Jason to let him take the trial upon himself, but in vain; Jason would yield to none of them. As they talked, there came to them one of the King's grandsons, whose life Jason once had saved, and he told them of Medea's magic power. There was nothing she could not do, he said, check the stars, even, and the moon. If she were persuaded to help, she could make Jason able to conquer the bulls and the dragon-teeth men.

It seemed the only plan that offered any hope, and they urged the prince to go back and try to win Medea over, not knowing that the God of Love had already done that.

Medea's Magic

She sat alone in her room, weeping and telling herself she was shamed forever because she cared so much for a stranger that she wanted to yield to a mad passion and go against her father. "Far better die," she said. She took in her hand a casket which held herbs for killing, but as she sat there with it, she thought of life and the delightful things that are in the world, and the sun seemed sweeter than ever before. She put the casket away, and, no longer wavering, she determined to use her power for the man she loved. She had a magic ointment which would make him who rubbed it on his body safe for that day; he could not be harmed by anything. The plant it was made from sprang up first when Prometheus' blood dripped down upon the earth. She put it in her bosom and went to find her nephew, the prince whom Jason had helped. She met him as he was looking for her to beg her to do just what she had already decided on. She agreed at once to all he said and sent him to the ship to tell Jason to meet her without delay in a certain place. As soon as he heard the message, Jason started, and as he went, Hera shed radiant grace upon him, so that all who saw him marveled at him. When he reached Medea, it seemed to her as if her heart left her to go to him; a dark mist clouded her eyes and she had no strength to move. The two stood face to face without a word, as lofty pine trees when the wind is still. Then again, when the wind stirs, they murmur; so these two also, stirred by the breath of love, were fated to tell out all their tale to each other.

He spoke first and implored her to be kind to him. He could not but have hope, he said, because her loveliness must surely mean that she excelled in gentle courtesy. She did not know how to speak to him; she wanted to pour out all she felt at once. Silently she drew the box of ointment from her bosom and gave it to him. She would have given her soul to him if he had asked her. And now both were fixing their eyes on the ground, abashed, and again were throwing glances at each other, smiling with love's desire.

At last Medea spoke and told him how to use the charm and that, when it was sprinkled on his weapons, it would make them as well as himself invincible for a day. If too many of the dragon-teeth men rushed to attack him, he must throw a stone into their midst, which would make them turn against each other and fight until all were killed. "I must go back to the palace now," she said. "But when you are once more safe at home, remember Medea, as I will remember you forever." He answered passionately, "Never by night and never by day will I forget you. If you will come to Greece, you shall be worshiped for what you have done for us, and nothing except death will come between us."

They parted, she to the palace to weep over her treachery to her father, he to the ship to send two of his comrades for the dragon's teeth. Meantime he made trial of the ointment, and at the touch of it a terrible, irresistible power entered into him, and the heroes all exulted. Yet, even so, when they reached the field where the King and the Colchians were waiting, and the bulls rushed out from their lair breathing forth flames of fire, terror overcame them. But Jason withstood the fearful creatures as a great rock in the sea withstands the waves. He forced first one and then the other down on its knees and fastened the yoke upon them, while all wondered at his mighty prowess. Over the field he drove them, pressing the plow down firmly and casting the dragon's teeth into the furrows. By the time the plowing was done, the crop was springing up, men bristling with arms who came rushing to attack him. Jason remembered Medea's words and flung a huge stone into their midst. With that, the warriors turned upon each other and fell beneath their own spears while the furrows ran with blood. So Jason's contest was ended in victory, bitter to King Æetes.

The King went back to the palace planning treachery against the heroes and vowing they should never have the Golden

Fleece. But Hera was working for them. She made Medea, all bewildered with love and misery, determine to fly with Jason. That night she stole out of the house and sped along the dark path to the ship, where they were rejoicing in their good fortune with no thought of evil. She fell on her knees before them and begged them to take her with them. They must get the Fleece at once, she told them, and then make all haste away or they would be killed. A terrible serpent guarded the Fleece, but she would lull it to sleep so that it would do them no harm. She spoke in anguish, but Jason rejoiced and raised her gently and embraced her and promised her she would be his own wedded wife when once they were back in Greece. Then, taking her on board, they went where she directed and reached the sacred grove where the Fleece hung. The guardian serpent was very terrible, but Medea approached it fearlessly, and, singing a sweet magical song, she charmed it to sleep. Swiftly Jason lifted the golden wonder from the tree it hung on, and, hurrying back, they reached the ship as dawn was breaking. The strongest were put at the oars and they rowed with all their might down the river to the sea.

The Murder of a Brother

By now what had happened was known to the King, and he sent his son in pursuit—Medea's brother, Apsyrtus. He led an army so great that it seemed impossible for the little band of heroes either to conquer it or to escape, but Medea saved them again, this time by a horrible deed. She killed her brother. Some say she sent him word that she was longing to go back to her home and that she had the Fleece for him if he would meet her that night at a certain spot. He came all unsuspecting and Jason struck him down, and his dark blood dyed his sister's silvery robe as she shrank away. With its leader dead, the army scattered in disorder, and the way to the sea lay open to the heroes.

Others say that Apsyrtus set sail on the *Argo* with Medea, although why he did so is not explained, and that it was the

King who pursued them. As his ship gained on them, Medea herself struck her brother down and, cutting him limb from limb, cast the pieces into the sea. The King stopped to gather them, and the *Argo* was saved.

By then the adventures of the Argonauts were almost over. One terrible trial they had while passing between the smooth, sheer rock of Scylla and the whirlpool of Charybdis, where the sea forever spouted and roared and the furious waves mounting up touched the very sky. But Hera had seen to it that sea nymphs should be at hand to guide them and send the ship on to safety.

Next came Crete—where they would have landed but for Medea. She told them that Talus lived there, the last man left of the ancient bronze race, a creature made all of bronze except one ankle where alone he was vulnerable. Even as she spoke, he appeared, terrible to behold, and threatened to crush the ship with rocks if they drew nearer. They rested on their oars, and Medea, kneeling, prayed to the hounds of Hades to come and destroy him. The dread powers of evil heard her. As the bronze man lifted a pointed crag to hurl it at the *Argo*, he grazed his ankle and the blood gushed forth until he sank and died. Then the heroes could land and refresh themselves for the voyage still before them.

The Murder of a Father

Upon reaching Greece they disbanded, each hero going to his home, and Jason with Medea took the Golden Fleece to Pelias. But they found that terrible deeds had been done there. Pelias had forced Jason's father to kill himself, and his mother had died of grief. Jason, bent upon punishing this wickedness, turned to Medea for the help which had never failed him. She brought about the death of Pelias by a cunning trick. To his daughters she said that she knew a secret, how to make the old young again; and to prove her words, she cut up before them a ram worn out with many years and put the pieces into a pot of boiling water. Then she uttered a charm, and in a moment out from the water sprang a lamb, which ran frisking away. The maidens were convinced. Medea gave Pelias a potent sleeping-draught and called upon his daughters to cut him into bits. With all their longing to make him young again, they could hardly force themselves to do so, but at last the dreadful task was done, the pieces in the water, and they looked to Medea to speak the magic words that would bring him back to them and to his youth. But she was gone—gone from the palace and from the city, and, horrified, they realized that they were their father's murderers. Jason was revenged, indeed.

Betrayed

There is a story, too, that Medea restored Jason's father to life and made him young again and that she gave to Jason the secret of perpetual youth. All that she did of evil and of good was done for him alone, and in the end, all the reward she got was that he turned traitor to her.

They came to Corinth after Pelias' death. Two sons were born to them, and all seemed well, even to Medea in her exile, lonely as exile must always be. But her great love for Jason made the loss of her family and her country seem to her a little thing. And then Jason showed the meanness that was in him, brilliant hero though he had seemed to be: he engaged himself to marry the daughter of the King of Corinth. It was a splendid marriage, and he thought of ambition only, never of love or of gratitude. In the first amazement of his treachery and in the passion of her anguish, Medea let fall words which made the King of Corinth fear she would do harm to his daughter—he must have been a singularly unsuspicious man not to have thought of that before—and he sent her word that she and her sons must leave the country at once. That was a doom almost as bad as death. A woman in exile with little helpless children had no protection for herself or them.

As she sat brooding over what she should do and thinking of her wrongs and her wretchedness—wishing for death to end the life she could no longer bear; sometimes remembering with tears her father and her home; sometimes shuddering at the stain nothing could wash out of her brother's blood, of Pelias', too; conscious above all of the wild, passionate devotion that had brought her to this evil and this misery—as she sat thus, Jason appeared before her. She looked at him; she did not speak. He was there beside her, yet she was far away from him, alone with her outraged love and her ruined life. His feelings had nothing in them to make him silent. He told her coldly that he had always known how uncontrolled her spirit was. If it had not been for her foolish, mischievous talk about his bride, she might have stayed on comfortably in Corinth. However, he had done his best for her. It was entirely through his efforts that she was only to be exiled, not killed. He had had a very hard time indeed to persuade the King, but he had spared no pains. He had come to her now because he was not a man to fail a friend, and he would see that she had plenty of gold and everything necessary for her journey.

This was too much. The torrent of Medea's wrongs burst forth. "You come to me?" she said—

> To me, of all the race of men?
> Yet it is well you came.
> For I shall ease the burden of my heart
> If I can make your baseness manifest.
> I saved you. Every man in Greece knows that.
> The bulls, the dragon-men, the serpent warder of the Fleece,
> I conquered them. I made you victor.
> I held the light that saved you.
> Father and home—I left them
> For a strange country.
> I overthrew your foes,
> Contrived for Pelias the worst of deaths.
> Now you forsake me.
> Where shall I go? Back to my father's house?
> To Pelias' daughters? I have become for you
> The enemy of all.

Myself, I had no quarrel with them.
Oh, I have had in you
A loyal husband, to be admired of men.
An exile now, O God, O God.
No one to help. I am alone.

His answer was that he had been saved not by her, but by Aphrodite, who had made her fall in love with him, and that she owed him a great deal for bringing her to Greece, a civilized country. Also that he had done very well for her in letting it be known how she had helped the Argonauts, so that people praised her. If only she could have had some common sense, she would have been glad of his marriage, as such a connection would have been profitable for her and the children, too. Her exile was her own fault only.

Medea's Revenge

Whatever else she lacked, Medea had plenty of intelligence. She wasted no more words upon him except to refuse his gold. She would take nothing, no help from him. Jason flung away angrily from her. "Your stubborn pride," he told her—

It drives away all those who would be kind.
But you will grieve the more for it.

From that moment Medea set herself to be revenged, as well she knew how.

By death, oh, by death, shall the conflict of life be decided,
Life's little day ended.

She determined to kill Jason's bride, and then—then? But she would not think of what else she saw before her. "Her death first," she said.

She took from a chest a most lovely robe. This she anointed with deadly drugs, and, placing it in a casket, she sent her sons with it to the new bride. They must ask her, she told them, to show that she accepted the gift by wearing it at once. The

Princess received them graciously and agreed. But no sooner had she put on the robe than a fearful, devouring fire enveloped her. She dropped dead; her very flesh had melted away.

When Medea knew the deed was done, she turned her mind to one still more dreadful. There was no protection for her children, no help for them anywhere. A slave's life might be theirs, nothing more. "I will not let them live for strangers to ill-use," she thought—

> To die by other hands more merciless than mine.
> No, I who gave them life will give them death.
> Oh, now no cowardice, no thought how young they are,
> How dear they are, how when they first were born—
> Not that—I will forget they are my sons
> One moment, one short moment—then forever sorrow.

When Jason came, full of fury for what she had done to his bride and determined to kill her, the two boys were dead, and Medea, on the roof of the house, was stepping into a chariot drawn by dragons. They carried her away through the air out of his sight as he cursed her, never himself, for what had come to pass.

Retold by Edith Hamilton

Baldur

Norse Myth

Norse myths are the myths of the Scandinavian peoples of northern Europe. The universe of Norse mythology has four major parts: Asgard, the high realm in the sky, home of the Æsir, or gods; Midgard, the middle realm on earth, home of human beings; Utgard (or Jötunheim), the outermost realm on the shores of the ocean, where fearsome giants dwell; and Helheim (or Niflheim), the dark underworld, home of the dead.

According to tradition, the Æsir must one day fight the forces of darkness. Until that final battle, however, they go about their work with high spirits, enjoying life in Asgard, keeping the evil giants in their place in Utgard, and protecting and guiding human beings in Midgard. This myth tells how all that changes.

Characters in "Baldur"

Baldur (bôl′dər): a son of Odin; the god of light; the best, wisest, and most loved of all the gods.

Frigga (frig′ə): the goddess of marriage; Odin's wife; the mother of Baldur.

Hermod (hʉr′mäd′): a son of Odin.

Hödur (hō′dər): the blind twin brother of Baldur.

Loki (lō′kē): one of the principal gods, a trickster who causes dissension among the other gods.

Odin (ō′din): the sky god and the chief god of Norse mythology.

Thor (thôr): the god of thunder, who wields the hammer Miölnir.

Valkyrior (val·kir′ē·ôr′): maidens who conduct the souls of those slain in battle to Valhalla, a great hall.

The Dream

Upon a summer's afternoon it happened that Baldur the Bright and Bold, beloved of men and Æsir, found himself alone in his palace of Broadblink. Thor was walking low down among the valleys, his brow heavy with summer heat; Frey and Gerda[1] sported on still waters in their cloud-leaf ship; Odin, for once, slept on the top of Air Throne; a noon-day stillness pervaded the whole earth; and Baldur in Broadblink, the wide-glancing, most sunlit of palaces, dreamed a dream.

Now the dream of Baldur was troubled. He knew not whence nor why; but when he awoke, he found that a most new and weighty care was within him. It was so heavy that Baldur could scarcely carry it, and yet he pressed it closely to his heart and said, "Lie there, and do not fall on any one but me." Then he rose up and walked out from the expanded splendour of his hall that he might seek his own mother, Frigga, and tell her what had happened to him. He found her in her crystal saloon, calm and kind, waiting to listen and ready to sympathise; so he walked up to her, his hands pressed closely on his heart, and lay down at her feet, sighing.

"What is the matter, dear Baldur?" asked Frigga, gently.

"I do not know, mother," answered he. "I do not know what the matter is, but I have a shadow in my heart."

"Take it out, then, my son, and let me look at it," replied Frigga.

"But I fear, mother, that if I do, it will cover the whole earth."

Then Frigga laid her hand upon the heart of her son that she might feel the shadow's shape. Her brow became clouded as she felt it; her parted lips grew pale, and she cried out, "Oh!

---

1. **Frey** (frā): the god of crops and prosperity; **Gerda:** his wife.

Baldur, my beloved son! The shadow is the shadow of death!"

Then said Baldur, "I will die bravely, my mother."

But Frigga answered, "You shall not die at all, for I will not sleep tonight until everything on earth has sworn to me that it will neither kill nor harm you."

So Frigga stood up and called to her everything on earth that had power to hurt or slay. First she called all metals to her; and heavy iron-ore came lumbering up the hill into the crystal hall, brass and gold, copper, silver, lead, and steel, and stood before the Queen, who lifted her right hand high in the air, saying, "Swear to me that you will not injure Baldur." And they all swore and went. Then she called to her all stones; and huge granite came with crumbling sand-stone, and white lime, and the round, smooth stones of the sea-shore, and Frigga raised her arm, saying, "Swear that you will not injure Baldur." And they swore and went. Then Frigga called to her the trees; and wide-spreading oak-trees, with tall ash and sombre firs, came rushing up the hill, with long branches, from which green leaves like flags were waving, and Frigga raised her hand and said, "Swear that you will not hurt Baldur." And they said, "We swear," and went. After this Frigga called to her the diseases, who came blown thitherward by poisonous winds on wings of pain and to the sound of moaning. Frigga said to them, "Swear." And they sighed, "We swear," then flew away. Then Frigga called to her all beasts, birds, and venomous snakes, who came to her and swore and disappeared. After this she stretched out her hand to Baldur, whilst a smile spread over her face, saying, "And now, my son, you cannot die."

But just then Odin came in, and when he had heard from Frigga the whole story, he looked even more mournful than she had done; neither did the cloud pass from his face when he was told of the oaths that had been taken.

"Why do you still look so grave, my lord?" demanded Frigga, at last. "Baldur cannot now die."

But Odin asked very gravely, "Is the shadow gone out of our son's heart, or is it still there?"

"It cannot be there," said Frigga, turning away her head resolutely and folding her hands before her.

But Odin looked at Baldur and saw how it was. The hands pressed to the heavy heart, the beautiful brow grown dim. Then immediately he arose, saddled Sleipnir, his eight-footed steed, mounted him, and, turning to Frigga, said, "I know of a dead Vala, Frigga, who, when she was alive, could tell what was going to happen; her grave lies on the east side of Helheim, and I am going there to awake her and ask whether any terrible grief is really coming upon us."

So saying, Odin shook the bridle in his hand, and the Eight-footed, with a bound, leapt forth, rushed like a whirlwind down the mountain of Asgard, and then dashed into a narrow defile between rocks.

Sleipnir went on through the defile a long way until he came to a place where the earth opened her mouth. There Odin rode in and down a broad, steep, slanting road which led him to the cavern Gnipa, and the mouth of the cavern Gnipa yawned upon Niflheim. Then thought Odin to himself, "My journey is already done." But just as Sleipnir was about to leap through the jaws of the pit, Garm, the voracious dog who was chained to the rock, sprang forward and tried to fasten himself upon Odin. Three times Odin shook him off, and still Garm, as fierce as ever, went on with the fight. At last Sleipnir leapt, and Odin thrust just at the same moment; then horse and rider cleared the entrance and turned eastward toward the dead Vala's grave, dripping blood along the road as they went, while the beaten Garm stood baying in the cavern's mouth.

When Odin came to the grave, he got off his horse and stood with his face northwards, looking through barred enclosures into the city of Helheim itself. The servants of Hela[2] were very busy there making preparations for some new guest—hanging gilded couches with curtains of anguish and splendid misery upon the walls. Then Odin's heart died within him, and he began to repeat mournful runes in a low tone to himself.

---

2. **Hela:** one of Loki's children. Her skin is half like the skin of a living person and half like the skin of a corpse, and she rules over Helheim, a huge abyss in the underworld populated by those dead who were not slain in battle.

The dead Vala turned heavily in her grave at the sound of his voice and, as he went on, sat bolt upright. "What man is this," she asked, "who dares disturb my sleep?"

Then Odin, for the first time in his life, said what was not true; the shadow of Baldur dead fell upon his lips, and he made answer, "My name is Vegtam, the son of Valtam."

"And what do you want from me?" asked the Vala.

"I want to know," replied Odin, "for whom Hela is making ready that gilded couch in Helheim."

"That is for Baldur the Beloved," answered the dead Vala. "Now go away, and let me sleep again, for my eyes are heavy."

But Odin said, "Only one word more. Is Baldur going to Helheim?"

"Yes, I've told you that he is," answered the Vala.

"Will he never come back to Asgard again?"

"If everything on earth should weep for him," answered she, "he will go back; if not, he will remain in Helheim."

Then Odin covered his face with his hands and looked into darkness.

"Do go away," said the Vala. "I'm so sleepy; I cannot keep my eyes open any longer."

But Odin raised his head and said again, "Only tell me this one thing. Just now, as I looked into darkness, it seemed to me as if I saw one on earth who would not weep for Baldur. Who was it?"

At this the Vala grew very angry and said, "How couldst *thou* see in darkness? I know of only one who, by giving away his eye, gained light. No Vegtam art thou, but Odin, chief of men."

At her angry words Odin became angry too and called out as loudly as ever he could, "No Vala art thou, nor wise woman, but rather the mother of three giants."

"Go, go!" answered the Vala, falling back in her grave. "No man shall waken me again until Loki have burst his chains and Ragnarök[3] be come." After this Odin mounted the Eight-footed once more and rode thoughtfully towards home.

---

3. **Ragnarök:** in Norse mythology, the end of the world, caused by a final conflict between the gods and the forces of evil. *Ragnarök* means "the judgment of the gods."

The Peacestead

When Odin came back to Asgard, Hermod took the bridle from his father's hand and told him that the rest of the Æsir were gone to the Peacestead—a broad, green plain which lay just outside the city. Now this was, in fact, the playground of the Æsir, where they practised trials of skill one with another and held tournaments and sham fights. These last were always conducted in the gentlest and most honourable manner, for the strongest law of the Peacestead was that no angry blow should be struck, or spiteful word spoken, upon the sacred field; and for this reason some have thought it might be well if children also had a Peacestead to play in.

Odin was too much tired by his journey from Helheim to go to the Peacestead that afternoon; so he turned away and shut himself up in his palace of Gladsheim. But when he was gone, Loki came into the city by another way and, hearing from Hermod where the Æsir were, set off to join them.

When he got to the Peacestead, Loki found that the Æsir were standing round in a circle shooting at something, and he peeped between the shoulders of two of them to find out what it was. To his surprise he saw Baldur standing in the midst, erect and calm, whilst his friends and brothers were aiming their weapons at him. Some hewed at him with their swords—others threw stones at him—some shot arrows pointed with steel, and Thor continually swung Miölnir at his head. "Well," said Loki to himself, "if this is the sport of Asgard, what must that of Jötunheim be? I wonder what Father Odin and Mother Frigga would say if they were here." But as Loki still looked, he became even more surprised, for the sport went on, and Baldur was not hurt. Arrows aimed at his very heart glanced back again untinged with blood. The stones fell down from his broad, bright brow and left no bruises there. Swords clave but did not wound him; Miölnir struck him, and he was not crushed. At this Loki grew perfectly furious with envy and hatred. "And why is Baldur to be so honoured," said he, "that even steel and stone shall not hurt him?" Then Loki changed himself into a little, dark, bent old woman, with a stick in his hand, and hobbled away from the Peacestead to Frigga's cool saloon. At the door he knocked with his stick.

"Come in!" said the kind voice of Frigga, and Loki lifted the latch.

Now when Frigga saw, from the other end of the hall, a little, bent, crippled old woman come hobbling up her crystal floor, she got up with true queenliness and met her half way, holding out her hand and saying in the kindest manner, "Pray sit down, my poor old friend, for it seems to me that you have come from a great way off."

"That I have, indeed," answered Loki in a tremulous, squeaking voice.

"And did you happen to see anything of the Æsir," asked Frigga, "as you came?"

"Just now I passed by the Peacestead and saw them at play."

"What were they doing?"

"Shooting at Baldur."

Then Frigga bent over her work with a pleased smile on her face. "And nothing hurt him?" she said.

"Nothing," answered Loki, looking keenly at her.

"No, nothing," murmured Frigga, still looking down and speaking half musingly to herself, "for all things have sworn to me that they will not."

"Sworn!" exclaimed Loki, eagerly. "What is that you say? Has everything sworn then?"

"Everything," answered she, "excepting, indeed, the little shrub mistletoe, which grows, you know, on the west side of Valhalla and to which I said nothing, because I thought it was too young to swear."

"Excellent!" thought Loki, and then he got up.

"You're not going yet, are you?" said Frigga, stretching out her hand and looking up at last into the eyes of the old woman.

"I'm quite rested now, thank you," answered Loki in his squeaky voice, and then he hobbled out at the door, which clapped after him and sent a cold gust into the room. Frigga shuddered and thought that a serpent was gliding down the back of her neck.

When Loki had left the presence of Frigga, he changed himself back to his proper shape and went straight to the west side of Valhalla, where the mistletoe grew. Then he opened his knife and cut off a large branch, saying these words: "Too young for Frigga's oaths, but not too weak for Loki's work." After which he set off for the Peacestead once more, the mistletoe in his hand. When he got there, he found that the Æsir were still at their sport, standing round, taking aim, and talking eagerly, and Baldur did not seem tired.

But there was one who stood alone, leaning against a tree, and who took no part in what was going on. This was Hödur, Baldur's blind twin-brother; he stood with his head bent downwards, silent, whilst the others were speaking, doing nothing when they were most eager; and Loki thought that there was a discontented expression on his face, just as if he were saying to himself, "Nobody takes any notice of me." So Loki went up to him and put his hand upon his shoulder.

"And why are you standing here all alone, my brave friend?" said he. "Why don't *you* throw something at Baldur? Hew at him with a sword, or show him some attention of that sort."

"I haven't got a sword," answered Hödur, with an impatient gesture, "and you know as well as I do, Loki, that Father Odin does not approve of my wearing warlike weapons, or joining in sham fights, because I am blind."

"Oh! Is that it?" said Loki. "Well, I only know *I* shouldn't like to be left out of everything. However, I've got a twig of mistletoe here which I'll lend you if you like; a harmless little twig enough, but I shall be happy to guide your arm if you would like to throw it, and Baldur might take it as a compliment from his twin-brother."

"Let me feel it," said Hödur, stretching out his uncertain hands.

"This way, this way, my dear friend," said Loki, giving him the twig. "Now, as hard as ever you can, to do *him honour*, throw!"

Hödur threw—Baldur fell, and the shadow of death covered the whole earth.

Baldur Dead

One after another they turned and left the Peacestead, those friends and brothers of the slain. One after another they turned and went towards the city; crushed hearts, heavy footsteps, no word amongst them, a shadow upon all. The shadow was in Asgard too—had walked through Frigga's hall and seated itself upon the threshold of Gladsheim. Odin had just come out to look at it, and Frigga stood by in mute despair as the Æsir came up.

"Loki did it! Loki did it!" they said at last in confused, hoarse whispers, and they looked from one to another, upon Odin, upon Frigga, upon the shadow which they saw before them and which they felt within. "Loki did it! Loki, Loki!" they went on saying, but it was no use repeating the name of Loki over and over again when there was another name they were too sad to utter which yet filled all their hearts—Baldur. Frigga said it first, and then they all went to look at him lying down so peacefully on the grass—dead, dead.

"Carry him to the funeral pyre!" said Odin, at length, and four of the Æsir stooped down and lifted their dead brother.

With scarcely any sound they carried the body tenderly to the sea-shore and laid it upon the deck of that majestic ship called Ringhorn, which had been *his.* Then they stood round waiting to see who would come to the funeral. Odin came, and on his shoulders sat his two ravens, whose croaking drew clouds down over the Asa's face, for Thought and Memory sang one sad song that day. Frigga came—Frey, Gerda, Freyja, Thor, Hœnir, Bragi, and Iduna. Heimdall came sweeping over the tops of the mountains on Golden Mane, his swift, bright steed. Ægir the Old groaned from under the deep and sent his daughters up to mourn around the dead. Frost-giants and mountain-giants came crowding round the rimy shores of Jötunheim to look across the sea upon the funeral of an Asa. Nanna came, Baldur's fair young wife; but when she saw the dead body of her husband, her own heart broke with grief, and the Æsir laid her beside him on the stately ship. After this Odin stepped forward and placed a ring on the breast of his son, whispering something at the same time in his ear; but when he and the rest of the Æsir tried to push Ringhorn into the sea before setting fire to it, they found that their hearts were so heavy they could lift nothing. So they beckoned to the giantess Hyrrokin to come over from Jötunheim and help them. She, with a single push, set the ship floating, and then, whilst Thor stood up, holding Miölnir high in the air, Odin lighted the funeral pile of Baldur and of Nanna.

So Ringhorn went out floating towards the deep, and the funeral fire burnt on. Its broad, red flame burst forth towards heaven; but when the smoke would have gone upward too, the winds came sobbing and carried it away.

Helheim

When at last the ship Ringhorn had floated out so far to sea that it looked like a dull, red lamp on the horizon, Frigga turned round and said, "Does any one of you, my children, wish to perform a noble action and win my love forever?"

"I do," cried Hermod, before any one else had time to open his lips.

"Go, then, Hermod," answered Frigga, "saddle Sleipnir with all speed, and ride down to Helheim; there seek out Hela, the stern mistress of the dead, and entreat her to send our beloved back to us once more."

Hermod was gone in the twinkling of an eye, not in at the mouth of the earth and through the steep cavern down which Odin went to the dead Vala's grave; he chose another way, though not a better one, for, go to Helheim how you will, the best is but a downward road, and so Hermod found it—downward, slanting, slippery, dark, and very cold. At last he came to the Giallar Bru—that sounding river which flows between the living and the dead and the bridge over which is paved with stones of glittering gold. Hermod was surprised to see gold in such a place; but as he rode over the bridge and looked down carefully at the stones, he saw that they were only tears which had been shed round the beds of the dying—only tears, and yet they made the way seem brighter. But when Hermod reached the other end of the bridge, he found the courageous woman who, for ages and ages, had been sitting there to watch the dead go by, and she stopped him, saying—

"What a noise you make. Who are you? Yesterday five troops of dead men went over the Giallar Bridge and did not shake it so much as you have done. Besides," she added, looking more closely at Hermod, "you are not a dead man at all. Your lips are neither cold nor blue. Why, then, do you ride on the way to Helheim?"

"I seek Baldur," answered Hermod. "Tell me, have you seen him pass?"

"Baldur," she said, "has ridden over the bridge; but there below, towards the north, lies the way to the Abodes of Death."

So Hermod went on the way until he came to the barred gates of Helheim itself. There he alighted, tightened his saddle-girths, remounted, clapped both spurs to his horse, and cleared the gate by one tremendous leap. Then Hermod found himself in a place where no living man had ever been before—the City of the Dead. Perhaps you think there is a great silence there, but you are mistaken. Hermod thought he had never in his life heard so much noise, for the echoes of all words were speaking together—words, some newly uttered and some ages old; but the dead men did not hear who flitted up and down the dark streets, for their ears had been stunned and become cold long since. Hermod rode on through the city until he came to the palace of Hela, which stood in the midst. Precipice was its threshold, the entrance-hall, Wide Storm, and yet Hermod was not too much afraid to seek the innermost rooms; so he went on to the banqueting-hall, where Hela sat at the head of her table and served her newest guests. Baldur, alas!, sat at her right-hand, and on her left his pale, young wife. When Hela saw Hermod coming up the hall, she smiled grimly but beckoned to him at the same time to sit down and told him that he might sup that night with her. It was a strange supper for a living man to sit down to. Hunger was the table; Starvation, Hela's knife; Delay, her man; Slowness, her maid; and Burning

Thirst, her wine. After supper Hela led the way to the sleeping apartments. "You see," she said, turning to Hermod, "I am very anxious about the comfort of my guests. Here are beds of unrest provided for all, hung with curtains of weariness, and look how all the walls are furnished with despair."

So saying, she strode away, leaving Hermod and Baldur together. The whole night they sat on those unquiet couches and talked. Hermod could speak of nothing but the past, and as he looked anxiously round the room, his eyes became dim with tears. But Baldur seemed to see a light far off, and he spoke of what was to come.

The next morning Hermod went to Hela and entreated her to let Baldur return to Asgard. He even offered to take his place in Helheim if she pleased, but Hela only laughed at this and said, "You talk a great deal about Baldur and boast how much every one loves him; I will prove now if what you have told me be true. Let everything on earth, living or dead, weep for Baldur and he shall go home again; but if *one* thing only refuse to weep, then let Helheim hold its own; he shall *not* go."

"Every one will weep willingly," said Hermod as he mounted Sleipnir and rode towards the entrance of the city. Baldur went with him as far as the gate and began to send messages to all his friends in Asgard, but Hermod would not listen to many of them.

"You will so soon come back to us," he said, "there is no use in sending messages."

So Hermod darted homewards, and Baldur watched him through the bars of Helheim's gateway as he flew along.

"Not soon, not soon," said the dead Asa, but still he saw the light far off and thought of what was to come.

Weeping

"Well, Hermod, what did she say?" asked the Æsir from the top of the hill as they saw him coming. "Make haste and tell us what she said." And Hermod came up.

"Oh! Is that all?" they cried as soon as he had delivered his message. "Nothing can be more easy"; and then they all hurried off to tell Frigga. She was weeping already, and in five minutes there was not a tearless eye in Asgard.

"But this is not enough," said Odin. "The whole earth must know of our grief that it may weep with us."

Then the father of the Æsir called to him his messenger maidens—the beautiful Valkyrior—and sent them out into all worlds with these three words on their lips: "Baldur is dead!" But the words were so dreadful that at first the messenger maidens could only whisper them in low tones as they went along: "Baldur is dead!" The dull, sad sounds flowed back on Asgard like a new river of grief, and it seemed to the Æsir as if they now wept for the first time—"Baldur is dead!"

"What is that the Valkyrior are saying?" asked the men and women in all the country round, and when they heard rightly, men left their labour and lay down to weep—women dropped the buckets they were carrying to the well and, leaning their faces over them, filled them with tears. The children crowded upon the doorsteps or sat down at the corners of the streets, crying as if their own mothers were dead.

The Valkyrior passed on. "Baldur is dead!" they said to the empty fields, and straightway the grass and the wild field-flowers shed tears. "Baldur is dead!" said the messenger maidens to the rocks and the stones, and the very stones began to weep. "Baldur is dead!" the Valkyrior cried, and even the old mammoth's bones, which had lain for centuries under the hills, burst into tears, so that small rivers gushed forth from every mountain's side. "Baldur is dead!" said the messenger maidens as they swept over silent sands, and all the shells wept pearls. "Baldur is dead!" they cried to the sea and to Jötunheim across the sea; and when the giants understood it, even they wept, whilst the sea rained spray to heaven. After this the Valkyrior stepped from one stone to another until they reached a rock that stood alone in the middle of the sea; then, all together, they bent forward over the edge of it, stooped down, and peeped over that they might tell the monsters of the deep. "Baldur is dead!" they said, and the sea monsters and the fish wept. Then the messenger maidens looked at one another and said, "Surely our work is done." So they twined their arms round one another's waists and set forth on the downward road to Helheim, there to claim Baldur from among the dead.

Now after he had sent forth his messenger maidens, Odin had seated himself on the top of Air Throne that he might see how the earth received his message. At first he watched the Valkyrior as they stepped forth north and south, and east and west, but soon the whole earth's steaming tears rose up like a great cloud and hid everything from him. Then he looked down through the cloud and said, "Are you all weeping?" Then Valkyrior heard the sound of his voice as they went all together down the slippery road, and they turned round, stretching out their arms towards Air Throne, their long hair falling back, whilst, with choked voices and streaming eyes, they answered, "The world weeps, Father Odin, the world and we."

After this they went on their way until they came to the end of the cave Gnipa, where Garm was chained and which yawned over Niflheim. "The world weeps," they said one to another by way of encouragement, for here the road was so dreadful; but just as they were about to pass through the mouth of Gnipa, they came upon a haggard witch named Thaukt, who sat in the entrance with her back to them and her face towards the abyss. "Baldur is dead! Weep, weep!" said the messenger maidens as they tried to pass her, but Thaukt made answer—

> What she doth hold,
> Let Hela keep;
> For naught care I,
> Though the world weep
> O'er Baldur's bale.
> Live he or die,
> With tearless eye
> Old Thaukt shall wail.

And with these words leaped into Niflheim with a yell of triumph.

"Surely that cry was the cry of Loki," said one of the maidens; but another pointed towards the city of Helheim, and there they saw the stern face of Hela looking over the wall.

"One has not wept," said the grim Queen, "and Helheim holds its own." So saying, she motioned the maidens away with her long, cold hand.

Then the Valkyrior turned and fled up the steep way to the foot of Odin's throne, like a pale snowdrift that flies before the storm.

After this a strong child, called Vali, was born in the city of Asgard. He was the youngest of Odin's sons—strong and cold as the icy January blast but full, also, as it is of the hope of the new year. When only a day old, he slew the blind Hödur by a single blow and then spent the rest of his life in trying to lift the shadow of death from the face of the weeping earth.

Retold by A. and E. Keary

Momotaro: Boy of the Peach

JAPANESE FOLK TALE

For generations, Japanese children have been enter-
tained—and instructed—by the folk tale about the hero
Momotaro. In some versions of the tale, Momotaro starts
out as a miniature baby enclosed in a peach pit; in others,
he is a full-sized toddler with extraordinary powers,
hiding inside a huge peach. In either case, Momotaro is
one of many heroes whose origins are certainly mysterious.

Once long, long ago, there lived a kind old man and a kind old woman in a small village in Japan.

One fine day they set out from their little cottage together. The old man went toward the mountains to cut some firewood for their kitchen, and the old woman went toward the river to do her washing.

When the old woman reached the shore of the river, she knelt down beside her wooden tub and began to scrub her clothes on a round, flat stone. Suddenly she looked up and saw something very strange floating down the shallow river. It was an enormous peach, bigger than the round wooden tub that stood beside the old woman.

Rumbley-bump and a-bumpety-bump . . . Rumbley-bump and a-bumpety-bump. The big peach rolled closer and closer over the stones in the stream.

"My gracious me!" the old woman said to herself. "In all my long life I have never seen a peach of such great size and beauty. What a fine present it would make for the old man. I do think I will take it home with me."

Then the old woman stretched out her hand just as far as she could, but no matter how hard she stretched, she couldn't reach the big peach.

"If I could just find a long stick, I would be able to reach it," thought the old woman, looking around, but all she could see were pebbles and sand.

"Oh, dear, what shall I do?" she said to herself. Then suddenly she thought of a way to bring the beautiful big peach to her side. She began to sing out in a sweet, clear voice:

> *The deep waters are salty!*
> *The shallow waters are sweet!*
> *Stay away from the salty water,*
> *And come where the water is sweet.*

She sang this over and over, clapping her hands in time to her song. Then, strangely enough, the big peach slowly began to bob along toward the shore where the water was shallow.

Rumbley-bump and a-bumpety-bump . . . Rumbley-bump and a-bumpety-bump. The big peach came closer and closer to the old woman and finally came to a stop at her feet.

The old woman was so happy she picked the big peach up very carefully and quickly carried it home in her arms. Then she waited for the old man to return so she could show him her lovely present. Toward evening the old man came home with a big pack of wood on his back.

"Come quickly, come quickly," the old woman called to him from the house.

"What is it? What is the matter?" the old man asked as he hurried to the side of the old woman.

"Just look at the fine present I have for you," said the old woman happily as she showed him the big round peach.

"My goodness! What a great peach! Where in the world did you buy such a peach as this?" the old man asked.

The old woman smiled happily and told him how she had found the peach floating down the river.

"Well, well, this is a fine present indeed," said the old man, "for I have worked hard today and I am very hungry."

Then he got the biggest knife they had so he could cut the big peach in half. Just as he was ready to thrust the sharp blade into the peach, he heard a tiny voice from inside.

"Wait, old man! Don't cut me!" it cried, and before the surprised old man and woman could say a word, the beautiful big peach broke in two, and a sweet little boy jumped out from inside. The old man and woman were so surprised they could only raise their hands and cry out, "Oh, oh! My goodness!"

Now the old man and woman had always wanted a child of their own, so they were very, very happy to find such a fine little boy, and decided to call him "Momotaro," which means boy-of-the-peach. They took very good care of the little boy and grew to love him dearly, for he was a fine young lad. They spent many happy years together, and before long Momotaro was fifteen years old.

One day Momotaro came before the old man and said, "You have both been good and kind to me. I am very grateful for all you have done, and now I think I am old enough to do some good for others too. I have come to ask if I may leave you."

"You wish to leave us, my son? But why?" asked the old man in surprise.

"Oh, I shall be back in a very short time," said Momotaro. "I wish only to go to the Island of the Ogres, to rid the land of those harmful creatures. They have killed many good people, and have stolen and robbed throughout the country. I wish to kill the ogres so they can never harm our people again."

"That is a fine idea, my son, and I will not stop you from going," said the old man.

So that very day Momotaro got ready to start out on his journey. The old woman prepared some millet cakes for him to take along on his trip, and soon Momotaro was ready to leave. The old man and woman were sad to see him go and called, "Be careful, Momotaro! Come back safely to us."

"Yes, yes, I shall be back soon," he answered. "Take care of yourselves while I am away," he added, and waved as he started down the path toward the forest.

He hurried along, for he was anxious to get to the Island of the Ogres. While he was walking through the cool forest where the grass grew long and high, he began to feel hungry. He sat down at the foot of a tall pine tree and carefully unwrapped the *furoshiki* which held his little millet cakes. "My, they smell good," he thought. Suddenly he heard the tall grass rustle and saw something stalking through the grass toward him. Momotaro blinked hard when he saw what it was. It was a dog as big as a calf! But Momotaro was not frightened, for the dog just said, "Momotaro-san, Momotaro-san, what is it you are eating that smells so good?"

"I'm eating a delicious millet cake which my good mother made for me this morning," he answered.

The dog licked his chops and looked at the cake with hungry eyes. "Please, Momotaro-san," he said, "just give me one of your millet cakes, and I will come along with you to the Island of the Ogres. I know why you are going there, and I can be of help to you."

"Very well, my friend," said Momotaro, "I will take you along with me." And he gave the dog one of his millet cakes to eat.

As they walked on, something suddenly leaped from the branches above and jumped in front of Momotaro. He stopped in surprise and found that it was a monkey who had jumped down from the trees.

"Greetings, Momotaro-san!" called the monkey happily. "I have heard that you are going to the Island of the Ogres to rid the land of these plundering creatures. Take me with you, for I wish to help you in your fight."

When the dog heard this, he growled angrily. "Grruff," he said to the monkey. "*I* am going to help Momotaro-san. We do not need the help of a monkey such as you! Out of our way! Grruff, grruff," he barked angrily.

"How dare you speak to me like that?" shrieked the monkey, and he leaped at the dog, scratching with his sharp claws. The dog and the monkey began to fight each other, biting, clawing, and growling. When Momotaro saw this, he pushed them apart and cried, "Here, here, stop it, you two! There is no reason why you both cannot go with me to the Island of the Ogres. I shall have two helpers instead of one!" Then he took another millet cake from his *furoshiki* and gave it to the monkey.

Now there were three of them going down the path to the edge of the woods—the dog in front, Momotaro in the middle, and the monkey walking in the rear. Soon they came to a big field, and just as they were about to cross it, a large pheasant hopped out in front of them. The dog jumped at it with a growl, but the pheasant fought back with such spirit that Momotaro ran over to stop the dog. "We could use a brave bird such as you to help us fight the ogres. We are on our way to their island this very day. How would you like to come along with us?"

"Oh, I would like that indeed, for I would like to help you rid the land of these evil and dangerous ogres," said the pheasant happily.

"Then here is a millet cake for you, too," said Momotaro, giving the pheasant a cake, just as he had the monkey and the dog.

Now there were four of them going to the Island of the Ogres, and as they walked down the path together, they became very good friends.

Before long they came to the water's edge and Momotaro found a boat big enough for all of them. They climbed in and headed for the Island of the Ogres. Soon they saw the island in the distance, wrapped in gray, foggy clouds. Dark stone walls rose up above towering cliffs, and large iron gates stood ready to keep out any who tried to enter.

Momotaro thought for a moment, then turned to the pheasant and said, "You alone can wing your way over their high walls and gates. Fly into their stronghold now, and do what you can to frighten them. We will follow as soon as we can."

So the pheasant flew far above the iron gates and stone walls and down onto the roof of the ogres' castle. Then he called to the ogres, "Momotaro-san has come to rid the land of you and your many evil deeds. Give up your stolen treasures now, and perhaps he will spare your lives!"

When the ogres heard this, they laughed and shouted, "HO,

HO, HO! We are not afraid of a little bird like you! We are not afraid of little Momotaro!"

The pheasant became very angry at this, and flew down, pecking at the heads of the ogres with his sharp, pointed beak. While the pheasant was fighting so bravely, the dog and monkey helped Momotaro to tear down the gates, and they soon came to the aid of the pheasant.

"Get away! Get away!" shouted the ogres, but the monkey clawed and scratched, the big dog growled and bit the ogres, and the pheasant flew about, pecking at their heads and faces. So fierce were they that soon the ogres began to run away. Half of them tumbled over the cliffs as they ran, and the others fell pell-mell into the sea. Soon only the Chief of the Ogres remained. He threw up his hands, and then bowed low to Momotaro. "Please spare me my life, and all our stolen treasures are yours. I promise never to rob or kill anyone again," he said.

Momotaro tied up the evil ogre, while the monkey, the dog, and the pheasant carried many boxes filled with jewels and treasures down to their little boat. Soon it was laden with all the treasures it could hold, and they were ready to sail toward home.

When Momotaro returned, he went from one family to another, returning the many treasures which the ogres had stolen from the people of the land.

"You will never again be troubled by the ogres of Ogre Island!" he said to them happily.

And they all answered, "You are a kind and brave lad, and we thank you for making our land safe once again."

Then Momotaro went back to the home of the old man and woman with his arms full of jewels and treasures from Ogre Island. The old man and woman were so glad to see him once again, and the three of them lived happily together for many, many years.

Retold by Yoshiko Uchida

The Return of Oisin

IRISH LEGEND

In Ireland's pre-Christian era, Celtic tribes shared a rich oral tradition, which included fantastic legends of superhuman men and women. Among the greatest heroes was Finn Mac Cool. He and his son Oisin (ōō·shēn') led the Fianna, a mighty brotherhood whose task was to hold the shores of Erin safe from invaders and to keep down raids and blood feuds among Erin's five kingdoms. The stories of Finn Mac Cool and his heroes are collected in the Fenian cycle of legends. One of these tells how Mac Cool built the Giant's Causeway, a strange rock formation on Ireland's northern coast, for the Fianna's use in traveling between Ireland and Scotland.

"The Return of Oisin" is set around A.D. 400, during a time of extraordinary change, when the Irish tribes were converted to Christianity by Patrick (called "Priest Patrick" in this tale). Though the Irish people were now Christian, they remembered the old "pagan" stories. They believed that their pre-Christian heroes—whom they called the "Fairy Kind"—had gone "underground."

Tyr-na-nOg, the place where Oisin has come from in this story, was, in the old stories, the land of the eternally young. It was believed to lie somewhere in the west.

In the Valley of the Thrushes, not far from where Dublin stands today, a crowd of men were trying to shift a great boulder from their tilled land, the village headman directing their efforts. The stone had been there as long as any of them could remember, or their grandfathers before them, and always they had grumbled at it because it got in the way of the plowing. But though one or two half-hearted attempts had been made to shift it, it still lay half embedded in the hillside, where it always had lain.

Now at last, they were really set upon getting rid of the thing, and every man in the village had gathered to lend his strength to the task.

But it seemed that their strength was all too little, for there they were heaving and straining and grunting and hauling, their faces crimson and the sweat running off them, and the great boulder not moving so much as a finger's breadth out of its bed.

And as they strained and struggled—and they getting nearer each moment to giving up—they saw riding toward them a horseman such as none of them had ever set eyes on before, save maybe in some glorious dream. Taller and mightier than any man of this world he was, and riding a foam-white stallion as far beyond mortal horses as he was beyond mortal men. His eyes were strangely dark, his fair hair like a sunburst about his head. A mantle of saffron silk flowed back from brooches of yellow gold that clasped it at his shoulders, and at his side hung a great golden-hilted sword.

"It is one of the Fairy Kind!" said an aged villager, making the sign of the horns with the two first fingers of his left hand.

"It is an archangel out of Heaven!" said a young one, and made the sign of the Cross.

The splendid being, man or fairy or angel, reined in his horse, and sat looking down at them with a puzzled pity on his face. "You wanted this shifting?" he said.

The headman drew nearer, greatly daring. "We did so, but it seems 'tis beyond our strength. Would you be lending us the power of your arm, now?"

"Surely," said the rider, and stooping from the saddle, set his hand under the boulder and gave a mighty heave. The boulder came out of the ground and went rolling over and over down the hillside like a shiny ball, and the watching villagers gave a great shout of wonder and admiration. But next moment their shouts turned to fearful and wondering dismay.

For as he heaved at the boulder, the rider's saddle girth had burst, so that he fell headlong to the ground. The moment the white stallion felt himself free, he neighed three times and set off at a tearing gallop toward the coast, and as he went, he seemed not merely to grow small with distance, but to lose shape and substance and fade into the summer air like a wisp of woodsmoke.

And there on the ground, where the splendid stranger had fallen, lay an old, old man, huge still, but with thin white beard and milky half-blind eyes, his silken mantle a patched and tattered cloak of coarsest homespun, his golden-hilted sword a rough ash stick such as a blind old beggar might use to support him and feel his way about the world. He half raised himself and peered about, then with a wild despairing cry, stretched all his length again burying his head in his arms.

In a little, seeing that nothing terrible seemed to have happened to any of themselves, some of the bolder of the villagers came closer and lifted him up and asked him who he was.

"I am Oisin the son of Finn Mac Cool," said the old man.

Then the villagers looked at each other, and the headman said, "If you mean who I think you mean, then you're as crazy as we must have been just now to be taking you for whatever it was we took you for."

"It was the sun in our eyes," said another man.

And they asked the old man a second time who he was.

"Why do you ask again, when I have already told you? I am Oisin the son of Finn Mac Cool, Captain of the Fianna of Erin."

"It is the sun on that bald head of yours," said the headman, kindly enough. "Finn Mac Cool and his heroes we have heard of, yes, but they have been dead these three hundred years."

Then the old man was silent a long while, his face bowed into his hands. At last he said, "How did they die?"

"At the Battle of Gavra, not so far from here at all. There is a green mound up there beside the battleground. I was hearing once it was the grave of one of them, called Osca. A great battle it was, and they do say that there were none but boys and old men left in Erin when the fighting was done."

"But Oisin did not die then," another put in. "No man knows the death of Oisin, but the harpers still sing the songs he made."

"But now Priest Patrick has come into Erin, and told us of the one true God, and Christ His Son, and the old days are done with, and we listen to them only as men listen to old tales that are half forgotten."

The old man seemed half-dazed, like one that has taken a blow between the eyes. Only he cried out once, harshly and near to choking, "Strong and without mercy is your new God! And He has much to answer for if He has slain the memory of Finn and Osca!"

Then the people were angry and cried "Sacrilege!" and some of them picked up the small surface stones of the field to throw at the old man. But the headman bade them let him be until Priest Patrick had seen him and told them what they should do.

So they took him to the old fortress of Drum Derg, where Patrick had at that time made his living place.

And Patrick listened to their account of how he had come to them, and how, with the sun in their eyes they had mistaken him for a young man and asked his aid in moving the great stone from their tilled land, and of what had happened after.

And Patrick was kind to the huge half-blind old beggar, and gave him a place for sleeping and a place for sitting by the fire, among his own Christian brotherhood.

And often the priest of the new God, and the old man who had been Oisin would talk together. And Oisin told wonderful stories of Finn and the Fianna and the High and Far-off Days, which Patrick bade one of his scribes to write down on pages of fair white sheepskin, lest they should be forgotten.

As time went by, Patrick came to believe that the old man was indeed Oisin the son of Finn Mac Cool, and one day he said to him, "It is upward of three hundred years since Finn and Osca and the flower of the Fianna died at Gavra. Tell me then, how is it that you have lived so long beyond your day and the days of your companions?"

So Oisin told him this last story: the story of how he had ridden hunting with the Fianna one summer morning among the lakes of Killarney, and how the Princess Niamh of the Golden Hair had come out of the West, and asked him to return to Tyr-na-nOg with her. And how he had taken leave of Finn and Osca and the rest, and mounted behind her on her white horse, and how they had headed westward again until they came to the sea, and headed westward still, leaving the companions of the Fianna behind them on the shore.

And when he reached that point in his story, Oisin buried his face in his hands and seemed to forget.

Then, to rouse him, and because he was a man of curiosity and interest in all things, Patrick said, "Success and benediction! Tell me what happened after that."

And Oisin raised his head again, and staring with half-blind eyes into the heart of the fire, as though he saw there all things happening again, he went on with his story.

"The white horse galloped across the waves as lightly as he had done across the green hills of Erin, and the wind overtook the waves, and we overtook the wind, and presently we passed into a golden haze through which there loomed half-seen islands with cities on their heights and palaces among leafy gardens. Once a fallow doe fled past us, chased by a milk-white hound with one blood-red ear; and once a maiden fled by on a bay horse, and she carrying a golden apple in her hand, and close behind her in hot pursuit, a young man on a white steed, a purple and crimson cloak flying from his shoulders, and a great sword naked in his hand.

"But the sky began to darken overhead, and the wind rose and began to blow in great gusts that roused the waves to fury and sent the spindrift flying like white birds over our heads, and the lightning leapt between the dark sky and darker sea, while the thunder boomed and crashed all about us. Yet still the white horse sped on, unafraid, as lightly and sweetly as over the summer seas that we had traversed before. And presently the wind died and the darkness rolled away and sunshine touched the racing seas with gold. And ahead of us, under the spreading lake of blue sky, lay the fairest land that ever I had seen. Green plains and distant hills were all bathed in a honey-wash of sunlight that flashed and sparkled from the lakes and streams that met every turn of the eye, and changed to gold the white walls of the beautiful palace which stood close beside the shore. Flowers were everywhere, and butterflies like dancing flames upon the air, and as soon as I saw it, I knew that this could be no place but Tyr-na-nOg, the Land of Youth.

"The white horse skimmed the waves toward the shore, and on the white sand we dismounted, and Niamh turned to me, most sweetly holding out her hands, and said, 'This is my own land. Everything I promised, you shall find here, and above all and before all, the love of Niamh of the Golden Hair.'

"Then there came toward us from the palace a troop of warriors, heroes and champions all, holding their shields reversed in token to me that they came in peace. And after them a gay and beautiful company led by the King of the land himself, in a robe of yellow silk, a golden crown blazing like the midsummer sun upon his head. And behind him came the Queen, most fair to see, and with a hundred maidens clustered all about her.

"They kissed their daughter joyfully and tenderly, and the King took my hand in his saying, 'A hundred thousand welcomes, brave Oisin.' Then turning with me to face all the host, he said, 'This is Oisin, from the far-off land of Erin, he who is to be the husband of Niamh of the Golden Hair. Bid him welcome, as I do.'

"Then all the host, nobles and warriors and maidens alike bade me welcome. And all together, Niamh and myself walking hand in hand in their midst, we went up to the palace, where a great feast was prepared.

"For ten days and nights we feasted, while the harpers made music sweeter than any heard in the world of men. I, Oisin, say that, I who was a harper among harpers of the world of men, in my time—and little birds as brightly colored as flowers flew and fluttered about the banquet house. And on the tenth day, Niamh and I were wed.

"I lived in the Land of Youth three years—I thought it was

three years—and I was happy as never man was happy before. But as the third year drew to a close, I began to think more and more of my father and my son, and of all the companions of my youth. Sometimes as we rode hunting, I would fancy that I heard the Fian hunting horn echoing through the woods, and think I recognised the deep baying of Bran and Skolawn among the belling of the milk-white Danann hounds. I began to fall into waking dreams, thinking how they would be hunting the woods of Slieve Bloom, or how the heroes would be telling old stories about the fire, in Almu of the White Walls, until it came to this—that Niamh asked me if I no longer loved her. I told her that she was the very life of my heart, and that I was happy as ever I had been in the Land of Youth, but the restlessness was on me, and I longed to see my father and my friends once more.

"Then Niamh kissed me and clung to me, and tried to turn my thoughts elsewhere. But still I half-heard the Fian hunting horn echoing through my dreams at night, and at last I begged leave of her and of the King her father, to visit my own land once more.

"The King gave me leave, though unwillingly, and Niamh said, 'It's not that I can be holding you while your heart draws you back to Erin, so I give you my leave also, though there's a shadow on my mind, and I fear that I shall never see you again.'

"I said, 'That is a foolish fear, for there's nothing that could keep me long from you. Only give me the white steed, for he knows the way and will bring me back safely to your side.'

"Then she said, 'I will give you the white steed, for indeed he knows the way. But listen now, and keep my words in your mind. Never once dismount from his back all the while you are in the world of men, for if you do, you can never come back to me. If once your feet touch the green grass of Erin, the way back to Tyr-na-nOg will be closed to you forever.'

"I promised that I would never dismount from the white steed, but remember always her words. And seeing her grief, which even my most faithful promise seemed not to touch, I was within a feather-weight of yielding to her and remaining always in Tyr-na-nOg; but the white horse stood ready, and the hunger was still on me, to see my father and my own land.

"So I mounted, and the horse set off at a gallop toward the shore. So again we sped across the sea, and the wind overtook the waves and we overtook the wind, and the shores of the Land of Youth sank into the golden mist behind us.

"Again it drifted all about us, that golden mist, and in the mist the towers and cities of the sea arose once more. And again the maiden with the golden apple in her hand fled past us on her bay horse, and the young horseman riding hard behind, his purple cloak streaming from his shoulders and his sword naked in his hand. And again the fallow doe fled by, hunted by the milk-white hound with one ear red as blood.

"So we came at last to the green shores of Erin.

"Gladly, once we were on land, I turned the horse's head toward Almu of the White Walls and rode on. And as I rode, I looked about me, seeking for familiar scenes and faces, and listening always for the sound of the Fian hunting horn. But all things seemed strangely altered, and nowhere did I hear or see any sign of my companions, and the folk who were tilling the ground were small and puny, so that they did not seem any more like countrymen of mine.

"I came at last through the woods to the open country around the Hill of Almu, and the hill was still there but overgrown with bushes and brambles, and on its broad flat crest, where the white walls of my father's dun had used to rise with its byres and barns and armorers' shops, the women's court and the guest quarters, and Finn's mighty mead-hall rising in the midst of all, were nothing but grassy hummocks grown over with elder and blackthorn and the arched sprays of the brambles, and the heather washing over all.

"Then horror fell upon me—though indeed I believed then that the dun was still there, but hidden from me by some enchantment of the Danann folk. And I flung wide my arms and shouted the names of Finn my father and Osca, and after them, the names of all the old brotherhood, Keelta, and Conan and Dering and the rest. Even Dearmid's name I shouted in that dreadful time. But no one answered, nothing moved save a thrush fluttering among the elder bushes. Then I thought that perhaps the hounds might hear me when men could not, and I shouted to Bran and Skolawn and strained my ears for an answering bark. But no sound came, save the hushing of a little wind through the hilltop grasses.

"So with the horror thick upon me, I wheeled the white horse and rode away from Almu, to search all Erin until I found my friends again, or some way out of the enchantment that held me captive. But everywhere I rode, I met only little puny people who gazed at me in wonder out of the faces of strangers, and in every household of the Fianna the brambles grew and the birds were at their nesting. So at last I came to the Glen of the Thrushes, where often I had hunted with Finn, and saw before me tilled land where I remembered only forest.

"And at the head of the tilled land a knot of these small and puny strangers were striving to shift a great stone that was in the way of the plowing. I rode closer, and they asked me for my help. And that was an easy thing to give, so I stooped in the saddle and set my hand under the stone and sent it rolling down the hillside. But with the strain of the heave my saddle girth broke, and I was flung to the ground, and my feet were on the green grass of Erin.

"Priest Patrick, the rest of my story they have told you!"

Retold by Rosemary Sutcliff

THE MAKING
OF
HEROES

Homer
(eighth century B.C.)

Little is known about Homer, the poet who wrote the *Iliad* and the *Odyssey*. In fact, no one knows for sure exactly who Homer was. The later Greeks believed he was a blind minstrel who came from the island of Chios. Some scholars think there must have been a different poet for each epic; some even think Homer was just a legend. On the whole, it seems most sensible to take the word of the Greeks themselves and to accept the existence of Homer, at least as an ideal model for a class of wandering bards or minstrels later called *rhapsodes* ("stitchers of songs"). These rhapsodes traveled about from community to community, singing of recent legendary events or of the doings of heroes, gods, and goddesses. They were the historians and entertainers, as well as the myth makers, of their time.

The Death of Hector
Book 22 of the Iliad

Homer

Long ago, Helen, the beautiful wife of Menelaus, king of
Sparta in Greece, ran away with Paris, a handsome young
prince of Troy (also known as Ilium), a city in Asia Minor
(modern-day Turkey). Outraged, Menelaus gathered
warriors from all over Greece and sailed to Troy, under the
command of his brother, Agamemnon, king of Mycenae,
to fetch his wife home and avenge the insult. The ten-year
conflict that resulted from this abduction of Helen is known
as the Trojan War. Most scholars believe that this legend
is based on a real war that occurred in the thirteenth
century B.C.

The events of the Iliad take place over several weeks
during the tenth year of the war. The story revolves
around two main characters: Achilles, the bravest and
most powerful warrior in the Greek army, and his enemy,
Hector, a prince of Troy and the most honorable warrior
of the Trojans.

Achilles has been angrily sitting out the war and sulking
in his tent because Agamemnon has stolen his captive, a
young woman from a town near Troy. But after his best
friend, Patroclus, who is wearing Achilles' armor, is killed
in combat by Hector, Achilles vows revenge. He returns
to the bloody field of battle and drives the Trojans to the
walls of their city. He is about to enter Troy when the god
Apollo, who favors the Trojans, intervenes. Disguising
himself as a Trojan, he lures Achilles into chasing him.

As Book 22 opens, the frightened Trojan warriors, taking advantage of Achilles' absence from the field, have taken refuge behind the high walls. One Trojan remains outside the city: Hector.

Characters in "The Death of Hector"

Greeks (also called Achaeans and Argives)

Achilles (ə·kil'ēz'): the son of King Peleus and the sea goddess Thetis; the mightiest of the Greek warriors.

Patroclus (pə·trō'kləs): a Greek warrior; the dearest friend of Achilles; has been killed in battle by Hector.

Trojans

Andromache (an·dräm'ə·kē): the wife of Hector.

Astyanax (as·tī'ə·naks'): the infant son of Hector and Andromache.

Hector (hek'tər): the son of Priam and Hecuba; the commander of the Trojan forces.

Hecuba (hek'yōō·bə): the queen of Troy; Priam's wife; the mother of Hector and Paris.

Priam (prī'əm): the king of Troy; the father of Hector and Paris.

Gods and Goddesses

Aphrodite (af'rə·dīt'ē): the goddess of love; sides with the Trojans during the war.

Apollo (ə·päl'ō): the god of poetry, music, archery, and prophecy; sides with the Trojans; also called **Phoebus.**

Athena (ə·thē'nə): the goddess of wisdom; takes the Greeks' side in the conflict.

So all through Troy the men who had fled like panicked
     fawns
were wiping off their sweat, drinking away their thirst,
leaning along the city's massive ramparts now
while Achaean troops, sloping shields to shoulders,
closed against the walls. But there stood Hector,
shackled fast by his deadly fate, holding his ground,
exposed in front of Troy and the Scaean Gates.
And now Apollo turned to taunt Achilles:
"Why are you chasing *me*? Why waste your speed?—

10   son of Peleus, you a mortal and I a deathless god.
You still don't know that I am immortal, do you?—
straining to catch me in your fury! Have you forgotten?
There's a war to fight with the Trojans you stampeded,
look, they're packed inside their city walls, but you,
you've slipped away out here. You can't kill *me*—
I can never die—it's not my fate!"

                                Enraged at that,
Achilles shouted in mid-stride, "You've blocked my way,
you distant, deadly Archer, deadliest god of all—
you made me swerve away from the rampart there.

20   Else what a mighty Trojan army had gnawed the dust
before they could ever straggle through their gates!
Now you've robbed me of great glory, saved their lives
with all your deathless ease. Nothing for you to fear,
no punishment to come. Oh I'd pay you back
if I only had the power at my command!"

    No more words—he dashed toward the city,
heart racing for some great exploit, rushing on
like a champion stallion drawing a chariot full tilt,
sweeping across the plain in easy, tearing strides—

30   so Achilles hurtled on, driving legs and knees.

    And old King Priam was first to see him coming,
surging over the plain, blazing like the star

that rears at harvest, flaming up in its brilliance,—
far outshining the countless stars in the night sky,
that star they call Orion's Dog—brightest of all
but a fatal sign emblazoned on the heavens,
it brings such killing fever down on wretched men.
So the bronze flared on his chest as on he raced—
and the old man moaned, flinging both hands high,
40 beating his head and groaning deep he called,
begging his dear son who stood before the gates,
unshakable, furious to fight Achilles to the death.
The old man cried, pitifully, hands reaching out to him,
"Oh Hector! Don't just stand there, don't, dear child,
waiting that man's attack—alone, cut off from friends!
You'll meet your doom at once, beaten down by Achilles,
so much stronger than you—that hard, headlong man.
Oh if only the gods loved him as much as I do . . .
dogs and vultures would eat his fallen corpse at once!—
50 with what a load of misery lifted from my spirit.
That man who robbed me of many sons, brave boys,
cutting them down or selling them off as slaves,
shipped to islands half the world away . . .
Even now there are two, Lycaon and Polydorus—
I cannot find them among the soldiers crowding Troy,
those sons Laothoë bore me, Laothoë queen of women.
But if they are still alive in the enemy's camp,
then we'll ransom them back with bronze and gold.
We have hoards inside the walls, the rich dowry
60 old and famous Altes presented with his daughter.
But if they're dead already, gone to the House of Death,
what grief to their mother's heart and mine—we gave
      them life.
For the rest of Troy, though, just a moment's grief
unless you too are battered down by Achilles.
Back, come back! Inside the walls, my boy!
Rescue the men of Troy and the Trojan women—
don't hand the great glory to Peleus' son,

bereft of your own sweet life yourself.

                        Pity me too!—
still in my senses, true, but a harrowed, broken man

70   marked out by doom—past the threshold of old age . . .
and Father Zeus will waste me with a hideous fate,
and after I've lived to look on so much horror!
My sons laid low, my daughters dragged away
and the treasure-chambers looted, helpless babies
hurled to the earth in the red barbarity of war . . .
my sons' wives hauled off by the Argives' bloody hands!
And I, I last of all—the dogs before my doors
will eat me raw, once some enemy brings me down
with his sharp bronze sword or spits me with a spear,

80   wrenching the life out of my body, yes, the very dogs
I bred in my own halls to share my table, guard my gates—
mad, rabid at heart they'll lap their master's blood
and loll before my doors.

                      Ah for a young man
all looks fine and noble if he goes down in war,
hacked to pieces under a slashing bronze blade—
he lies there dead . . . but whatever death lays bare,
all wounds are marks of glory. When an old man's killed
and the dogs go at the gray head and the gray beard
and mutilate the genitals—that is the cruelest sight
in all our wretched lives!"

90   So the old man groaned
and seizing his gray hair tore it out by the roots
but he could not shake the fixed resolve of Hector.
And his mother wailed now, standing beside Priam,
weeping freely, loosing her robes with one hand
and holding out her bare breast with the other,
her words pouring forth in a flight of grief and tears:
"Hector, my child! Look—have some respect for *this*!
Pity your mother too, if I ever gave you the breast
to soothe your troubles, remember it now, dear boy—

100 beat back that savage man from safe inside the walls!
Don't go forth, a champion pitted against him—

merciless, brutal man. If he kills you now,
how can I ever mourn you on your deathbed?—
dear branch in bloom, dear child I brought to birth!—
Neither I nor your wife, that warm, generous woman . . .
Now far beyond our reach, now by the Argive ships
the rushing dogs will tear you, bolt your flesh!"

So they wept, the two of them crying out
to their dear son, both pleading time and again
110 but they could not shake the fixed resolve of Hector.
No, he waited Achilles, coming on, gigantic in power.
As a snake in the hills, guarding his hole, awaits a man—
bloated with poison, deadly hatred seething inside him,
glances flashing fire as he coils round his lair . . .
so Hector, nursing his quenchless fury, gave no ground,
leaning his burnished shield against a jutting wall,
but harried still, he probed his own brave heart:
"No way out. If I slip inside the gates and walls,
Polydamas will be first to heap disgrace on me—
120 he was the one who urged me to lead our Trojans
back to Ilium just last night, the disastrous night
Achilles rose in arms like a god. But did I give way?
Not at all. And how much better it would have been!
Now my army's ruined, thanks to my own reckless pride,
I would die of shame to face the men of Troy
and the Trojan women trailing their long robes . . .
Someone less of a man than I will say, 'Our Hector—
staking all on his own strength, he destroyed his army!'
So they will mutter. So now, better by far for me
130 to stand up to Achilles, kill him, come home alive
or die at his hands in glory out before the walls.
But wait—what if I put down my studded shield
and heavy helmet, prop my spear on the rampart
and go forth, just as I am, to meet Achilles,
noble Prince Achilles . . .
why, I could promise to give back Helen, yes,
and all her treasures with her, all those riches

Paris once hauled home to Troy in the hollow ships—
and they were the cause of all our endless fighting—
140 Yes, yes, return it all to the sons of Atreus now
to haul away, and then, at the same time, divide
the rest with all the Argives, all the city holds,
and then I'd take an oath for the Trojan royal council
that we will hide nothing! Share and share alike the hoards
our handsome citadel stores within its depths and—
Why debate, my friend? Why thrash things out?
I must not go and implore him. He'll show no mercy,
no respect for me, my rights—he'll cut me down
straight off—stripped of defenses like a woman
150 once I have loosed the armor off my body.
No way to parley with that man—not now—
not from behind some oak or rock to whisper,
like a boy and a young girl, lovers' secrets
a boy and girl might whisper to each other . . .
Better to clash in battle, now, at once—
see which fighter Zeus awards the glory!"

So he wavered,
waiting there, but Achilles was closing on him now
like the god of war, the fighter's helmet flashing,
over his right shoulder shaking the Pelian ash spear,
160 that terror, and the bronze around his body flared
like a raging fire or the rising, blazing sun.
Hector looked up, saw him, started to tremble,
nerve gone, he could hold his ground no longer,
he left the gates behind and away he fled in fear—
and Achilles went for him, fast, sure of his speed
as the wild mountain hawk, the quickest thing on wings,
launching smoothly, swooping down on a cringing dove
and the dove flits out from under, the hawk screaming
over the quarry, plunging over and over, his fury
170 driving him down to beak and tear his kill—
so Achilles flew at him, breakneck on in fury
with Hector fleeing along the walls of Troy,
fast as his legs would go. On and on they raced,
passing the lookout point, passing the wild fig tree

tossed by the wind, always out from under the ramparts
down the wagon trail they careered until they reached
the clear running springs where whirling Scamander
rises up from its double wellsprings bubbling strong—
and one runs hot and the steam goes up around it,
180   drifting thick as if fire burned at its core
but the other even in summer gushes cold
as hail or freezing snow or water chilled to ice . . .
And here, close to the springs, lie washing-pools
scooped out in the hollow rocks and broad and smooth
where the wives of Troy and all their lovely daughters
would wash their glistening robes in the old days,
the days of peace before the sons of Achaea came . . .
Past these they raced, one escaping, one in pursuit
and the one who fled was great but the one pursuing
190   greater, even greater—their pace mounting in speed
since both men strove, not for a sacrificial beast
or oxhide trophy, prizes runners fight for, no,
they raced for the life of Hector breaker of horses.
Like powerful stallions sweeping round the post for trophies,
galloping full stretch with some fine prize at stake,
a tripod, say, or woman offered up at funeral games
for some brave hero fallen—so the two of them
whirled three times around the city of Priam,
sprinting at top speed while all the gods gazed down,
200   and the father of men and gods broke forth among them now:
"Unbearable—a man I love, hunted round his own city walls
and right before my eyes. My heart grieves for Hector.
Hector who burned so many oxen in my honor, rich cuts,
now on the rugged crests of Ida, now on Ilium's heights.
But now, look, brilliant Achilles courses him round
the city of Priam in all his savage, lethal speed.
Come, you immortals, think this through. Decide.
Either we pluck the man from death and save his life
or strike him down at last, here at Achilles' hands—
for all his fighting heart."
210   But immortal Athena,
her gray eyes wide, protested strongly: "Father!

Lord of the lightning, king of the black cloud,
what are you saying? A man, a mere mortal,
his doom sealed long ago? You'd set him free
from all the pains of death?
                                        Do as you please—
but none of the deathless gods will ever praise you."

And Zeus who marshals the thunderheads replied,
"Courage, Athena, third-born of the gods, dear child.
Nothing I said was meant in earnest, trust me,
220   I mean you all the good will in the world. Go.
Do as your own impulse bids you. Hold back no more."

So he launched Athena already poised for action—
down the goddess swept from Olympus' craggy peaks.

And swift Achilles kept on coursing Hector, nonstop
as a hound in the mountains starts a fawn from its lair,
hunting him down the gorges, down the narrow glens
and the fawn goes to ground, hiding deep in brush
but the hound comes racing fast, nosing him out
until he lands his kill. So Hector could never throw
230   Achilles off his trail, the swift racer Achilles—
time and again he'd make a dash for the Dardan Gates,
trying to rush beneath the rock-built ramparts, hoping
men on the heights might save him, somehow, raining spears
but time and again Achilles would intercept him quickly,
heading him off, forcing him out across the plain
and always sprinting along the city side himself—
endless as in a dream . . .
when a man can't catch another fleeing on ahead
and he can never escape nor his rival overtake him—
240   so the one could never run the other down in his speed
nor the other spring away. And how could Hector have fled
the fates of death so long? How unless one last time,
one final time Apollo had swept in close beside him,

driving strength in his legs and knees to race the wind?
And brilliant Achilles shook his head at the armies,
never letting them hurl their sharp spears at Hector—
someone might snatch the glory, Achilles come in second.
But once they reached the springs for the fourth time,
then Father Zeus held out his sacred golden scales:
250   in them he placed two fates of death that lays men low—
one for Achilles, one for Hector breaker of horses—
and gripping the beam mid-haft the Father raised it high
and down went Hector's day of doom, dragging him down
to the strong House of Death—and god Apollo left him.
Athena rushed to Achilles, her bright eyes gleaming,
standing shoulder-to-shoulder, winging orders now:
"At last our hopes run high, my brilliant Achilles—
Father Zeus must love you—
we'll sweep great glory back to Achaea's fleet,
260   we'll kill this Hector, mad as he is for battle!
No way for him to escape us now, no longer—
not even if Phoebus the distant deadly Archer
goes through torments, pleading for Hector's life,
groveling over and over before our storming Father Zeus.
But you, you hold your ground and catch your breath
while I run Hector down and persuade the man
to fight you face-to-face."
                              So Athena commanded
and he obeyed, rejoicing at heart—Achilles stopped,
leaning against his ashen spearshaft barbed in bronze.
270   And Athena left him there, caught up with Hector at once,
and taking the build and vibrant voice of Deiphobus
stood shoulder-to-shoulder with him, winging orders:
"Dear brother, how brutally swift Achilles hunts you—
coursing you round the city of Priam in all his lethal speed!
Come, let us stand our ground together—beat him back."

     "Deiphobus!"—Hector, his helmet flashing, called out to her—
"dearest of all my brothers, all these warring years,
of all the sons that Priam and Hecuba produced!

Now I'm determined to praise you all the more,
280   you who dared—seeing me in these straits—
to venture out from the walls, all for *my* sake,
while the others stay inside and cling to safety."

   The goddess answered quickly, her eyes blazing,
True, dear brother—how your father and mother both
implored me, time and again, clutching my knees,
and the comrades round me begging me to stay!
Such was the fear that broke them, man for man,
but the heart within me broke with grief for you.
Now headlong on and fight! No letup, no lance spared!
290   So now, now we'll *see* if Achilles kills us both
and hauls our bloody armor back to the beaked ships
or *he* goes down in pain beneath your spear."

   Athena luring him on with all her immortal cunning—
and now, at last, as the two came closing for the kill
it was tall Hector, helmet flashing, who led off:
"No more running from you in fear, Achilles!
Not as before. Three times I fled around
the great city of Priam—I lacked courage then
to stand your onslaught. Now my spirit stirs me
300   to meet you face-to-face. Now kill or be killed!
Come, we'll swear to the gods, the highest witnesses—
the gods will oversee our binding pacts. I swear
I will never mutilate you—merciless as you are—
if Zeus allows me to last it out and tear your life away.
But once I've stripped your glorious armor, Achilles,
I will give your body back to your loyal comrades.
Swear you'll do the same."
                     A swift dark glance
and the headstrong runner answered, "Hector, stop!
You unforgivable, you . . . don't talk to me of pacts.
310   There are no binding oaths between men and lions—
wolves and lambs can enjoy no meeting of the minds—

they are all bent on hating each other to the death.
So with you and me. No love between us. No truce
till one or the other falls and gluts with blood
Ares who hacks at men behind his rawhide shield.
Come, call up whatever courage you can muster.
Life or death—now prove yourself a spearman,
a daring man of war! No more escape for you—
Athena will kill you with my spear in just a moment.
320 Now you'll pay at a stroke for all my comrades' grief,
all you killed in the fury of your spear!"

                                      With that,
shaft poised, he hurled and his spear's long shadow flew
but seeing it coming, glorious Hector ducked away,
crouching down, watching the bronze tip fly past
and stab the earth—but Athena snatched it up
and passed it back to Achilles
and Hector the gallant captain never saw her.
He sounded out a challenge to Peleus' princely son:
"You missed, look—the great godlike Achilles!
330 So you knew nothing at all from Zeus about my death—
and yet how sure you were! All bluff, cunning with words,
that's all you are—trying to make me fear you,
lose my nerve, forget my fighting strength.
Well, you'll never plant your lance in my back
as I flee *you* in fear—plunge it through my chest
as I come charging in, if a god gives you the chance!
But now it's for you to dodge *my* brazen spear—
I wish you'd bury it in your body to the hilt.
How much lighter the war would be for Trojans then
340 if you, their greatest scourge, were dead and gone!"

    Shaft poised, he hurled and his spear's long shadow flew
and it struck Achilles' shield—a dead-center hit—
but off and away it glanced and Hector seethed,
his hurtling spear, his whole arm's power poured
in a wasted shot. He stood there, cast down . . .
he had no spear in reserve. So Hector shouted out

to Deiphobus bearing his white shield—with a ringing
     shout
he called for a heavy lance—
                              but the man was nowhere
       near him,
vanished—
               yes and Hector knew the truth in his heart
350 and the fighter cried aloud, "My time has come
At last the gods have called me down to death.
I thought he was at my side, the hero Deiphobus—
he's safe inside the walls, Athena's tricked me blind.
And now death, grim death is looming up beside me,
no longer far away. No way to escape it now. This,
this was their pleasure after all, sealed long ago—
Zeus and the son of Zeus, the distant deadly Archer—
though often before now they rushed to my defense.
So now I meet my doom. Well let me die—
360 but not without struggle, not without glory, no,
in some great clash of arms that even men to come
will hear of down the years!"
                              And on that resolve
he drew the whetted sword that hung at his side,
tempered, massive, and gathering all his force
he swooped like a soaring eagle
launching down from the dark clouds to earth
to snatch some helpless lamb or trembling hare.
So Hector swooped now, swinging his whetted sword
and Achilles charged too, bursting with rage, barbaric,
370 guarding his chest with the well-wrought blazoned shield,
head tossing his gleaming helmet, four horns strong
and the golden plumes shook that the god of fire
drove in bristling thick along its ridge.
Bright as that star amid the stars in the night sky,
star of the evening, brightest star that rides the heavens,
so fire flared from the sharp point of the spear Achilles
brandished high in his right hand, bent on Hector's death,
scanning his splendid body—where to pierce it best?

The rest of his flesh seemed all encased in armor,
380 burnished, brazen—*Achilles'* armor that Hector stripped
from strong Patroclus when he killed him—true,
but one spot lay exposed,
where collarbones lift the neckbone off the shoulders,
the open throat, where the end of life comes quickest—*there*
as Hector charged in fury brilliant Achilles drove his spear
and the point went stabbing clean through the tender neck
but the heavy bronze weapon failed to slash the windpipe—
Hector could still gasp out some words, some last reply . . .
he crashed in the dust—
                    godlike Achilles gloried over him:
390 "Hector—surely you thought when you stripped Patroclus' armor
that you, you would be safe! Never a fear of me—
far from the fighting as I was—you fool!
Left behind there, down by the beaked ships
his great avenger waited, a greater man by far—
that man was I, and I smashed your strength! And you—
the dogs and birds will maul you, shame your corpse
while Achaeans bury my dear friend in glory!"

Struggling for breath, Hector, his helmet flashing,
said, "I beg you, beg you by your life, your parents—
400 don't let the dogs devour me by the Argive ships!
Wait, take the princely ransom of bronze and gold,
the gifts my father and noble mother will give you—
but give my body to friends to carry home again,
so Trojan men and Trojan women can do me honor
with fitting rites of fire once I am dead."

Staring grimly, the proud runner Achilles answered,
"Beg no more, you fawning dog—begging me by my parents!
Would to god my rage, my fury would drive me now
to hack your flesh away and eat you raw—
410 such agonies you have caused me! Ransom?
No man alive could keep the dog-packs off you,
not if they haul in ten, twenty times that ransom

and pile it here before me and promise fortunes more—
no, not even if Dardan Priam should offer to weigh out
your bulk in gold! Not even then will your noble mother
lay you on your deathbed, mourn the son she bore . . .
The dogs and birds will rend you—blood and bone!"

At the point of death, Hector, his helmet flashing,
said, "I know you well—I see my fate before me.
420 Never a chance that I could win you over . . .
Iron inside your chest, that heart of yours.
But now beware, or my curse will draw god's wrath
upon your head, that day when Paris and lord Apollo—
for all your fighting heart—destroy you at the Scaean Gates!"

Death cut him short. The end closed in around him.
Flying free of his limbs
his soul went winging down to the House of Death,
wailing his fate, leaving his manhood far behind, ·
his young and supple strength. But brilliant Achilles
430 taunted Hector's body, dead as he was, "Die, die!
For my own death, I'll meet it freely—whenever Zeus
and the other deathless gods would like to bring it on!"

With that he wrenched his bronze spear from the corpse,
laid it aside and ripped the bloody armor off the back.
And the other sons of Achaea, running up around him,
crowded closer, all of them gazing wonder-struck
at the build and marvelous, lithe beauty of Hector.
And not a man came forward who did not stab his body,
glancing toward a comrade, laughing: "Ah, look here—
440 how much softer he is to handle now, this Hector,
than when he gutted our ships with roaring fire!"

Standing over him, so they'd gloat and stab his body.
But once he had stripped the corpse the proud runner Achilles
took his stand in the midst of all the Argive troops
and urged them on with a flight of winging orders:

"Friends—lords of the Argives, O my captains!
Now that the gods have let me kill this man
who caused us agonies, loss on crushing loss—
more than the rest of all their men combined—
450   come, let us ring their walls in armor, test them,
see what recourse the Trojans still may have in mind.
Will they abandon the city heights with this man fallen?
Or brace for a last, dying stand though Hector's gone?
But wait—what am I saying? Why this deep debate?
Down by the ships a body lies unwept, unburied—
Patroclus . . . I will never forget him,
not as long as I'm still among the living
and my springing knees will lift and drive me on.
Though the dead forget their dead in the House of Death,
I will remember, even there, my dear companion.
460   Now,
come, you sons of Achaea, raise a song of triumph!
Down to the ships we march and bear this corpse on high—
we have won ourselves great glory. We have brought
magnificent Hector down, that man the Trojans
glorified in their city like a god!"
                                        So he triumphed
and now he was bent on outrage, on shaming noble Hector.
Piercing the tendons, ankle to heel behind both feet,
he knotted straps of rawhide through them both,
lashed them to his chariot, left the head to drag
470   and mounting the car, hoisting the famous arms aboard,
he whipped his team to a run and breakneck on they flew,
holding nothing back. And a thick cloud of dust rose up
from the man they dragged, his dark hair swirling round
that head so handsome once, all tumbled low in the dust—
since Zeus had given him once to his enemies now
to be defiled in the land of his own fathers.

      So his whole head was dragged down in the dust.
And now his mother began to tear her hair . . .
she flung her shining veil to the ground and raised

480   a high, shattering scream, looking down at her son.
     Pitifully his loving father groaned and round the king
     his people cried with grief and wailing seized the city—
     for all the world as if all Troy were torched and smoldering
     down from the looming brows of the citadel to her roots.
     Priam's people could hardly hold the old man back,
     frantic, mad to go rushing out the Dardan Gates.
     He begged them all, groveling in the filth,
     crying out to them, calling each man by name,
     "Let go, my friends! Much as you care for me,
490   let me hurry out of the city, make my way,
     all on my own, to Achaea's waiting ships!
     I must implore that terrible, violent man . . .
     Perhaps—who knows?—he may respect my age,
     may pity an old man. He has a father too,
     as old as I am—Peleus sired him once,
     Peleus reared him to be the scourge of Troy
     but most of all to me—he made my life a hell.
     So many sons he slaughtered, just coming into bloom . . .
     but grieving for all the rest, one breaks my heart the most
500   and stabbing grief for him will take me down to Death—
     my Hector—would to god he had perished in my arms!
     Then his mother who bore him—oh so doomed,
     she and I could glut ourselves with grief."

     So the voice of the king rang out in tears,
     citizens wailed in answer, and noble Hecuba
     led the wives of Troy in a throbbing chant of sorrow:
     "O my child—my desolation! How can I go on living?
     What agonies must I suffer now, now *you* are dead and gone?
     You were my pride throughout the city night and day—
510   a blessing to us all, the men and women of Troy:
     throughout the city they saluted you like a god.
     You, you were their greatest glory while you lived—
     now death and fate have seized you, dragged you down!"

     Her voice rang out in tears, but the wife of Hector

had not heard a thing. No messenger brought the truth
of how her husband made his stand outside the gates.
She was weaving at her loom, deep in the high halls,
working flowered braiding into a dark red folding robe.
And she called her well-kempt women through the house
520   to set a large three-legged cauldron over the fire
so Hector could have his steaming hot bath
when he came home from battle—poor woman,
she never dreamed how far he was from bathing,
struck down at Achilles' hands by blazing-eyed Athena.
But she heard the groans and wails of grief from the rampart now
and her body shook, her shuttle dropped to the ground,
she called out to her lovely waiting women, "Quickly—
two of you follow me—I must see what's happened.
That cry—that was Hector's honored mother I heard!
530   My heart's pounding, leaping up in my throat,
the knees beneath me paralyzed—Oh I know it . . .
something terrible's coming down on Priam's children.
Pray god the news will never reach my ears!
Yes but I dread it so—what if great Achilles
has cut my Hector off from the city, daring Hector,
and driven him out across the plain, and all alone?—
He may have put an end to that fatal headstrong pride
that always seized my Hector—never hanging back
with the main force of men, always charging ahead,
giving ground to no man in his fury!"
540   So she cried,
dashing out of the royal halls like a madwoman,
her heart racing hard, her women close behind her.
But once she reached the tower where soldiers massed
she stopped on the rampart, looked down and saw it all—
saw him dragged before the city, stallions galloping,
dragging Hector back to Achaea's beaked warships—
ruthless work. The world went black as night
before her eyes, she fainted, falling backward,
gasping away her life breath . . .
550   She flung to the winds her glittering headdress,

the cap and the coronet, braided band and veil,
all the regalia golden Aphrodite gave her once,
the day that Hector, helmet aflash in sunlight,
led her home to Troy from her father's house
with countless wedding gifts to win her heart.
But crowding round her now her husband's sisters
and brothers' wives supported her in their midst,
and she, terrified, stunned to the point of death,
struggling for breath now and coming back to life,
560 burst out in grief among the Trojan women: "O Hector—
I am destroyed! Both born to the same fate after all!
You, you at Troy in the halls of King Priam—
I at Thebes, under the timberline of Placos,
Eetion's house . . . He raised me as a child,
that man of doom, his daughter just as doomed—
would to god he'd never fathered *me*!

                      Now you go down
to the House of Death, the dark depths of the earth,
and leave me here to waste away in grief, a widow
lost in the royal halls—and the boy only a baby,
570 the son we bore together, you and I so doomed.
Hector, what help are you to him, now you are dead?—
what help is he to you? Think, even if he escapes
the wrenching horrors of war against the Argives,
pain and labor will plague him all his days to come.
Strangers will mark his lands off, stealing his estates.
The day that orphans a youngster cuts him off from friends.
And he hangs his head low, humiliated in every way . . .
his cheeks stained with tears, and pressed by hunger
the boy goes up to his father's old companions,
580 tugging at one man's cloak, another's tunic,
and some will pity him, true,
and one will give him a little cup to drink,
enough to wet his lips, not quench his thirst.
But then some bully with both his parents living
beats him from the banquet, fists and abuses flying:
'You, get out—you've got no father feasting with us here!'

And the boy, sobbing, trails home to his widowed mother . . .
Astyanax!
                        And years ago, propped on his father's knee,
he would only eat the marrow, the richest cuts of lamb,
590   and when sleep came on him and he had quit his play,
cradled warm in his nurse's arms he'd drowse off,
snug in a soft bed, his heart brimmed with joy.
Now what suffering, now he's lost his father—
                                                    Astyanax!
The Lord of the City, so the Trojans called him,
because it was you, Hector, you and you alone
who shielded the gates and the long walls of Troy.
But now by the beaked ships, far from your parents,
glistening worms will wriggle through your flesh,
once the dogs have had their fill of your naked corpse—
600   though we have such stores of clothing laid up in the halls,
fine things, a joy to the eye, the work of women's hands.
Now, by god, I'll burn them all, blazing to the skies!
No use to you now, they'll never shroud your body—
but they will be your glory
burned by the Trojan men and women in your honor!"

Her voice rang out in tears and the women wailed in answer.

Translated from the Greek by Robert Fagles

Virgil
(70–19 B.C.)

Universally acknowledged as the greatest of Roman poets, Virgil expressed in his poetry two major themes—a majestic vision of world order and peace in his epic poem the *Aeneid* and an abiding love for the simple joys and rewards of nature and honest toil in his earlier poems. Born Publius Vergilius Maro to a farming family near the town of Mantua, he grew up in a region that was considered part of Gaul (modern-day France) and did not officially become part of Italy until he was a young man. His father sent him to Rome to study law, philosophy, and literature with young men of nobler birth.

Virgil was born into a time of political upheaval that drove him away from public life and made him seek refuge in his life-long love of the land. When he was in his mid-twenties, the Roman leader Julius Caesar was assassinated, and Rome was rocked by a civil war that lasted for years. Caesar's assassins fought against forces led by Caesar's friend Mark Antony and by Caesar's nephew and heir, Octavian. Then Antony and Octavian fought with each other, prolonging the strife for another decade. During the civil wars, Virgil lived almost as a recluse in his rural home, where he began to write poetry idealizing rural life. His *Eclogues*, a collection of ten pastoral poems, established his reputation.

When Virgil was about forty, Octavian became Rome's sole ruler. The reign of Octavian, who is better known by his honorary title Augustus ("revered one"), ushered in one of the longest eras of peace and order in Rome's history. Octavian's rule made a tremendous difference in the life of Virgil. He turned from glorifying country life to a much grander project: creating a national Roman epic on the order of the *Iliad* and the *Odyssey*. He planned to set down the story of Aeneas, the ancestor of the legendary founder of Rome, Romulus. It was also his intention that his epic creation would be the pride and joy of Augustus's reign.

Virgil worked long and hard on his *Aeneid* for the last ten years of his life. In a letter he complained bitterly that the project was driving him almost insane. As he was dying, he even begged his friends to burn the manuscript he had labored so long to write, because it was not in finished form and he was not satisfied with it. Fortunately, the emperor Augustus, who recognized the value of the poem both as literature and as favorable propaganda for himself, refused to comply with the poet's last wish and preserved the *Aeneid* for future generations. And so the work that made Virgil miserable during his final years also gave him immortality.

The Fall of Troy
from Book 2 of the Aeneid

Virgil

The events of the Aeneid *take place near the end of the Trojan War in the thirteenth century* B.C. *For ten long years, the Greeks have camped outside Troy, unable to break through the walls. Finally, they resort to a trick. They conceal a group of warriors inside a huge wooden horse. Then the Greek army pretends to sail away. The Trojans fall for the trick. Thinking that the Greeks have finally given up the battle, they surge joyfully out of their city walls and, spotting the huge horse, think that it is a tribute to the gods. Opening the massive gates of Troy, they wheel the horse and its hidden cargo into the city.*

That night, when the Trojans are asleep, the warriors get out of the horse and open the city gates, and the Greek army pours in. Most of the Trojans are slaughtered.

As this episode opens, Aeneas, a warrior on the Trojan side, is fleeing from the burning city. The Trojan king, Priam, and his sons are dead. Most of Aeneas's men have been killed. Filled with horror at the destruction he sees about him, the warrior comes upon Helen, whose elopement with Paris caused the war. She is hiding near the altar of Vesta, goddess of the hearth and home.

Characters in "The Fall of Troy"

Aeneas (i·nē'əs): the son of the goddess Venus and Anchises.

Anchises (an·kī'sēz'): the father of Aeneas; the king of Dardania; an ally of his second cousin, Priam, the king of Troy.

Creusa (krē·yōō'sə): a daughter of Priam; the sister of Hector; the wife of Aeneas.

Helen (hel'ən): the wife of Menelaus; seduced and abducted by Paris, a prince of Troy, thereby causing the ten-year war.

Iulus (yōōl'əs): the son of Aeneas and Creusa; an ancestor of Julius Caesar; also called **Ascanius.**

Pyrrhus (pir'əs): the son of Achilles; has killed King Priam.

Grim horror, then, came home to me. I saw
My father when I saw the king, the life
Going out with the cruel wound. I saw Creusa
Forsaken, my abandoned home, Iulus,
My little son. I looked around. They all
Had gone, exhausted, flung down from the walls,
Or dead in the fire, and I was left alone.
    And I saw Helen, hiding, of all places,
At Vesta's shrine, and clinging there in silence,
10 But the bright flames lit the scene. That hated woman,
Fearing both Trojan anger and Greek vengeance,
A common fury to both lands, was crouching
Beside the altar. Anger flared up in me
For punishment and vengeance. Should she then,
I thought, come home to Sparta safe, uninjured
Walk through Mycenae, a triumphant queen?
See husband, home, parents and children, tended

By Trojan slave-girls? This, with Priam fallen
And Troy burnt down, and the shore soaked in blood?
20   Never! No memorable name, I knew,
Was won by punishing women, yet, for me,
There might be praise for the just abolition
Of this unholiness, and satisfaction
In vengeance for the ashes of my people.
All this I may have said aloud, in frenzy,
As I rushed on, when to my sight there came
A vision of my lovely mother, radiant
In the dark night, a goddess manifest,
As tall and fair as when she walks in heaven.
30   She caught me by the hand and stopped me:—"Son,
What sorrow rouses this relentless anger,
This violence? Do you care for me no longer?
Consider others first, your aged father,
Anchises; is your wife Creusa living?
Where is Iulus? Greeks are all around them,
Only my love between them, fire and sword.
It is not for you to blame the Spartan woman,
Daughter of Tyndareus, or even Paris.
The gods are the ones, the high gods are relentless.
40   It is they who bring this power down, who topple
Troy from the high foundation. Look! Your vision
Is mortal dull, I will take the cloud away—
Fear not a mother's counsel. Where you see
Rock torn from rock, and smoke and dust in billows,
Neptune is working, plying the trident, prying
The walls from their foundations. And see Juno,
Fiercest of all, holding the Scaean gates,
Girt with the steel, and calling from the ships
Implacable companions. On the towers—
50   Turn, and be certain—Pallas takes command
Gleaming with Gorgon and storm-cloud. Even Jove,
Our father, nerves the Greeks with fire and spirit,
And spurs the other gods against the Trojans.
Hasten the flight, my son; no other labor

Waits for accomplishment. I promise safety
Until you reach your father's house." She had spoken
And vanished in the thickening night of shadows.
Dread shapes come into vision, mighty powers,
Great gods at war with Troy, which, so it seemed,
60 Was sinking as I watched, with the same feeling
As when on mountain-tops you see the loggers
Hacking an ash-tree down, and it always threatens
To topple, nodding a little, and the leaves
Trembling when no wind stirs, and dies of its wounds
With one long loud last groan, and dirt from the ridges
Heaves up as it goes down with roots in air.
Divinity my guide, I leave the roof-top,
I pass unharmed through enemies and blazing,
Weapons give place to me, and flames retire.

70   At last I reached the house, I found my father,
The first one that I looked for. I meant to take him
To the safety of the hills, but he was stubborn,
Refusing longer life or barren exile,
Since Troy was dead. "You have the strength," he told me,
"You are young enough, take flight. For me, had heaven
Wanted to save my life, they would have spared
This home for me. We have seen enough destruction,
More than enough, survived a captured city.
Speak to me as a corpse laid out for burial,
80 A quick farewell, and go. Death I shall find
With my own hand; the enemy will pity,
Or look for spoil. The loss of burial
Is nothing at all. I have been living too long
Hated by gods and useless, since the time
Jove blasted me with lightning wind and fire."
He would not move, however we wept, Creusa,
Ascanius, all the house, insistent, pleading
That he should not bring all to ruin with him.
He would not move, he would not listen. Again
90 I rush to arms, I pray for death; what else

Was left to me? "Dear father, were you thinking
I could abandon you, and go? what son
Could bear a thought so monstrous? If the gods
Want nothing to be left of so great a city,
If you are bound, or pleased, to add us all
To the wreck of Troy, the way is open for it—
Pyrrhus will soon be here; from the blood of Priam
He comes; he slays the son before the father,
The sire at the altar-stone; O my dear mother,

100   Was it for this you saved me, brought me through
The fire and sword, to see our enemies
Here in the very house, and wife and son
And father murdered in each other's blood?
Bring me my arms; the last light calls the conquered.
Let me go back to the Greeks, renew the battle,
We shall not all of us die unavenged."
Sword at my side, I was on the point of going,
Working the left arm into the shield. Creusa
Clung to me on the threshold, held my feet,

110   And made me see my little son:—"Dear husband,
If you are bent on dying, take us with you,
But if you think there is any hope in fighting,
And you should know, stay and defend the house!
To whom are we abandoned, your father and son,
And I, once called your wife?" She filled the house
With moaning outcry. And then something happened,
A wonderful portent. Over Iulus' head,
Between our hands and faces, there appeared
A blaze of gentle light; a tongue of flame,

120   Harmless and innocent, was playing over
The softness of his hair, around his temples.
We were afraid, we did our best to quench it
With our own hands, or water, but my father
Raised joyous eyes to heaven, and prayed aloud:—
"Almighty Jupiter, if any prayer
Of ours has power to move you, look upon us,
Grant only this, if we have ever deserved it,

Grant us a sign, and ratify the omen!"
He had hardly spoken, when thunder on the left
130 Resounded, and a shooting star from heaven
Drew a long trail of light across the shadows.
We saw it cross above the house, and vanish
In the woods of Ida, a wake of gleaming light
Where it had sped, and a trail of sulphurous odor.
This was a victory: my father rose
In worship of the gods and the holy star,
Crying: "I follow, son, wherever you lead;
There is no delay, not now; Gods of my fathers,
Preserve my house, my grandson; yours the omen,
140 And Troy is in your keeping. O my son,
I yield, I am ready to follow." But the fire
Came louder over the walls, the flames rolled nearer
Their burning tide. "Climb to my shoulders, father,
It will be no burden, so we are together,
Meeting a common danger or salvation.
Iulus, take my hand; Creusa, follow
A little way behind. Listen, you servants!
You will find, when you leave the city, an old temple
That once belonged to Ceres; it has been tended
150 For many years with the worship of our fathers.
There's a little hill there, and a cypress tree;
And that's where we shall meet, one way or another.
And one thing more: you, father, are to carry
The holy objects and the gods of the household,
My hands are foul with battle and blood, I could not
Touch them without pollution."

                       I bent down
And over my neck and shoulders spread the cover
Of a tawny lion-skin, took up my burden;
Little Iulus held my hand, and trotted,
160 As best he could, beside me; Creusa followed.
We went on through the shadows. I had been
Brave, so I thought, before, in the rain of weapons
And the cloud of massing Greeks. But now I trembled

At every breath of air, shook at a whisper,
Fearful for both my burden and companion.
    I was near the gates, and thinking we had made it,
But there was a sound, the tramp of marching feet,
And many of them, it seemed; my father, peering
Through the thick gloom, cried out:—"Son, they are coming!
170 Flee, flee! I see their shields, their gleaming bronze."
Something or other took my senses from me
In that confusion. I turned aside from the path,
I do not know what happened then. Creusa
Was lost; she had missed the road, or halted, weary,
For a brief rest. I do not know what happened,
She was not seen again; I had not looked back,
Nor even thought about her, till we came
To Ceres' hallowed home. The count was perfect,
Only one missing there, the wife and mother.
180 Whom did I not accuse, of gods and mortals,
Then in my frenzy? What worse thing had happened
In the city overthrown? I left Anchises,
My son, my household gods, to my companions,
In a hiding-place in the valley; and I went back
Into the city again, wearing my armor,
Ready, still one more time, for any danger.
I found the walls again, the gate's dark portals,
I followed my own footsteps back, but terror,
Terror and silence were all I found. I went
190 On to my house. She might, just might, have gone there.
Only the Greeks were there, and fire devouring
The very pinnacles. I tried Priam's palace;
In the empty courtyards Phoenix and Ulysses
Guarded the spoils piled up at Juno's altar.
They had Trojan treasure there, loot from the altars,
Great drinking-bowls of gold, and stolen garments,
And human beings. A line of boys and women
Stood trembling there.
    I took the risk of crying through the shadows,
200 Over and over, "Creusa!" I kept calling,

"Creusa!" and "Creusa!" but no answer.
No sense, no limit, to my endless rushing
All through the town; and then at last I saw her,
Or thought I did, her shadow a little taller
Than I remembered. And she spoke to me
Beside myself with terror:—"O dear husband,
What good is all this frantic grief? The gods
Have willed it so, Creusa may not join you
Out of this city; Jupiter denies it.

210 Long exile lies ahead, and vast sea-reaches
The ships must furrow, till you come to land
Far in the West; rich fields are there, and a river
Flowing with gentle current; its name is Tiber.
And happy days await you there, a kingdom,
A royal wife. Banish the tears of sorrow
Over Creusa lost. I shall never see
The arrogant houses of the Myrmidons,
Nor be a slave to any Grecian woman;
I am a Dardan woman; I am the wife

220 Of Venus' son; it is Cybele who keeps me
Here on these shores. And now farewell, and love
Our son." I wept, there was more to say; she left me,
Vanishing into empty air. Three times
I reached out toward her, and three times her image
Fled like the breath of a wind or a dream on wings.
The night was over; I went back to my comrades.

    I was surprised to find so many more
Had joined us, ready for exile, pitiful people,
Mothers, and men, and children, streaming in

230 From everywhere, looking for me to lead them
Wherever I would. Over the hills of Ida
The morning-star was rising; in the town
The Danaans held the gates, and help was hopeless.
I gave it up, I lifted up my father,
Together we sought the hills.

Translated from the Latin by Rolfe Humphries

Miguel de Cervantes
(1547–1616)

Miguel de Cervantes Saavedra, Spain's greatest writer, struggled with poverty all his life. He died, still impoverished, around the time of the death of his great (and much more prosperous) English contemporary, William Shakespeare. The epitaph Cervantes wrote for himself could also be the epitaph for his hero, Don Quijote:

> For if he like a madman lived,
> At least he like a wise one died.

Cervantes' own life was a tale of poverty, woe, and imprisonment. Born the son of a wandering apothecary (pharmacist) near Madrid, Cervantes was probably not formally educated, but he read widely. Because prospects in civilian life seemed dim, Cervantes enlisted in the army. He fought bravely in the naval Battle of Lepanto but was so badly wounded that his left hand was crippled for the rest of his life, earning him the nickname *El manco de Lepanto*—"the crippled man of Lepanto."

Seeking military promotion, Cervantes took a sea voyage to a new posting, accompanied by his brother. But his hopes for advancement were cruelly mocked when he and his brother were captured at sea by pirates and held as slaves in Algeria. During the five years he was captive, Cervantes became known among the other prisoners for his bravery in leading several escape attempts. He was finally freed when his family borrowed money to pay the ransom. Over the next few years, Cervantes married, worked as a tax collector, and wrote stories, plays, and poems, but he was never financially secure. At forty, he was thrown into prison, largely because of the debts his family had taken on in order to ransom him from the pirates.

According to legend, it was while he was in prison that Cervantes conceived the story of Don Quijote, a poor, aging landowner whose mind becomes unhinged from reading too many romantic tales of chivalry. As he teeters on the edge of insanity, Quijote becomes convinced that he also is a knight-errant (a wandering knight who braves dangers to do good deeds), even though knighthood's flower withered years ago.

The History of That Ingenious Gentleman Don Quijote de La Mancha took the form of a parody, or humorous imitation, of the old knightly romances. Published when Cervantes was fifty-eight, Part I of the book caused an immediate sensation. The first edition sold out, and pirated, or illegally printed, copies began to appear everywhere. Six editions were printed the first year; within ten years, the book had been translated into English and French. Soon everyone in Europe was laughing at the droll adventures of the ridiculous but touching Don Quijote. Someone even tried to capitalize on Cervantes' success with a bogus sequel. When Cervantes came out with his own Part II in 1615, a year before he died, the sequel pleased readers hungry for more of the addled old knight's adventures. The second installment of Don Quijote's adventures is widely regarded as even better than the first.

By the end of his life, Cervantes was famous, but he was still poor. Until the nineteenth century, authors were at the mercy of publishers, and so it was his publisher and not Cervantes who grew wealthy from *Don Quijote*'s popularity. Cervantes died in poverty on April 22, 1616. To his family, he left only a little money and many debts. To the world, he left a comic masterpiece that earned the wounded man of Lepanto another and more enduring title: "Father of the Modern Novel."

Tilting at Windmills
from **The History of That Ingenious Gentleman Don Quijote de La Mancha**

Miguel de Cervantes

An elderly nobleman named Alonso Quijana, dazzled by the old stories of knights who rescue maidens in distress and slay giants, decides to join the knightly ranks and rid the world of evil. Calling himself Don Quijote, he polishes up a suit of rusty armor, puts on a cardboard helmet, saddles up a bony old horse (which he names "Rocinante"), and hobbles off in search of glory.

One of his first tasks is to find a damsel to whom he can dedicate his life and good deeds. He chooses a farm girl in the neighborhood, named Aldonza Lorenzo. Blind to her rough edges, the old gentleman renames the girl Dulcinea del Toboso (because the name suggests a princess).

On his first expedition, the old man has himself "knighted" by a bewildered innkeeper. But as he sets off on his adventures, he is beaten by a mule driver and taken home, where he is treated like a lunatic. His books are all taken away, and everyone hopes that the lunacy will pass.

from Chapter Seven

The second expedition of our good knight, Don Quijote de La Mancha

During this time, too, Don Quijote sought out a farmer, a neighbor of his and a good man (if we can use that term for anyone who's poor) but not very well endowed from the neck up. To make a long story short, he piled so many words on him, coaxing him, making him promises, that the poor fellow agreed to ride out with him and serve as his squire. Among other things, Don Quijote told him he ought to be delighted to join the quest because you could never tell when an adventure might earn them, in two shakes of a lamb's tail, a whole island, and Don Quijote would leave him there to be its governor. Because of promises like this, and many more of the same sort, Sancho Panza—which was the farmer's name—left his wife and children and agreed to become his neighbor's squire.

Don Quijote promptly set to work hunting up money and, selling something here, pawning something there, making one bad bargain after another, he managed to put together a fair-sized sum. He also wangled a small shield for himself (borrowed from a friend) and, patching up his helmet as best he could, warned his squire of the exact day and hour at which he planned to ride out, so Sancho could make sure he had everything he was going to need. And above all else Don Quijote advised him to bring along saddlebags, which Sancho said he would do, and he'd bring a very fine donkey, too, because he hadn't had much practice getting places on foot. Don Quijote had some doubts about the donkey, trying to remember if there had ever been a knight errant whose squire rode along on an ass, but couldn't recall a single one. In spite of which he decided to take Sancho with him, intending to arrange a more honorable mount as soon as he had the chance, by seizing a horse from the first ill-mannered knight he bumped into. He got some shirts ready, and as many other things as he could, following the advice the innkeeper had given him, and all of this having been arranged without either Sancho Panza saying goodbye to his wife and children, or Don Quijote to his niece and his housekeeper, one night they rode out of the village without anyone seeing them, and rode so far that, by dawn, they thought it would be impossible to find them, even if a search were made.

Sancho Panza jogged along on his donkey like some biblical patriarch, carrying his saddlebags and his leather wine bottle, wanting very badly to see himself the governor of an island, as his master had promised. Don Quijote had decided to go in the very same direction, and along the very same road, as on his first expedition, which led through the fields of Montiel, which he crossed with less difficulty than the last time, for it was early morning and the sun's rays came slanting down and did not tire them out. Then Sancho Panza said to his master:

"Now be careful, your grace, sir knight errant, you don't forget that island you promised me, because no matter how big it is I'll know how to govern it."

To which Don Quijote answered:

"You must know, Sancho Panza my friend, that it used to be very common, in ancient times, for knights errant to make their squires governor of whatever islands or regions they conquered, and I am resolved not to neglect this gracious custom—indeed, I intend to improve on it, for occasionally, and I suspect most of the time, they waited until their squires had grown old and fed up with such service, enduring bad days and even worse nights, and then gave them a title—count, or more often marquis of some valley or province, more or less. But if you and I both live, it could be that in less than a week I'll have conquered a kingdom to which others pay allegiance, which would be just right for crowning you ruler of one of those subordinate domains. Nor should you think this in any way remarkable, for no one can possibly foresee or even imagine the way the world turns for such knights, so it could easily happen that I will be able to grant you still more than my promise."

"So," said Sancho Panza, "if I become a king, by one of those miracles your grace is talking about, at the very least my old lady, Teresa, would get to be a queen, and my kids would be princes."

"But who could possibly doubt it?" answered Don Quijote.

"I doubt it," replied Sancho Panza, "because it seems to me that, even if God let crowns come raining down all over the earth, none would land on my wife's head. You see, señor, she wouldn't be worth two cents as a queen. She might make a better countess, but it wouldn't be easy, even with God's help."

"Put yourself in God's hands, Sancho," said Don Quijote,

"and He will give both you and your wife what it is best you should each have. But don't so lower your spirit that you'll be satisfied with less than a provincial governorship."

"I won't, my lord," answered Sancho, "especially since I've got a master like your grace, who understands just what's best for me and what I can handle."

Chapter Eight

The great success won by our brave Don Quijote in his dreadful, unimaginable encounter with two windmills, plus other honorable events well worth remembering

Just then, they came upon thirty or forty windmills, which (as it happens) stand in the fields of Montiel, and as soon as Don Quijote saw them he said to his squire:

"Destiny guides our fortunes more favorably than we could have expected. Look there, Sancho Panza, my friend, and see those thirty or so wild giants, with whom I intend to do battle and to kill each and all of them, so with their stolen booty we can begin to enrich ourselves. This is noble, righteous warfare, for it is wonderfully useful to God to have such an evil race wiped from the face of the earth."

"What giants?" asked Sancho Panza.

"The ones you can see over there," answered his master, "with the huge arms, some of which are very nearly two leagues long."

"Now look, your grace," said Sancho, "what you see over there aren't giants, but windmills, and what seem to be arms are just their sails, that go around in the wind and turn the millstone."

"Obviously," replied Don Quijote, "you don't know much about adventures. Those are giants—and if you're frightened, take yourself away from here and say your prayers, while I go charging into savage and unequal combat with them."

Saying which, he spurred his horse, Rocinante, paying no attention to the shouts of Sancho Panza, his squire, warning him that without any question it was windmills and not giants he was going to attack. So utterly convinced was he they were giants, indeed, that he neither heard Sancho's cries nor noticed, close as he was, what they really were, but charged on, crying:

"Flee not, oh cowards and dastardly creatures, for he who attacks you is a knight alone and unaccompanied."

Just then the wind blew up a bit, and the great sails began to stir, which Don Quijote saw and cried out:

"Even should you shake more arms than the giant Briareo himself, you'll still have to deal with me."

As he said this, he entrusted himself with all his heart to his lady Dulcinea, imploring her to help and sustain him at such a critical moment, and then, with his shield held high and his spear braced in its socket, and Rocinante at a full gallop, he charged directly at the first windmill he came to, just as a sudden swift gust of wind sent its sail swinging hard around, smashing the spear to bits and sweeping up the knight and his horse, tumbling them all battered and bruised to the ground. Sancho Panza came rushing to his aid, as fast as his donkey could run, but when he got to his master, found him unable to move, such a blow had he been given by the falling horse.

"God help me!" said Sancho. "Didn't I tell your grace to be careful what you did, that these were just windmills, and anyone who could ignore that had to have windmills in his head?"

"Silence, Sancho, my friend," answered Don Quijote. "Even more than other things, war is subject to perpetual change. What's more, I think the truth is that the same Frestón the magician, who stole away my room and my books, transformed these giants into windmills, in order to deprive me of the glory of vanquishing them, so bitter is his hatred of me. But in the end, his evil tricks will have little power against my good sword."

"God's will be done," answered Sancho Panza.

Then, helping his master to his feet, he got him back up on Rocinante, whose shoulder was half dislocated. After which, discussing the adventure they'd just experienced, they followed the road toward Lápice Pass, for there, said Don Quijote, they couldn't fail to find adventures of all kinds, it being a well-traveled highway. But having lost his lance, he went along very sorrowfully, as he admitted to his squire, saying:

"I remember having read that a certain Spanish knight named Diego Pérez de Vargas, having lost his sword while fighting in a lost cause, pulled a thick bough, or a stem, off an oak tree, and did such things with it, that day, clubbing down so many Moors that ever afterwards they nicknamed him Machuca [Clubber], and indeed from that day on he and all his descendants bore the name Vargas y Machuca. I tell you this because, the first oak tree I come to, I plan to pull off a branch like that, one every bit as good as the huge stick I can see in my mind, and I propose to perform such deeds with it that you'll be thinking yourself blessed, having the opportunity to see them, and being a living witness to events that might otherwise be unbelievable."

"It's in God's hands," said Sancho. "I believe everything is exactly the way your grace says it is. But maybe you could sit a little straighter, because you seem to be leaning to one side, which must be because of the great fall you took."

"True," answered Don Quijote, "and if I don't say anything about the pain it's because knights errant are never supposed to complain about a wound, even if their guts are leaking through it."

"If that's how it's supposed to be," replied Sancho, "I've got nothing to say. But Lord knows I'd rather your grace told me, any time something hurts you. Me, I've got to groan, even if it's the smallest little pain, unless that rule about knights errant not complaining includes squires, too."

Don Quijote couldn't help laughing at his squire's simplicity, and cheerfully assured him he could certainly complain any time he felt like it, voluntarily or involuntarily, since in all his reading about knighthood and chivalry he'd never come across anything to the contrary. Sancho said he thought it was dinner-time. His master replied that, for the moment, he himself had no need of food, but Sancho should eat whenever he wanted to. Granted this permission, Sancho made himself as comfortable as he could while jogging along on his donkey and, taking out of his saddlebags what he had put in them, began eating as he rode, falling back a good bit behind his master, and from time to time tilting up his wine-skin with a pleasure so intense that the fanciest barman in Málaga might have envied him. And as he rode along like this, gulping quietly away, none of the promises his master had made were on his mind, nor did he feel in the least troubled or afflicted—in fact, he was thoroughly relaxed about this adventure-hunting business, no matter how dangerous it was supposed to be.

In the end, they spent that night sleeping in a wood, and Don Quijote pulled a dry branch from one of the trees, to serve him, more or less, as a lance, fitting onto it the spearhead he'd taken off the broken one. Nor did Don Quijote sleep, that whole night long, meditating on his lady Dulcinea—in order to fulfill what he'd read in his books, namely, that knights always spent long nights out in the woods and other uninhabited places, not sleeping, but happily mulling over memories of their ladies. Which wasn't the case for Sancho Panza: with his stomach full, and not just with chicory water, his dreams swept him away, nor would he have bothered waking up, for all the sunlight shining full on his face, or the birds singing—brightly, loudly greeting the coming of the new day—if his master hadn't called to him. He got up and, patting his wineskin, found it a lot flatter than it had been the night before, which grieved his heart, since it didn't look as if they'd be making up the shortage any time soon. Don Quijote had no interest in breakfast, since, as we have said, he had been sustaining himself with delightful memories. They returned to the road leading to Lápice Pass, which they could see by about three that afternoon.

"Here," said Don Quijote as soon as he saw it, "here, brother Sancho Panza, we can get our hands up to the elbows in adventures. But let me warn you: even if you see me experiencing the greatest dangers in the world, never draw your sword to defend me, unless of course you see that those who insult me are mere rabble, people of low birth, in which case you may be permitted to help me. But if they're knights, the laws of knight-hood make it absolutely illegal, without exception, for you to help me, unless you yourself have been ordained a knight."

"Don't worry, your grace," answered Sancho Panza. "You'll find me completely obedient about this, especially since I'm a very peaceful man—I don't like getting myself into quarrels and fights. On the other hand, when it comes to someone lay-ing a hand on me, I won't pay much attention to those laws, because whether they're divine or human they permit any man to defend himself when anyone hurts him."

"To be sure," answered Don Quijote. "But when it comes to helping me against other knights, you must restrain your nat-ural vigor."

"And that's what I'll do," replied Sancho. "I'll observe this rule just as carefully as I keep the sabbath."

While they were talking, they could see, coming down the road, two Benedictine friars, mounted on a pair of camels—or, at least, the mules they rode on were every bit as big. Like well-bred travelers, they were wearing dust-goggles and carrying parasols. Behind them there was a coach with four or five out-riders, mounted on mules, and two young muledrivers on foot. The coach contained, as became clear later on, a Basque lady on her way to Seville to join her husband, who was sailing for the Indies to take up a post of some distinction. The friars were not her traveling companions, although they were on the same road, but as soon as Don Quijote saw them he said to his squire:

"If I'm not mistaken, this is going to be the most famous ad-venture ever heard of, for those black forms over there must be, and indeed they are, there's no doubt about it, magicians who are spiriting away a princess in that coach, so I need to exert every bit of my strength to undo such wrongdoing."

"This is going to be worse than the windmills," said Sancho. "Now look, your grace, those are Benedictine friars, and the coach has got to belong to some well-bred lady. Listen to me: watch out, you'd better be careful—don't be fooled by the devil."

"But haven't I already told you, Sancho," answered Don Quijote, "that you don't know anything about adventures?

What I tell you is the truth, as you'll see in a moment."

Saying which, he galloped ahead and set himself in the middle of the road, right in the friars' path, and as soon as he thought they were close enough to hear what he said, he called out:

"You masked devils, you monsters! Release this very moment the noble princesses you are carrying off against their will, or else prepare yourself to die on the spot, as fit punishment for your evil deeds."

The friars pulled back on the reins and gaped—as much at Don Quijote's appearance as at what he said, to which they responded:

"Sir knight, we're not masked devils nor are we monsters, we're just two Benedictine monks riding down the road, and whether or not there are any kidnapped princesses in that coach, we have no idea."

"Don't waste soothing words on me," said Don Quijote. "I know you, you lying scum."

And without waiting for any further response, he spurred Rocinante and, lance at the ready, rushed at the first friar with such fearless courage that, had the man not dropped off the mule, he would have been thrown to the ground and probably badly wounded, if not already stone dead. The second monk, seeing how his companion had been treated, dug his spurs into his huge mule and began to gallop over the fields, faster than any wind.

Seeing the friar fall, Sancho Panza fairly leapt off his mule, went over to him, and started pulling off his robes. Just then the two young muledrivers, the friars' servants, came up and asked him why he was pulling those clothes off. Sancho told them this was his legitimate prize, as spoils of the battle won by his master, Don Quijote. The muledrivers, who had no sense of humor, and knew nothing about either booty or battle, saw that Don Quijote had already ridden on past and was speaking to the people in the coach, so they jumped on Sancho and knocked him to the ground and, barely leaving a hair in his beard, beat him and kicked him, leaving him stretched out on the ground, senseless and half-dead. Then, without losing a moment, they helped the friar to mount again—terrified, trembling, his face white as a sheet. And as soon as he was up on his mule, he spurred it right after his companion, who was waiting, a good way off, wondering how this sudden violent outburst would conclude. And then, without waiting to see how the whole affair might end, the two of them rode off down the road, making more signs of the cross than if the devil himself had been right behind them.

As we have said, Don Quijote was speaking to the lady in the coach, saying to her:

"My lady, your beauteousness is now enabled to dispose of yourself exactly as you most please, since your proud kidnappers lie in the dust, overthrown by this strong arm of mine. And lest you worry yourself about the name of your liberator, know that I am called Don Quijote de La Mancha, knight errant and soldier of fortune, and captive to the matchless and most beautiful lady, Doña Dulcinea del Toboso. In acknowledgment of the kindness I have extended to you, I ask only that you direct yourself to Toboso and present yourself to that lady on my behalf, telling her what part I have had in your liberation."

One of the mounted pages accompanying the coach, a Basque, had been listening to everything Don Quijote said, and seeing that the knight did not intend to allow the coach to continue on its way, declaring that it must turn around and go back to Toboso, rode over to Don Quijote, took hold of his lance, and said to him, in bad Spanish (and worse Basque), approximately as follows:

"Go away, wrong riding knight. By the God that made me, if you no leave coach, as I am Basque I kill you."

Don Quijote understood him very well indeed, and replied with perfect calm:

"Were you a knight, as to be sure you are not, I would already have punished you for your stupidity and insolence, you miserable creature."

To which the Basque responded:

"I no knight? I swear to God as I Christian you lie. You put down spear and draw sword, and we find out pretty damned soon who get bell onto cat. Basque on ground be gentleman on sea, by the devil, and you liar who think say other thing."

"And so, said the noble knight Agrajes, we shall see," answered Don Quijote.

And tossing his spear to the ground, he drew his sword, raised his shield, and attacked the Basque, determined to kill him. Seeing him come, the Basque would have preferred to get down from his mule, which was a rented animal he could not trust, but had no choice except to draw his own sword. Still, he was lucky enough to find himself near the coach, so he grabbed a cushion to use as a shield, and they had at it, exactly as if they'd been mortal enemies. The others tried to settle the quarrel, but couldn't, because the Basque kept saying in his broken Spanish that if they didn't let him finish his fight he'd kill his mistress and everyone else who got in his way. The lady in the coach, astonished and terrified by what she saw, directed the coachman to drive off a bit, and from that distance prepared to watch the harsh battle—and as that struggle went on, the Basque gave Don Quijote a great blow high on the shoulder, swinging over his shield, and had our knight not been in armor the thrust would have split him down to the waist. Feeling the weight of this colossal blow, Don Quijote cried out, at the top of his lungs:

"Oh lady of my soul, Dulcinea, flower of all beauty, help this knight of yours, who, to please your great goodness, now finds himself in this difficult situation!"

He said all this, and tightened his grip on his sword, and held the shield high in front of him, and attacked the Basque, all at the same time, having made up his mind to trust everything to a single blow.

Seeing him come at him this way, with such determination, the Basque perfectly well understood our knight's courage, and made up his mind to do exactly the same thing. So he held himself ready, behind his upraised coach cushion, but could not turn his mule an inch in any direction, for the animal, totally exhausted and not meant for these particular games, couldn't so much as lift a hoof.

So, as we've said, there came Don Quijote right at the wary

Basque, his sword raised high, resolved to cut the man in half, and the Basque awaited him, his sword too lifted high, and sheltering behind his cushion, and everyone around was terrified, waiting to find out what would come of the tremendous blows which each of them was threatening for the other, and the lady in the coach and all the rest of her servants were saying a thousand prayers and making vows to every holy image and sacred shrine in all of Spain, if only God would save their fellow, and them too, from the immense danger in which they found themselves.

But the trouble with all this is that, at this exact point, at these exact words, the original author of this history left the battle suspended in mid-air, excusing himself on the grounds that he himself could not find anything more written on the subject of these exploits of Don Quijote than what has already been set down. Now it's true that I, your second author, found it hard to believe that such a fascinating tale could have been simply consigned to the dust, nor that there wouldn't be clever people in La Mancha, curious to find out if in their archives, or in other documents, there wasn't something more about this famous knight. And so, with this idea in mind, I was not without hope that I'd dig up the ending of this pleasant story, which, were the judgment of Heaven favorable, I proposed to narrate as, in fact, you may hereafter find it narrated in Part Two.

Translated from the Spanish by Burton Raffel

Leo Tolstoy
(1828–1910)

When Count Leo Nikolayevich Tolstoy died, he may have been the most famous man in the Western world. A great writer and a prominent social reformer, he is still, to this day, a giant of Russian literature.

Tolstoy was born into wealth and aristocracy. Orphaned at age nine, he and his brothers and sister were raised by aunts on the family estate. As Tolstoy grew into young manhood, he at first led an aimless life, piling up gambling debts and frittering away much of his inheritance.

Seeking adventure, Tolstoy joined the army and fought bravely during the Crimean War. But this experience exposed the wealthy young man to a degree of suffering he had never seen before. He returned home a more serious person, even opening a school on his estate for his serfs' children. Tolstoy became obsessed with social and spiritual reform.

Tolstoy's long-suffering wife, Sonya Bers, bore her husband thirteen children, recopied his illegible manuscripts, and took over the management of his estate. It was Sonya who enabled him to write his greatest novels, *War and Peace* and *Anna Karenina*.

By age fifty, Tolstoy had reached a moral and spiritual crisis. Aspiring to be holy and to do good, he found his best models not in other writers and philosophers, but in Russia's self-sufficient peasants. He condemned private ownership of property, capitalism, the Russian Orthodox Church, and Russia's czarist government. Tolstoy even repudiated his two great novels for their "bourgeois" preoccupation with the aristocracy. He transferred management of his estate to his family, renounced smoking, drinking, and eating meat, and engaged in manual labor so that he would not profit from the toil of others. He turned from complex tales of unhappy upper-class people to stories about the virtues of love and honest labor.

Visitors from all over the world came to Tolstoy's home to honor the great man. He tried to live the simple life, but fame and public attention got in the way. Finally, at eighty-two, Tolstoy resolved to seek a place where he could live a poor, reclusive life. He fled his home and family in secret one night, with his doctor and his youngest daughter. At a remote railroad station, the fugitives got off the train, and Tolstoy, by then ill with a high fever, was taken to the stationmaster's house. There, Tolstoy died of pneumonia.

His death was announced in headlines all over the world, and his fame outlived his attempt to escape it. Although Tolstoy was a pacifist and a Christian, the Communist leaders of Russia, like their czarist predecessors, never banned his books. His rural grave is a major tourist attraction, and his house in Moscow is now the Tolstoy Museum.

Alyosha the Pot
Leo Tolstoy

A lyosha was a younger brother. He was nicknamed "the Pot," because once, when his mother sent him with a pot of milk for the deacon's wife, he stumbled and broke it. His mother thrashed him soundly, and the children in the village began to tease him, calling him "the Pot." Alyosha the Pot: and this is how he got his nickname.

Alyosha was a skinny little fellow, lop-eared—his ears stuck out like wings—and with a large nose. The children always teased him about this, too, saying "Alyosha has a nose like a gourd on a pole!"

There was a school in the village where Alyosha lived, but reading and writing and such did not come easy for him, and besides there was no time to learn. His older brother lived with a merchant in town, and Alyosha had begun helping his father when still a child. When he was only six years old, he was already watching over his family's cow and sheep with his younger sister in the common pasture. And long before he was grown, he had started taking care of their horses day and night. From his twelfth year he plowed and carted. He hardly had the strength for all these chores, but he did have a certain manner—he was always cheerful. When the children laughed at him, he fell silent or laughed himself. If his father cursed him, he stood quietly and listened. And when they finished and ignored him again, he smiled and went back to whatever task was before him.

When Alyosha was nineteen years old, his brother was taken into the army; and his father arranged for Alyosha to take his brother's place as a servant in the merchant's household. He was given his brother's old boots and his father's cap and coat and was taken into town. Alyosha was very pleased with his new clothes, but the merchant was quite dissatisfied with his appearance.

"I thought you would bring me a young man just like Semyon," said the merchant, looking Alyosha over carefully. "But you've brought me such a sniveller. What's he good for?"

"Ah, he can do anything—harness and drive anywhere you like. And he's a glutton for work. Only looks like a stick. He's really very wiry."

"That much is plain. Well, we shall see."

"And above all he's a meek one. Loves to work."

"Well, what can I do? Leave him."

And so Alyosha began to live with the merchant.

The merchant's family was not large. There were his wife, his old mother and three children. His older married son, who had only completed grammar school, was in business with his father. His other son, a studious sort, had been graduated from the high school and was for a time at the university, though he had been expelled and now lived at home. And there was a daughter, too, a young girl in the high school.

At first they did not like Alyosha. He was too much the peasant and was poorly dressed. He had no manners and addressed everyone familiarly as in the country. But soon they grew used to him. He was a better servant than his brother and was always very responsive. Whatever they set him to do he did willingly and quickly, moving from one task to another without stopping. And at the merchant's, just as at home, all the work was given to Alyosha. The more he did, the more everyone heaped upon him. The mistress of the household and her old mother-in-law, and the daughter, and the younger son, even the merchant's clerk and the cook—all sent him here and sent him there and ordered him to do everything that they could think of. The only thing that Alyosha ever heard was "Run do this, fellow," or "Alyosha, fix this up now," or "Did you forget, Alyosha? Look here, fellow, don't you forget!" And Alyosha ran, and fixed, and looked, and did not forget, and managed to do everything and smiled all the while.

Alyosha soon wore out his brother's boots, and the merchant scolded him sharply for walking about in tatters with his bare feet sticking out and ordered him to buy new boots in the market. These boots were truly new, and Alyosha was very happy with them; but his feet remained old all the same, and by evening they ached so from running that he got mad at them. Alyosha was afraid that when his father came to collect his wages, he would be very annoyed that the master had deducted the cost of the new boots from his pay.

In winter Alyosha got up before dawn, chopped firewood, swept out the courtyard, fed grain to the cow and the horses and watered them. Afterwards, he lit the stoves, cleaned the boots and coats of all the household, got out the samovars and polished them. Then, either the clerk called him into the shop to take out the wares or the cook ordered him to knead the dough and to wash the pans. And later he would be sent into town with a message, or to the school for the daughter, or to fetch lamp oil or something else for the master's old mother. "Where have you been loafing, you worthless thing?" one would say to him, and then another. Or among themselves they would say, "Why go yourself? Alyosha will run for you. Alyosha, Alyosha!" And Alyosha would run.

Alyosha always ate breakfast on the run and was seldom in time for dinner. The cook was always chiding him, because he never took meals with the others, but for all that she did feel sorry for him and always left him something hot for dinner and for supper.

Before and during holidays there was a lot more work for Alyosha, though he was happier during holidays, because then everyone gave him tips, not much, only about sixty kopeks usually; but it was his own money, which he could spend as he chose. He never laid eyes on his wages, for his father always came into town and took from the merchant Alyosha's pay, giving him only the rough edge of his tongue for wearing out his brother's boots too quickly. When he had saved two rubles altogether from tips, Alyosha bought on the cook's advice a red knitted sweater. When he put it on for the first time and looked down at himself, he was so surprised and delighted that he just stood in the kitchen gaping and gulping.

Alyosha said very little, and when he did speak, it was always to say something necessary abruptly and briefly. And when he was told to do something or other or was asked if he could do it, he always answered without the slightest hesitation, "I can do it." And he would immediately throw himself into the job and do it.

Alyosha did not know how to pray at all. His mother had once taught him the words, but he had forgot even as she spoke. Nonetheless, he did pray, morning and evening, but simply, just with his hands, crossing himself.

Thus Alyosha lived for a year and a half, and then, during the second half of the second year, the most unusual experience of his life occurred. This experience was his sudden discovery, to his complete amazement, that besides those relationships between people that arise from the need that one may have for another, there also exist other relationships that are completely different: not a relationship that a person has with another because that other is needed to clean boots, to run errands or to harness horses; but a relationship that a person has with another who is in no way necessary to him, simply because that other one wants to serve him and to be loving to him. And he discovered, too, that he, Alyosha, was just such a person. He realized all this through the cook Ustinja. Ustinja was an orphan, a young girl yet, and as hard a worker as Alyosha. She began to feel sorry for Alyosha, and Alyosha for the first time in his life felt that he himself, not his services, but he himself was needed by another person. When his mother had been kind to him or had felt sorry for him, he took no notice of it, because it seemed to him so natural a thing, just the same as if he felt sorry for himself. But suddenly he realized that Ustinja, though completely a stranger, felt sorry for him, too. She always left him a pot of kasha with butter, and when he ate, she sat with him, watching him with her chin propped upon her fist. And when he looked up at her and she smiled, he, too, smiled.

It was all so new and so strange that at first Alyosha was frightened. He felt that it disturbed his work, his serving, but he was nonetheless very happy. And when he happened to look down and notice his trousers, which Ustinja had mended for him, he would shake his head and smile. Often while he was working or running an errand, he would think of Ustinja and mutter warmly, "Ah, that Ustinja!" Ustinja helped him as best she could, and he helped her. She told him all about her life, how she had been orphaned when very young, how an old aunt had taken her in, how this aunt later sent her into town to work, how the merchant's son had tried stupidly to seduce her, and how she put him in his place. She loved to talk, and he found listening to her very pleasant. Among other things he heard that in town it often happened that peasant boys who came to serve in households would marry the cooks. And once she asked him if his parents would marry him off soon. He replied that he didn't know and that there was no one in his village whom he wanted.

"What, then, have you picked out someone else?" she asked.

"Yes. I'd take you. Will you?"

"O Pot, my Pot, how cunningly you put it to me!" she said, cuffing him playfully on the back with her ladle.

At Shrovetide Alyosha's old father came into town again to collect his son's wages. The merchant's wife had found out that Alyosha planned to marry Ustinja, and she was not at all pleased. "She will just get pregnant, and then what good will she be!" she complained to her husband.

The merchant counted out Alyosha's money to his father. "Well, is my boy doing all right by you?" asked the old man. "I told you he was a meek one, would do anything you say."

"Meek or no, he's done something stupid. He has got it into his head to marry the cook. And I will not keep married servants. It doesn't suit us."

"Eh, that little fool! What a fool! How can he think to do such a stupid thing! But don't worry over it. I'll make him forget all that nonsense."

The old man walked straight into the kitchen and sat down

at the table to wait for his son. Alyosha was, as always, running an errand, but he soon came in all out of breath.

"Well, I thought you were a sensible fellow, but what nonsense you've thought up!" Alyosha's father greeted him.

"I've done nothing."

"What d'you mean nothing! You've decided to marry. I'll marry you when the time comes, and I'll marry you to whoever I want, not to some town slut."

The old man said a great deal more of the same sort. Alyosha stood quietly and sighed. When his father finished, he smiled.

"So I'll forget about it," he said.

"See that you do right now," the old man said curtly as he left.

When his father had gone and Alyosha remained alone with Ustinja, who had been standing behind the kitchen door listening while his father was talking, he said to her: "Our plan won't work out. Did you hear? He was furious, won't let us."

Ustinja began to cry quietly into her apron. Alyosha clucked his tongue and said, "How could I not obey him? Look, we must forget all about it."

In the evening, when the merchant's wife called him to close the shutters, she said to him, "Are you going to obey your father and forget all this nonsense about marrying?"

"Yes. Of course. I've forgot it," Alyosha said quickly, then smiled and immediately began weeping.

From that time Alyosha did not speak again to Ustinja about marriage and lived as he had before.

One morning during Lent the clerk sent Alyosha to clear the snow off the roof. He crawled up onto the roof, shovelled it clean and began to break up the frozen snow near the gutters when his feet slipped out from under him and he fell headlong with his shovel. As ill luck would have it, he fell not into the snow, but onto an entry-way with an iron railing. Ustinja ran up to him, followed by the merchant's daughter.

"Are you hurt, Alyosha?"

"Yes. But it's nothing. Nothing."

He wanted to get up, but he could not and just smiled. Others came and carried him down into the yard-keeper's lodge. An orderly from the hospital arrived, examined him and asked where he hurt. "It hurts all over," he replied. "But it's nothing. Nothing. Only the master will be annoyed. Must send word to Papa."

Alyosha lay abed for two full days, and then, on the third day, they sent for a priest.

"You're not going to die, are you?" asked Ustinja.

"Well, we don't all live forever. It must be some time," he answered quickly, as always. "Thank you, dear Ustinja, for feeling sorry for me. See, it's better they didn't let us marry, for nothing would have come of it. And now all is fine."

He prayed with the priest, but only with his hands and with his heart. And in his heart he felt that if he was good here, if he obeyed and did not offend, then there all would be well.

He said little. He only asked for something to drink and smiled wonderingly. Then he seemed surprised at something, and stretched out and died.

Translated from the Russian by S. A. Carmack

Nelson Mandela
(1918–   )

Nelson Mandela was born to be a leader. The great-grandson of a king and the son of a village headman, he began life in a small village in Thembuland, in the Transkei territory of South Africa, eight years after the country became a British colony. Mandela's original African name was Rolihlahla, which means "troublemaker"—a prophetic choice, according to members of his family. (When he started school, an African teacher renamed him "Nelson," presumably in honor of the British naval hero Lord Horatio Nelson.)

Mandela remembers his childhood as a happy balance of discipline and love. When he was about ten, his father died, and the boy became the ward of the Thembu king. He was raised with the king's son and prepared to become an adviser to the royal family of the Thembu tribe. At missionary school, however, Mandela was exposed for the first time to customs other than those of the Thembu tribe, and his horizons widened. Opting not to join the Thembu tribal leadership, he instead earned a law degree and opened the first black law partnership in South Africa when he was twenty-four.

Two years later, the young lawyer took a step that changed the course of his life: He joined the African National Congress, a black nationalist movement. The ANC actively advocated the end of apartheid (ə·pär'tāt'), the inhuman South African system of laws that mandated racial separation. As a result of his activities with the ANC, Mandela was tried for treason but finally acquitted. At first, Mandela supported the ANC in its nonviolent resistance to the government's apartheid policies. Then, as a result of the massacre of unarmed African resisters by the police at Sharpeville and the banning of the ANC in 1960, Mandela became an advocate of violence to sabotage the white government's authority. He was imprisoned, and when the police found an arsenal of ammunition and bombs in an ANC hideout, Mandela was tried for treason again and this time was sentenced to life imprisonment.

During his time in prison, Mandela became a symbol of the black liberation movement in South Africa, and his prison writings were published throughout the world. Finally, in 1990, the ANC was recognized, and after twenty-seven years in prison, Mandela was released. In the following year, Mandela was elected president of the ANC and agreed to end the organization's use of violence to oppose the government. During these years, as a result of negotiations led by Mandela, the government finally put an end to apartheid. In 1994, when South Africa held the first elections in which all races could vote, the ANC won a majority, and Mandela became the first black president of his country. He was seventy-six years old.

from Long Walk to Freedom
Nelson Mandela

In 1994, Mandela published his autobiography, Long
Walk to Freedom. *In it, he chronicles the three stages
of his life—first as a law-abiding citizen, then as an
outlaw and prisoner opposing government policies, and
lastly as a freed man and the president of his country.*

*In this excerpt from the end of the book, Mandela
discusses the deep and lasting effect that apartheid
policies have had on him as a human being and on his
country and its people.*

The policy of apartheid created a deep and lasting wound
in my country and my people. All of us will spend many
years, if not generations, recovering from that profound hurt.
But the decades of oppression and brutality had another, un-
intended effect, and that was that it produced the Oliver
Tambos, the Walter Sisulus, the Chief Luthuäs, the Yusuf
Dadoos, the Bram Fischers, the Robert Sobukwes of our time—
men of such extraordinary courage, wisdom, and generosity
that their like may never be known again. Perhaps it requires
such depth of oppression to create such heights of character.
My country is rich in the minerals and gems that lie beneath
its soil, but I have always known that its greatest wealth is its
people, finer and truer than the purest diamonds.

It is from these comrades in the struggle that I learned the
meaning of courage. Time and again, I have seen men and
women risk and give their lives for an idea. I have seen men
stand up to attacks and torture without breaking, showing a
strength and resiliency that defies the imagination. I learned
that courage was not the absence of fear, but the triumph over

it. I felt fear myself more times than I can remember, but I hid it behind a mask of boldness. The brave man is not he who does not feel afraid, but he who conquers that fear.

I never lost hope that this great transformation would occur. Not only because of the great heroes I have already cited, but because of the courage of the ordinary men and women of my country. I always knew that deep down in every human heart, there is mercy and generosity. No one is born hating another person because of the color of his skin, or his background, or his religion. People must learn to hate, and if they can learn to hate, they can be taught to love, for love comes more naturally to the human heart than its opposite. Even in the grimmest times in prison, when my comrades and I were pushed to our limits, I would see a glimmer of humanity in one of the guards, perhaps just for a second, but it was enough to reassure me and keep me going. Man's goodness is a flame that can be hidden but never extinguished.

We took up the struggle with our eyes wide open, under no illusion that the path would be an easy one. As a young man, when I joined the African National Congress, I saw the price my comrades paid for their beliefs, and it was high. For myself, I have never regretted my commitment to the struggle, and I was always prepared to face the hardships that affected me personally. But my family paid a terrible price, perhaps too dear a price for my commitment.

In life, every man has twin obligations—obligations to his family, to his parents, to his wife and children; and he has an obligation to his people, his community, his country. In a civil and humane society, each man is able to fulfill those obligations according to his own inclinations and abilities. But in a country like South Africa, it was almost impossible for a man of my birth and color to fulfill both of those obligations. In South Africa, a man of color who attempted to live as a human being was punished and isolated. In South Africa, a man who tried to fulfill his duty to his people was inevitably ripped from his family and his home and was forced to live a life apart, a twilight existence of secrecy and rebellion. I did not in the beginning choose to place my people above my family, but in attempting to serve my people, I found that I was prevented from fulfilling my obligations as a son, a brother, a father, and a husband.

In that way, my commitment to my people, to the millions of South Africans I would never know or meet, was at the expense of the people I knew best and loved most. It was as simple and yet as incomprehensible as the moment a small child asks her father, "Why can you not be with us?" And the father must utter the terrible words: "There are other children like you, a great many of them . . ." and then one's voice trails off.

I was not born with a hunger to be free. I was born free—free in every way that I could know. Free to run in the fields near my mother's hut, free to swim in the clear stream that ran through my village, free to roast mealies under the stars and ride the broad backs of slow-moving bulls. As long as I obeyed my father and abided by the customs of my tribe, I was not troubled by the laws of man or God.

It was only when I began to learn that my boyhood freedom was an illusion, when I discovered as a young man that my freedom had already been taken from me, that I began to hunger for it. At first, as a student, I wanted freedom only for myself, the transitory freedoms of being able to stay out at night, read what I pleased, and go where I chose. Later, as a young man in Johannesburg, I yearned for the basic and honorable freedoms of achieving my potential, of earning my keep, of marrying and having a family—the freedom not to be obstructed in a lawful life.

But then I slowly saw that not only was I not free, but my brothers and sisters were not free. I saw that it was not just my freedom that was curtailed, but the freedom of everyone who looked like I did. That is when I joined the African National Congress, and that is when the hunger for my own freedom became the greater hunger for the freedom of my people. It was this desire for the freedom of my people to live their lives with dignity and self-respect that animated my life, that transformed a frightened young man into a bold one, that drove a law-abiding attorney to become a criminal, that turned a family-loving husband into a man without a home, that forced a life-loving man to live like a monk. I am no more virtuous or self-sacrificing than the next man, but I found that I could not even enjoy the poor and limited freedoms I was allowed when I knew my people were not free. Freedom is indivisible; the chains on any one of my people were the chains on all of them, the chains on all of my people were the chains on me.

It was during those long and lonely years that my hunger for the freedom of my own people became a hunger for the freedom of all people, white and black. I knew as well as I knew anything that the oppressor must be liberated just as surely as the oppressed. A man who takes away another man's freedom is a prisoner of hatred, he is locked behind the bars of prejudice and narrow-mindedness. I am not truly free if I am taking away someone else's freedom, just as surely as I am not free when my freedom is taken from me. The oppressed and the oppressor alike are robbed of their humanity.

When I walked out of prison, that was my mission, to liberate the oppressed and the oppressor both. Some say that has now been achieved. But I know that that is not the case. The truth is that we are not yet free; we have merely achieved the freedom to be free, the right not to be oppressed. We have not taken the final step of our journey, but the first step on a longer and even more difficult road. For to be free is not merely to cast off one's chains, but to live in a way that respects and enhances the freedom of others. The true test of our devotion to freedom is just beginning.

I have walked that long road to freedom. I have tried not to falter; I have made missteps along the way. But I have discovered the secret that after climbing a great hill, one only finds that there are many more hills to climb. I have taken a moment here to rest, to steal a view of the glorious vista that surrounds me, to look back on the distance I have come. But I can rest only for a moment, for with freedom come responsibilities, and I dare not linger, for my long walk is not yet ended.

THE WORLD
OF
IRONY

Guy de Maupassant
(1850–1893)

Few writers have ever worked harder to master their craft, or succeeded more spectacularly, than Guy de Maupassant. Over a century after his death, his stories still set a standard of excellence for writers of short fiction.

Maupassant was born into a family of rural merchants in the French province of Normandy, which later became the setting for much of his fiction. His parents separated when he was young, and he was raised by his mother, who encouraged him to write from an early age. More encouragement came from the many artists and writers among the family's friends, including the great novelist Gustave Flaubert.

In school, Maupassant was known as something of a rebel. In his late teens, he joined the French army, accepting the discipline of army life and serving during the Franco-Prussian War. Afterward he entered law school. In his free time, he kept writing.

When Maupassant moved to Paris to take a job with the government, he reestablished contact with Flaubert. Flaubert invited Maupassant to join a group of several prominent Realist writers who met at his house to discuss literature. Under the influence of his new friends, Maupassant began focusing on realistic prose fiction. Flaubert wanted his young protégé to understand that good writing depends on seeing things anew rather than recording what others have thought. Flaubert was also strict about word choice: "Whatever you want to say, there is only one word to express it, only one verb to give it movement, only one adjective to qualify it."

When his story "Ball of Fat" won critical acclaim in 1880, Maupassant turned all his energy to writing. Within only a few years, he became enormously popular. For eleven years, he wrote at a hectic pace, producing nearly three hundred stories and six novels. In 1883 alone, he turned out two novels and seventy short stories. Periodicals snapped up his stories.

Maupassant's stories are known for their minute realistic details, their concentration on essentials, and their ironic plot twists. The conciseness of the stories stems partly from the fact that they were originally published in newspapers, which severely restricted their length. Maupassant used the restrictions to his advantage: By the deft selection of details, he gives individuality to characters who also represent distinct social types. Maupassant's stories also reveal a bitter attitude toward life. He was especially hard on middle-class "respectability," sentimentality, reactionaries, and women.

By his late thirties, Maupassant was nearly blind from overwork and disease. Painkilling drugs made his health worse. His short story "The Horla," which has been called one of the most terrifying stories of madness ever written, foretold Maupassant's own fate. The end of 1891 brought a complete mental breakdown, from which he never recovered. The great writer died in a Paris asylum before his forty-third birthday.

The Piece of String
Guy de Maupassant

On all the roads around Goderville the peasants and their wives were making their way toward the little town, for it was market day. The men were plodding along, their bodies leaning forward with every movement of their long bandy legs—legs deformed by hard work, by the pressure of the plow which also raises the left shoulder and twists the spine, by the spreading of the knees required to obtain a firm stance for reaping, and by all the slow, laborious tasks of country life. Their blue starched smocks, shining as if they were varnished, and decorated with a little pattern in white embroidery on the collar and cuffs, bellied out around their bony frames like balloons ready to fly away, with a head, two arms and two feet sticking out of each one.

Some were leading a cow or a calf by a rope, while their wives hurried the animal on by whipping its haunches with a leafy branch. The women carried large baskets on their arms from which protruded the heads of chickens or ducks. And they walked with a shorter, brisker step than their husbands, their gaunt, erect figures wrapped in skimpy little shawls pinned across their flat chests and their heads wrapped in tight-fitting white coifs topped with bonnets.

Then a cart went by, drawn at a trot by a small horse, with two men sitting side by side bumping up and down and a woman at the back holding on to the sides to lessen the jolts.

The square in Goderville was crowded with a confused mass of animals and human beings. The horns of the bullocks, the tall beaver hats of the well-to-do peasants, and the coifs of the peasant women stood out above the throng. And the high-pitched, shrill, yapping voices made a wild, continuous din, dominated now and then by a great deep-throated roar of laughter from a jovial countryman or the long lowing of a cow tied to the wall of a house.

Everywhere was the smell of cowsheds and milk and manure, of hay and sweat, that sharp, unpleasant odor of men and animals which is peculiar to people who work on the land.

Maître Hauchecorne of Bréauté had just arrived in Goderville and was making his way toward the market square when he caught sight of a small piece of string on the ground. Maître Hauchecorne, a thrifty man like all true Normans, reflected that anything which might come in useful was worth picking up, so he bent down—though with some difficulty, for he suffered from rheumatism. He picked up the piece of thin cord and was about to roll it up carefully when he noticed Maître Malandain, the saddler, standing at his door watching him. They had had a quarrel some time before over a halter and they had remained on bad terms ever since, both of them being the sort to nurse a grudge. Maître Hauchecorne felt a little shamefaced at being seen by his enemy like this, picking a bit of string up out of the muck. He hurriedly concealed his find, first under his smock, then in his trouser pocket; then he pretended to go on looking for something on the ground which he couldn't find, before continuing on his way to the square, leaning forward, bent double by his rheumatism.

He was promptly lost in the noisy slow-moving crowd, in which everyone was engaged in endless and excited bargaining. The peasants were prodding the cows, walking away and coming back in an agony of indecision, always afraid of being taken in and never daring to make up their minds, watching the vendor's eyes, and perpetually trying to spot the man's trick and the animal's defect.

After putting their big baskets down at their feet, the women had taken out their fowls, which now lay on the ground, tied by their legs, their eyes terrified and their combs scarlet. They listened to the offers they were made and either stuck to their price, hard-faced and impassive, or else, suddenly deciding to accept the lower figure offered, shouted after the customer who was slowly walking away: "All right, Maître Anthime, it's yours."

Then, little by little, the crowd in the square thinned out, and as the Angelus rang for noon, those who lived too far away to go home disappeared into the various inns.

At Jourdain's the main room was crowded with people eating, while the vast courtyard was full of vehicles of all sorts—carts, gigs, wagons, tilburies, and indescribable shandrydans, yellow with dung, broken down and patched together, raising their shafts to heaven like a pair of arms, or else heads down and bottoms up.

Close to the people sitting at table, the bright fire blazing in the huge fireplace was scorching the backs of the row on the right. Three spits were turning, carrying chickens, pigeons, and legs of mutton; and a delicious smell of meat roasting and gravy trickling over browning flesh rose from the hearth, raising people's spirits and making their mouths water.

All the aristocracy of the plow took its meals at Maître Jourdain's. Innkeeper and horse dealer, he was a cunning rascal who had made his pile.

Dishes were brought in and emptied, as were the jugs of yellow cider. Everybody talked about the business he had done, what he had bought and sold. News and views were exchanged about the crops. The weather was good for the greens but rather damp for the wheat.

All of a sudden the roll of a drum sounded in the courtyard in front of the inn. Except for one or two who showed no interest, everybody jumped up and ran to the door or windows with his mouth still full and his napkin in his hand.

After finishing his roll on the drum, the town crier made the following pronouncement, speaking in a jerky manner and pausing in the wrong places: "Let it be known to the inhabitants of Goderville, and in general to all—persons present at the market that there was lost this morning, on the Beuzeville road, between—nine and ten o'clock, a black leather wallet containing five hundred francs and some business documents. Anybody finding the same is asked to bring it immediately—

to the town hall or to return it to Maître Fortuné Houlbrèque of Manneville. There will be a reward of twenty francs."

Then the man went away. The dull roll of the drum and the faint voice of the town crier could be heard once again in the distance.

Everybody began talking about the incident, estimating Maître Houlbrèque's chances of recovering or not recovering his wallet.

The meal came to an end.

They were finishing their coffee when the police sergeant appeared at the door and asked: "Is Maître Hauchecorne of Bréauté here?"

Maître Hauchecorne, who was sitting at the far end of the table, replied: "Yes, here I am."

The sergeant went on: "Maître Hauchecorne, will you be good enough to come with me to the town hall? The Mayor would like to have a word with you."

The peasant, surprised and a little worried, tossed down his glass of brandy, stood up, and even more bent than in the morning, for the first few steps after a rest were especially difficult, set off after the sergeant, repeating: "Here I am, here I am."

The Mayor was waiting for him, sitting in an armchair. He was the local notary, a stout, solemn individual, with a penchant for pompous phrases.

"Maître Hauchecorne," he said, "you were seen this morning, on the Beuzeville road, picking up the wallet lost by Maître Houlbrèque of Manneville."

The peasant gazed in astonishment at the Mayor, already frightened by this suspicion which had fallen upon him, without understanding why.

"Me? I picked up the wallet?"

"Yes, you."

"Honest, I don't know nothing about it."

"You were seen."

"I were seen? Who seen me?"

"Monsieur Malandain, the saddler."

Then the old man remembered, understood, and flushed with anger.

"So he seen me, did he, the bastard! He seen me pick up this bit of string, Mayor—look!"

And rummaging in his pocket, he pulled out the little piece of string.

But the Mayor shook his head incredulously.

"You'll never persuade me, Maître Hauchcorne, that Monsieur Malandain, who is a man who can be trusted, mistook that piece of string for a wallet."

The peasant angrily raised his hand and spat on the floor as proof of his good faith, repeating: "But it's God's truth, honest it is! Not a word of it's a lie, so help me God!"

The Mayor went on: "After picking up the object you even went on hunting about in the mud for some time to see whether some coin might not have fallen out."

The old fellow was almost speechless with fear and indignation.

"Making up . . . making up . . . lies like that to damn an honest man! Making up lies like that!"

In spite of all his protestations, the Mayor did not believe him.

He was confronted with Maître Malandain, who repeated and maintained his statement. They hurled insults at each other for an hour. Maître Hauchecorne was searched, at his own request. Nothing was found on him.

Finally the Mayor, not knowing what to think, sent him away, warning him that he was going to report the matter to the public prosecutor and ask for instructions.

The news had spread. As he left the town hall, the old man was surrounded by people who questioned him with a curiosity which was sometimes serious, sometimes ironical, but in which there was no indignation. He started telling the story of the piece of string. Nobody believed him. Everybody laughed.

As he walked along, other people stopped him, and he stopped his acquaintances, repeating his story and his protestations over and over again, and showing his pockets turned inside out to prove that he had got nothing.

Everybody said: "Get along with you, you old rascal!"

And he lost his temper, irritated, angered, and upset because nobody would believe him. Not knowing what to do, he simply went on repeating his story.

Darkness fell. It was time to go home. He set off with three of his neighbors to whom he pointed out the place where he had picked up the piece of string; and all the way home he talked of nothing else.

In the evening he took a turn round the village of Bréauté in order to tell everybody his story. He met with nothing but incredulity.

He felt ill all night as a result.

The next day, about one o'clock in the afternoon, Marius Paumelle, a laborer on Maître Breton's farm at Ymauville, returned the wallet and its contents to Maître Houlbrèque of Manneville.

The man claimed to have found the object on the road; but, as he could not read, he had taken it home and given it to his employer.

The news spread round the neighborhood and reached the ears of Maître Hauchecorne. He immediately went out and about repeating his story, this time with its sequel. He was triumphant.

"What really got my goat," he said, "wasn't so much the thing itself, if you see what I mean, but the lies. There's nothing worse than being blamed on account of a lie."

He talked about his adventure all day; he told the story to people he met on the road, to people drinking in the inn, to people coming out of church the following Sunday. He stopped total strangers and told it to them. His mind was at rest now, and yet something still bothered him without his knowing exactly what it was. People seemed to be amused as they listened to him. They didn't appear to be convinced. He had the impression that remarks were being made behind his back.

The following Tuesday he went to the Goderville market, simply because he felt an urge to tell his story.

Malandain, standing at his door, burst out laughing when he saw him go by. Why?

He accosted a farmer from Criquetot, who didn't let him finish his story, but gave him a dig in the ribs and shouted at him: "Go on, you old rogue!" Then he turned on his heels.

Maître Hauchecorne was taken aback and felt increasingly uneasy. Why had he been called an old rogue?

Once he had sat down at table in Jourdain's inn, he started explaining the whole business all over again.

A horse dealer from Montivilliers called out to him: "Get along with you, you old rascal! I know your little game with the bit of string."

Hauchecorne stammered: "But they found the wallet!"

The other man retorted: "Give over, Grandpa! Him as brings a thing back isn't always him as finds it. But mum's the word!"

The peasant was speechless. At last he understood. He was being accused of getting an accomplice to return the wallet.

He tried to protest, but the whole table burst out laughing.

He couldn't finish his meal and went off in the midst of jeers and laughter.

He returned home ashamed and indignant, choking with anger and embarrassment, all the more upset in that he was quite capable, with his Norman cunning, of doing what he was accused of having done, and even of boasting of it as a clever trick. He dimly realized that, since his duplicity was widely known, it was impossible to prove his innocence. And the injustice of the suspicion cut him to the quick.

Then he began telling the story all over again, making it longer every day, adding fresh arguments at every telling, more energetic protestations, more solemn oaths, which he thought out and prepared in his hours of solitude, for he could think of nothing else but the incident of the piece of string. The more complicated his defense became, and the more subtle his arguments, the less people believed him.

"Them's a liar's arguments," people used to say behind his back.

Realizing what was happening, he ate his heart out, exhausting himself in futile efforts.

He started visibly wasting away.

The local wags now used to get him to tell the story of the piece of string to amuse them, as people get an old soldier to talk about his battles. His mind, seriously affected, began to give way.

Towards the end of December he took to his bed.

He died early in January, and in the delirium of his death agony he kept on protesting his innocence, repeating over and over again: "A bit of string . . . a little bit of string . . . look, Mayor, here it is . . ."

Translated from the French by Roger Colet

Nadine Gordimer
(1923–   )

Shortly after winning the 1991 Nobel Prize in literature, Nadine Gordimer commented, "I began to write . . . out of a sense of wonderment about life . . . trying to make sense out of the mystery of life. That hasn't changed in all the years that I've been writing. That is the starting point of everything that I write."

Gordimer was born in Springs, a small town near Johannesburg, on the gold-mining ridge that has yielded much of South Africa's wealth. Gordimer grew up in a middle-class family in a repressive colonial society that imitated European conventions and values. She has said that she spent a great deal of her childhood reading because the atmosphere was so dull.

At the age of nine, considered sickly, Gordimer was taken out of school for a time. It was then that she started writing. At fifteen she published her first story in a Johannesburg weekly journal. Her first internationally published short-story collection, *The Soft Voice of the Serpent*, appeared in 1952. ("The Train from Rhodesia" is taken from that collection.)

The characters in Gordimer's stories and novels are shaped in part by apartheid, South Africa's harshly maintained separation of races. For over forty years, Gordimer's fiction became a quiet but insistent force in the struggle against apartheid.

Perhaps one of Gordimer's greatest achievements is her ability to treat South Africa's problems from a literary rather than a political perspective. "I don't understand politics except in terms of what politics does to influence lives," Gordimer once explained. "What interests me is the infinite variety of effects apartheid has on men and women."

Although Gordimer is respected around the world, she was a thorn in the side of her own country's government when apartheid was still in effect. Three of her novels were banned in

South Africa. Nevertheless, Gordimer has always considered herself an "intensely loyal" South African. She has said, "I care deeply for my country. If I didn't, I wouldn't still be here."

The Train from Rhodesia
Nadine Gordimer

The train came out of the red horizon and bore down to-wards them over the single straight track.

The stationmaster came out of his little brick station with its pointed chalet roof, feeling the creases in his serge uniform in his legs as well. A stir of preparedness rippled through the squatting native venders waiting in the dust; the face of a carved wooden animal, eternally surprised, stuck out of a sack. The stationmaster's barefoot children wandered over. From the grey mud huts with the untidy heads that stood within a dec-orated mud wall, chickens, and dogs with their skin stretched like parchment over their bones, followed the piccanins down to the track. The flushed and perspiring west cast a reflection, faint, without heat, upon the station, upon the tin shed marked "Goods," upon the walled kraal, upon the grey tin house of the stationmaster and upon the sand, that lapped all around from sky to sky, cast little rhythmical cups of shadow, so that the sand became the sea, and closed over the children's black feet softly and without imprint.

The stationmaster's wife sat behind the mesh of her veranda. Above her head the hunk of a sheep's carcass moved slightly, dangling in a current of air.

They waited.

The train called out, along the sky; but there was no answer; and the cry hung on: I'm coming ... I'm coming ...

The engine flared out now, big, whisking a dwindling body behind it; the track flared out to let it in.

Creaking, jerking, jostling, gasping, the train filled the station.

Here, let me see that one—the young woman curved her body farther out of the corridor window. Missus? smiled the old man, looking at the creatures he held in his hand. From a piece of string on his grey finger hung a tiny woven basket; he lifted it, questioning. No, no, she urged, leaning down towards him, across the height of the train towards the man in the piece of old rug; that one, that one, her hand commanded. It was a lion, carved out of soft dry wood that looked like spongecake; heraldic, black and white, with impressionistic detail burnt in. The old man held it up to her still smiling, not from the heart, but at the customer. Between its vandyke teeth, in the mouth opened in an endless roar too terrible to be heard, it had a black tongue. Look, said the young husband, if you don't mind! And round the neck of the thing, a piece of fur (rat? rabbit? meerkat?); a real mane, majestic, telling you somehow that the artist had delight in the lion.

All up and down the length of the train in the dust the artists sprang, walking bent, like performing animals, the better to exhibit the fantasy held towards the faces on the train. Buck, startled and stiff, staring with round black and white eyes. More lions, standing erect, grappling with strange, thin, elongated warriors who clutched spears and showed no fear in their slits of eyes. How much, they asked from the train, how much?

Give me penny, said the little ones with nothing to sell. The dogs went and sat, quite still, under the dining car, where the train breathed out the smell of meat cooking with onion.

A man passed beneath the arch of reaching arms meeting grey-black and white in the exchange of money for the staring wooden eyes, the stiff wooden legs sticking up in the air; went along under the voices and the bargaining, interrogating the wheels. Past the dogs; glancing up at the dining car where he could stare at the faces, behind glass, drinking beer, two by two, on either side of a uniform railway vase with its pale dead flower. Right to the end, to the guard's van, where the stationmaster's children had just collected their mother's two loaves of bread; to the engine itself, where the stationmaster and the driver stood talking against the steaming complaint of the resting beast.

The man called out to them, something loud and joking. They turned to laugh, in a twirl of steam. The two children careered over the sand, clutching the bread, and burst through the iron gate and up the path through the garden in which nothing grew.

Passengers drew themselves in at the corridor windows and turned into compartments to fetch money, to call someone to look. Those sitting inside looked up: suddenly different, caged faces, boxed in, cut off after the contact of outside. There was an orange a piccanin would like . . . What about that chocolate? It wasn't very nice . . .

A girl had collected a handful of the hard kind, that no one liked, out of the chocolate box, and was throwing them to the dogs, over at the dining car. But the hens darted in and swallowed the chocolates, incredibly quick and accurate, before they had even dropped in the dust, and the dogs, a little bewildered, looked up with their brown eyes, not expecting anything.

—No, leave it, said the young woman, don't take it . . .

Too expensive, too much, she shook her head and raised her voice to the old man, giving up the lion. He held it high where she had handed it to him. No, she said, shaking her head. Three-and-six? insisted her husband, loudly. Yes baas! laughed the old man. *Three-and-six?*—the young man was incredulous. Oh leave it—she said. The young man stopped. Don't you want it? he said, keeping his face close to the old man. No, never mind, she said, leave it. The old native kept his head on one side, looking at them sideways, holding the lion. Three-and-six, he murmured, as old people repeat things to themselves.

The young woman drew her head in. She went into the coupé and sat down. Out of the window, on the other side, there was nothing; sand and bush; a thorn tree. Back through the open doorway, past the figure of her husband in the corridor, there was the station, the voices, wooden animals waving, running feet. Her eye followed the funny little valance of scrolled wood that outlined the chalet roof of the station; she thought of the lion and smiled. That bit of fur round the neck. But the wooden buck, the hippos, the elephants, the baskets that already bulked out of their brown paper under the seat and on the luggage rack! How will they look at home? Where will you put them? What will they mean away from the places you found them? Away from the unreality of the last few weeks? The young man outside. But he is not part of the unreality; he is for good now. Odd ... somewhere there was an idea that he, that living with him, was part of the holiday, the strange places.

Outside, a bell rang. The stationmaster was leaning against the end of the train, green flag rolled in readiness. A few men who had got down to stretch their legs sprang onto the train, clinging to the observation platforms, or perhaps merely standing on the iron step, holding the rail; but on the train, safe from the one dusty platform, the one tin house, the empty sand.

There was a grunt. The train jerked. Through the glass the beer drinkers looked out, as if they could not see beyond it. Behind the fly-screen, the stationmaster's wife sat facing back at them beneath the darkening hunk of meat.

There was a shout. The flag drooped out. Joints not yet co-ordinated, the segmented body of the train heaved and bumped back against itself. It began to move; slowly the scrolled chalet moved past it, the yells of the natives, running alongside, jetted up into the air, fell back at different levels. Staring wooden faces waved drunkenly, there, then gone, questioning for the last time at the windows. Here, one-and-six baas!—As one automatically opens a hand to catch a thrown ball, a man fumbled wildly down his pocket, brought up the shilling and sixpence and threw them out; the old native, gasping, his skinny toes splaying the sand, flung the lion.

The piccanins were waving, the dogs stood, tails uncertain, watching the train go: past the mud huts, where a woman turned to look up from the smoke of the fire, her hand pausing on her hip.

The stationmaster went slowly in under the chalet.

The old native stood, breath blowing out the skin between his ribs, feet tense, balanced in the sand, smiling and shaking his head. In his opened palm, held in the attitude of receiving, was the retrieved shilling and sixpence.

The blind end of the train was being pulled helplessly out of the station.

The young man swung in from the corridor, breathless. He was shaking his head with laughter and triumph. Here! he said. And waggled the lion at her. One-and-six!

What? she said.

He laughed. I was arguing with him for fun, bargaining— when the train had pulled out already, he came tearing after . . . One-and-six Baas! So there's your lion.

She was holding it away from her, the head with the open jaws, the pointed teeth, the black tongue, the wonderful ruff of fur facing her. She was looking at it with an expression of not seeing, of seeing something different. Her face was drawn up, wryly, like the face of a discomforted child. Her mouth lifted nervously at the corner. Very slowly, cautious, she lifted her finger and touched the mane, where it was joined to the wood.

But how could you, she said. He was shocked by the dismay of her face.

Good Lord, he said, what's the matter?

If you wanted the thing, she said, her voice rising and breaking with the shrill impotence of anger, why didn't you buy it in the first place? If you wanted it, why didn't you pay for it? Why didn't you take it decently, when he offered it? Why did you have to wait for him to run after the train with it, and give him one-and-six? One-and-six!

She was pushing it at him, trying to force him to take the lion. He stood astonished, his hands hanging at his sides.

But you wanted it! You liked it so much?

—It's a beautiful piece of work, she said fiercely, as if to protect it from him.

You liked it so much! You said yourself it was too expensive—

Oh *you*—she said, hopeless and furious. *You* . . . She threw the lion on to the seat.

He stood looking at her.

She sat down again in the corner and, her face slumped in her hands, stared out of the window. Everything was turning round inside her. One-and-six. One-and-six. One-and-six for the wood and the carving and the sinews of the legs and the switch of the tail. The mouth open like that and the teeth. The black tongue, rolling, like a wave. The mane round the neck. To give one-and-six for that. The heat of shame mounted through her legs and body and sounded in her ears like the sound of sand pouring. Pouring, pouring. She sat there, sick. A weariness, a tastelessness, the discovery of a void made her hands slacken their grip, atrophy emptily, as if the hour was not worth their grasp. She was feeling like this again. She had thought it was something to do with singleness, with being alone and belonging too much to oneself.

She sat there not wanting to move or speak, or to look at anything, even; so that the mood should be associated with nothing, no object, word or sight that might recur and so re-call the feeling again . . . Smuts blew in grittily, settled on her hands. Her back remained at exactly the same angle, turned against the young man sitting with his hands drooping be-tween his sprawled legs, and the lion, fallen on its side in the corner.

The train had cast the station like a skin. It called out to the sky, I'm coming, I'm coming; and again, there was no answer.

Doris Lessing
(1919–   )

"The important part of writing," says Doris Lessing, "is living. You have to live in such a way that your writing emerges from it." Lessing's writing has consistently illuminated possibilities for personal, social, and political change.

Lessing was born in Persia (now Iran) to British parents who wanted to escape what they considered England's narrowness and provincialism. When she was five, her father gave up his job as a bank manager in Tehran and bought a farm in Rhodesia (now the independent country of Zimbabwe). The nearest neighbor was miles away, and Lessing's childhood there was horribly lonely. Only as an adult did Lessing realize that this solitude had fostered a fine education: Loneliness led her to read the classics of European and American literature.

Even in childhood, Lessing was aware of the injustices in colonial Africa's racial policies. Her family's 3,000-acre farm employed some thirty to fifty black African laborers, each of them earning the equivalent of about $1.50 a month and all of them living in mud huts with no sanitation. The capital city of Salisbury (now Harare) had a white population of about ten thousand and a larger black population that was exploited and oppressed. By the time she was in her twenties, Lessing had entered radical politics.

At the age of thirty, Lessing left Africa for England with her two-year-old son and the finished manuscript of her first novel, *The Grass Is Singing*, which traces a complex relationship between a white farmer's wife and her black servant. It quickly commanded attention as one of the earliest novels about Africa's racial problems.

Lessing's subsequent work continued to draw on her early life in Rhodesia and on her political awareness. *African Stories*

(1964) takes place in the Africa of her childhood; *Children of Violence* (1952–1969), a series of five novels, follows the aptly named Martha Quest, who—like her creator—spends her childhood in Africa and her mature life in postwar Britain.

Lessing is acclaimed for her brilliant experiments with form and genre. *The Golden Notebook* (1962) is structured as a series of notebooks kept by the novel's protagonist. In it, Lessing combines fiction, parody, and factual reporting to explore her concerns with politics, mental illness, and the problems of women in modern life. Her five-volume series *Canopus in Argos: Archives* (1979–1983) is a sequence of visionary fantasies set in outer space.

Doris Lessing believes that a writer should be "an instrument of change." Effecting positive change "is not merely a question of preventing evil," she maintains, "but of strengthening a vision of a good which may defeat the evil."

A Sunrise on the Veld
Doris Lessing

A veld *is a flat African grassland with scattered islands of bushes and trees. In this story, the veld provides a setting for the passage from childhood innocence to the beginnings of adult responsibility, a coming of age triggered by the irony of an unexpected discovery.*

Every night that winter he said aloud into the dark of the pillow: Half-past four! Half-past four! till he felt his brain had gripped the words and held them fast. Then he fell asleep at once, as if a shutter had fallen; and lay with his face turned to the clock so that he could see it first thing when he woke.

It was half-past four to the minute, every morning. Triumphantly pressing down the alarm-knob of the clock, which the dark half of his mind had outwitted, remaining vigilant all night and counting the hours as he lay relaxed in sleep, he huddled down for a last warm moment under the clothes, playing with the idea of lying abed for this once only. But he played with it for the fun of knowing that it was a weakness he could defeat without effort; just as he set the alarm each night for the delight of the moment when he woke and stretched his limbs, feeling the muscles tighten, and thought: Even my brain—even that! I can control every part of myself.

Luxury of warm rested body, with the arms and legs and fingers waiting like soldiers for a word of command! Joy of knowing that the precious hours were given to sleep voluntarily!—for he had once stayed awake three nights running, to prove that he could, and then worked all day, refusing even to admit that he was tired; and now sleep seemed to him a servant to be commanded and refused.

The boy stretched his frame full-length, touching the wall at his head with his hands, and the bedfoot with his toes; then he sprung out, like a fish leaping from water. And it was cold, cold.

He always dressed rapidly, so as to try and conserve his night-warmth till the sun rose two hours later; but by the time he had on his clothes his hands were numbed and he could scarcely hold his shoes. These he could not put on for fear of waking his parents, who never came to know how early he rose.

As soon as he stepped over the lintel, the flesh of his soles contracted on the chilled earth, and his legs began to ache with cold. It was night: the stars were glittering, the trees standing black and still. He looked for signs of day, for the greying of the edge of a stone, or a lightening in the sky where the sun would rise, but there was nothing yet. Alert as an animal he crept past the dangerous window, standing poised with his hand on the sill for one proudly fastidious moment, looking in at the stuffy blackness of the room where his parents lay.

Feeling for the grass-edge of the path with his toes, he reached inside another window further along the wall, where his gun had been set in readiness the night before. The steel was icy, and numbed fingers slipped along it, so that he had to hold it in the crook of his arm for safety. Then he tiptoed to the room where the dogs slept, and was fearful that they might have been tempted to go before him; but they were waiting, their haunches crouched in reluctance at the cold, but ears and swinging tails greeting the gun ecstatically. His warning undertone kept them secret and silent till the house was a hundred yards back: then they bolted off into the bush, yelping excitedly. The boy imagined his parents turning in their beds and muttering: Those dogs again! before they were dragged back in sleep; and he smiled scornfully. He always looked back over his shoulder at the house before he passed a wall of trees that shut it from sight. It looked so low and small, crouching there under a tall and brilliant sky. Then he turned his back on it, and on the frowsting sleepers, and forgot them.

He would have to hurry. Before the light grew strong he must be four miles away; and already a tint of green stood in the hollow of a leaf, and the air smelled of morning and the stars were dimming.

He slung the shoes over his shoulder, veld *skoen* that were crinkled and hard with the dews of a hundred mornings. They would be necessary when the ground became too hot to bear. Now he felt the chilled dust push up between his toes, and he let the muscles of his feet spread and settle into the shapes of the earth; and he thought: I could walk a hundred miles on feet like these! I could walk all day, and never tire!

He was walking swiftly through the dark tunnel of foliage that in day-time was a road. The dogs were invisibly ranging the lower travelways of the bush, and he heard them panting. Sometimes he felt a cold muzzle on his leg before they were off again, scouting for a trail to follow. They were not trained, but free-running companions of the hunt, who often tired of the long stalk before the final shots, and went off on their own pleasure. Soon he could see them, small and wild-looking in a wild strange light, now that the bush stood trembling on the verge of colour, waiting for the sun to paint earth and grass afresh.

The grass stood to his shoulders; and the trees were showering a faint silvery rain. He was soaked; his whole body was clenched in a steady shiver.

Once he bent to the road that was newly scored with animal trails, and regretfully straightened, reminding himself that the pleasure of tracking must wait till another day.

He began to run along the edge of a field, noting jerkily how it was filmed over with fresh spiderweb, so that the long reaches of great black clods seemed netted in glistening grey. He was using the steady lope he had learned by watching the natives, the run that is a dropping of the weight of the body from one foot to the next in a slow balancing movement that never tires, nor shortens the breath; and he felt the blood pulsing down his legs and along his arms, and the exultation and pride of body mounted in him till he was shutting his teeth hard against a violent desire to shout his triumph.

Soon he had left the cultivated part of the farm. Behind him the bush was low and black. In front was a long vlei, acres of long pale grass that sent back a hollowing gleam of light to a satiny sky. Near him thick swathes of grass were bent with the weight of water, and diamond drops sparkled on each frond.

The first bird woke at his feet and at once a flock of them sprang into the air calling shrilly that day had come; and suddenly, behind him, the bush woke into song, and he could hear the guinea fowl calling far ahead of him. That meant they would now be sailing down from their trees into thick grass, and it was for them he had come: he was too late. But he did not mind. He forgot he had come to shoot. He set his legs wide, and balanced from foot to foot, and swung his gun up and down in both hands horizontally, in a kind of improvised exercise, and let his head sink back till it was pillowed in his neck muscles, and watched how above him small rosy clouds floated in a lake of gold.

Suddenly it all rose in him: it was unbearable. He leapt up into the air, shouting and yelling wild, unrecognisable noises. Then he began to run, not carefully, as he had before, but madly, like a wild thing. He was clean crazy, yelling mad with the joy of living and a superfluity of youth. He rushed down the vlei under a tumult of crimson and gold, while all the birds of the world sang about him. He ran in great leaping strides, and shouted as he ran, feeling his body rise into the crisp rushing air and fall back surely on to sure feet; and thought briefly, not believing that such a thing could happen to him, that he could break his ankle any moment, in this thick tangled grass. He cleared bushes like a duiker, leapt over rocks; and finally came to a dead stop at a place where the ground fell abruptly away below him to the river. It had been a two-mile-long dash through waist-high growth, and he was breathing hoarsely and could no longer sing. But he poised on a rock and looked down at stretches of water that gleamed through stooping trees, and thought suddenly, I am fifteen! Fifteen! The words came new to him; so that he kept repeating them wonderingly, with swelling excitement; and he felt the years of his life with his hands, as if he were counting marbles, each one hard and separate and compact, each one a wonderful shining thing. That was what he was: fifteen years of this rich soil, and this slow-moving water, and air that smelt like a challenge whether it was warm and sultry at noon, or as brisk as cold water, like it was now.

There was nothing he couldn't do, nothing! A vision came to him, as he stood there, like when a child hears the word "eternity" and tries to understand it, and time takes possession of the mind. He felt his life ahead of him as a great and wonderful thing, something that was his; and he said aloud with the blood rising to his head: all the great men of the world have been as I am now, and there is nothing I can't become, nothing I can't do; there is no country in the world I cannot make part of myself, if I choose. I contain the world. I can make of it what I want. If I choose, I can change everything that is going to happen: it depends on me, and what I decide now.

The urgency, and the truth and the courage of what his voice was saying exulted him so that he began to sing again at the top of his voice, and the sound went echoing down the river gorge. He stopped for the echo, and sang again: stopped and shouted. That was what he was!—he sang, if he chose; and the world had to answer him.

And for minutes he stood there, shouting and singing and waiting for the lovely eddying sound of the echo; so that his own new strong thoughts came back and washed round his head, as if someone were answering him and encouraging him; till the gorge was full of soft voices clashing back and forth from rock to rock over the river. And then it seemed as if there was a new voice. He listened, puzzled, for it was not his own. Soon he was leaning forward, all his nerves alert, quite still: somewhere close to him there was a noise that was no joyful bird, nor tinkle of falling water, nor ponderous movement of cattle.

There it was again. In the deep morning hush that held his future and his past, was a sound of pain, and repeated over and over: it was a kind of shortened scream, as if someone, something, had no breath to scream. He came to himself, looked about him, and called for the dogs. They did not appear: they had gone off on their own business, and he was alone. Now he was clean sober, all the madness gone. His heart beating fast, because of that frightened screaming, he stepped carefully off the rock and went towards a belt of trees. He was moving cautiously, for not so long ago he had seen a leopard in just this spot.

At the edge of the trees he stopped and peered, holding his gun ready; he advanced, looking steadily about him, his eyes narrowed. Then, all at once, in the middle of a step, he faltered, and his face was puzzled. He shook his head impatiently, as if he doubted his own sight.

There, between two trees, against a background of gaunt black rocks, was a figure from a dream, a strange beast that was horned and drunken-legged, but like something he had never even imagined. It seemed to be ragged. It looked like a small buck that had black ragged tufts of fur standing up irregularly all over it, with patches of raw flesh beneath . . . but the patches of rawness were disappearing under moving black and came again elsewhere; and all the time the creature screamed, in small gasping screams, and leaped drunkenly from side to side, as if it were blind.

Then the boy understood: it *was* a buck. He ran closer, and again stood still, stopped by a new fear. Around him the grass was whispering and alive. He looked wildly about, and then down. The ground was black with ants, great energetic ants that took no notice of him, but hurried and scurried towards the fighting shape, like glistening black water flowing through the grass.

And, as he drew in his breath and pity and terror seized him, the beast fell and the screaming stopped. Now he could hear nothing but one bird singing, and the sound of the rustling, whispering ants.

He peered over at the writhing blackness that jerked convulsively with the jerking nerves. It grew quieter. There were small twitches from the mass that still looked vaguely like the shape of a small animal.

It came into his mind that he should shoot it and end its pain; and he raised the gun. Then he lowered it again. The buck could no longer feel; its fighting was a mechanical protest of the nerves. But it was not that which made him put down the gun. It was a swelling feeling of rage and misery and protest that expressed itself in the thought: if I had not come it would have died like this: so why should I interfere? All over the bush things like this happen; they happen all the time; this is how life goes on, by living things dying in anguish. He gripped the gun between his knees and felt in his own limbs the myriad swarming pain of the twitching animal that could no longer feel, and set his teeth, and said over and over again under his breath: I can't stop it. I can't stop it. There is nothing I can do.

He was glad that the buck was unconscious and had gone past suffering so that he did not have to make a decision to kill it even when he was feeling with his whole body: this is what happens, this is how things work.

It was right—that was what he was feeling. *It was right and nothing could alter it.*

The knowledge of fatality, of what has to be, had gripped him and for the first time in his life; and he was left unable to make any movement of brain or body, except to say: "Yes, yes. That is what living is." It had entered his flesh and his bones and grown into the furthest corners of his brain and would never leave him. And at that moment he could not have performed the smallest action of mercy, knowing as he did, having lived on it all his life, the vast unalterable, cruel veld, where at any moment one might stumble over a skull or crush the skeleton of some small creature.

Suffering, sick, and angry, but also grimly satisfied with his new stoicism, he stood there leaning on his rifle, and watched the seething black mound grow smaller. At his feet, now, were ants trickling back with pink fragments in their mouths, and there was a fresh acid smell in his nostrils. He sternly controlled the uselessly convulsing muscles of his empty stomach, and reminded himself: the ants must eat too! At the same time he found that the tears were streaming down his face, and his clothes were soaked with the sweat of that other creature's pain.

The shape had grown small. Now it looked like nothing recognisable. He did not know how long it was before he saw the blackness thin, and bits of white showed through, shining in the sun—yes, there was the sun, just up, glowing over the rocks. Why, the whole thing could not have taken longer than a few minutes.

He began to swear, as if the shortness of the time was in itself unbearable, using the words he had heard his father say. He strode forward, crushing ants with each step, and brushing them off his clothes, till he stood above the skeleton, which lay sprawled under a small bush. It was clean-picked. It might have been lying there years, save that on the white bone were pink fragments of gristle. About the bones ants were ebbing away, their pincers full of meat.

The boy looked at them, big black ugly insects. A few were standing and gazing up at him with small glittering eyes.

"Go away!" he said to the ants, very coldly. "I am not for you—not just yet, at any rate. Go away." And he fancied that the ants turned and went away.

He bent over the bones and touched the sockets in the skull; that was where the eyes were, he thought incredulously, remembering the liquid dark eyes of a buck. And then he bent the slim foreleg bone, swinging it horizontally in his palm.

That morning, perhaps an hour ago, this small creature had been stepping proud and free through the bush, feeling the chill on its hide even as he himself had done, exhilarated by it. Proudly stepping the earth, tossing its horns, frisking a pretty white tail, it had sniffed the cold morning air. Walking like kings and conquerors it had moved through this freeheld bush, where each blade of grass grew for it alone, and where the river ran pure sparkling water for its slaking.

And then—what had happened? Such a swift surefooted thing could surely not be trapped by a swarm of ants?

The boy bent curiously to the skeleton. Then he saw that the back leg that lay uppermost and strained out in the tension of death, was snapped midway in the thigh, so that broken bones jutted over each other uselessly. So that was it! Limping into the ant-masses it could not escape, once it had sensed the danger. Yes, but how had the leg been broken? Had it fallen perhaps? Impossible, a buck was too light and graceful. Had some jealous rival horned it?

What could possibly have happened? Perhaps some Africans had thrown stones at it, as they do, trying to kill it for meat, and had broken its leg. Yes, that must be it.

Even as he imagined the crowd of running, shouting natives and the flying stones, and the leaping buck, another picture came into his mind. He saw himself, on any one of these bright ringing mornings, drunk with excitement, taking a snap shot at some half-seen buck. He saw himself with the gun lowered, wondering whether he had missed or not; and thinking at last that it was late, and he wanted his breakfast, and it was not worth while to track miles after an animal that would very likely get away from him in any case.

For a moment he would not face it. He was a small boy again, kicking sulkily at the skeleton, hanging his head, refusing to accept the responsibility.

Then he straightened up, and looked down at the bones with an odd expression of dismay, all the anger gone out of him. His mind went quite empty: all around him he could see trickles of ants disappearing into the grass. The whispering noise was faint and dry, like the rustling of a cast snakeskin.

At last he picked up his gun and walked homewards. He was telling himself half defiantly that he wanted his breakfast. He was telling himself that it was getting very hot, much too hot to be out roaming the bush.

Really, he was tired. He walked heavily, not looking where he put his feet. When he came within sight of his home he stopped, knitting his brows. There was something he had to think out. The death of that small animal was a thing that concerned him, and he was by no means finished with it. It lay at the back of his mind uncomfortably.

Soon, the very next morning, he would get clear of everybody and go to the bush and think about it.

Chinua Achebe
(1930–   )

Chinua Achebe was born and raised in the traditional Igbo (or Ibo) village of Ogidi when Nigeria was still a British colony. Much of Achebe's work draws on his childhood experiences in this village, the ancestral home of his father.

During his five years at the University of Ibaden, Achebe began to question the colonial-era notion that African culture was inferior to European culture. He knew that Africans had their own stories to tell and for that reason began writing short stories with an African focus. His first novel, *Things Fall Apart* (1958), won international acclaim, opening many Westerners' eyes to the cultural heritage of Africa and to the destructive effects of colonialism on individual Africans. His novels focus on life in Nigeria—sometimes presented as a fictionalized nation—from the arrival of early English missionaries, through years of colonial rule, to a post-independence era rife with corruption and political turmoil.

In 1967, civil war erupted in Nigeria when the Igbo attempted to secede and form a new republic called Biafra. The Biafran cause ultimately failed, and by the time the war ended in 1970, several million people had died, many of them starving in refugee camps. Several of the stories in Achebe's collection *Girls at War* (1972) reflect events of the war years and their aftermath. "Civil Peace" is one of these.

Civil Peace
Chinua Achebe

Chinua Achebe experienced firsthand the brutal civil war that erupted when Biafra attempted to secede from Nigeria. In this story, set during the first months after Biafra's defeat, Achebe reveals the ironies of the lawless and chaotic "peace" that ensued.

Jonathan Iwegbu counted himself extraordinarily lucky. "Happy survival!" meant so much more to him than just a current fashion of greeting old friends in the first hazy days of peace. It went deep to his heart. He had come out of the war with five inestimable blessings—his head, his wife Maria's head and the heads of three out of their four children. As a bonus he also had his old bicycle—a miracle too but naturally not to be compared to the safety of five human heads.

The bicycle had a little history of its own. One day at the height of the war it was commandeered "for urgent military action." Hard as its loss would have been to him he would still have let it go without a thought had he not had some doubts about the genuineness of the officer. It wasn't his disreputable rags, nor the toes peeping out of one blue and one brown canvas shoes, nor yet the two stars of his rank done obviously in a hurry in biro, that troubled Jonathan; many good and heroic soldiers looked the same or worse. It was rather a certain lack of grip and firmness in his manner. So Jonathan, suspecting he might be amenable to influence, rummaged in his raffia bag and produced the two pounds with which he had been going to buy firewood which his wife, Maria, retailed to camp officials for extra stock-fish and corn meal, and got his bicycle back. That night he buried it in the little clearing in the bush where the dead of the camp, including his own youngest son, were buried. When he dug it up again a year later after the surrender all it needed was a little palm-oil greasing. "Nothing puzzles God," he said in wonder.

He put it to immediate use as a taxi and accumulated a small pile of Biafran money ferrying camp officials and their families across the four-mile stretch to the nearest tarred road. His standard charge per trip was six pounds and those who had the money were only glad to be rid of some of it in this way. At the end of a fortnight he had made a small fortune of one hundred and fifteen pounds.

Then he made the journey to Enugu and found another miracle waiting for him. It was unbelievable. He rubbed his eyes and looked again and it was still standing there before him. But, needless to say, even that monumental blessing must be accounted also totally inferior to the five heads in the family. This newest miracle was his little house in Ogui Overside. Indeed nothing puzzles God! Only two houses away a huge concrete edifice some wealthy contractor had put up just before the war was a mountain of rubble. And here was Jonathan's little zinc house of no regrets built with mud blocks quite intact! Of course the doors and windows were missing and five sheets off the roof. But what was that? And anyhow he had returned to Enugu early enough to pick up bits of old zinc and wood and soggy sheets of cardboard lying around the neighbourhood before thousands more came out of their forest holes looking for the same things. He got a destitute carpenter with one old hammer, a blunt plane and a few bent and rusty nails in his tool bag to turn this assortment of wood, paper and metal into door and window shutters for five Nigerian shillings or fifty Biafran pounds. He paid the pounds, and moved in with his overjoyed family carrying five heads on their shoulders.

His children picked mangoes near the military cemetery and sold them to soldiers' wives for a few pennies—real pennies this time—and his wife started making breakfast akara balls for neighbours in a hurry to start life again. With his family earnings he took his bicycle to the villages around and bought fresh palm-wine which he mixed generously in his rooms with the water which had recently started running again in the public tap down the road, and opened up a bar for soldiers and other lucky people with good money.

At first he went daily, then every other day and finally once a week, to the offices of the Coal Corporation where he used to be a miner, to find out what was what. The only thing he did find out in the end was that that little house of his was even a greater blessing than he had thought. Some of his fellow ex-miners who had nowhere to return at the end of the day's waiting just slept outside the doors of the offices and cooked what meal they could scrounge together in Bournvita tins. As the weeks lengthened and still nobody could say what was what Jonathan discontinued his weekly visits altogether and faced his palm-wine bar.

But nothing puzzles God. Came the day of the windfall when after five days of endless scuffles in queues and counter-queues in the sun outside the Treasury he had twenty pounds counted into his palms as ex gratia award for the rebel money he had turned in. It was like Christmas for him and for many others like him when the payments began. They called it (since few could manage its proper official name) *egg-rasher.*

As soon as the pound notes were placed in his palm Jonathan simply closed it tight over them and buried fist and money inside his trouser pocket. He had to be extra careful because he had seen a man a couple of days earlier collapse into near-madness in an instant before that oceanic crowd because no sooner had he got his twenty pounds than some heartless ruffian picked it off him. Though it was not right that a man in such an extremity of agony should be blamed yet many in the queues that day were able to remark quietly on the victim's carelessness, especially after he pulled out the innards of his pocket and revealed a hole in it big enough to pass a thief's head. But of course he had insisted that the money had been in the other pocket, pulling it out too to show its comparative wholeness. So one had to be careful.

Jonathan soon transferred the money to his left hand and pocket so as to leave his right free for shaking hands should the need arise, though by fixing his gaze at such an elevation as to miss all approaching human faces he made sure that the need did not arise, until he got home.

He was normally a heavy sleeper but that night he heard all the neighbourhood noises die down one after another. Even the night watchman who knocked the hour on some metal somewhere in the distance had fallen silent after knocking one o'clock. That must have been the last thought in Jonathan's mind before he was finally carried away himself. He couldn't have been gone for long, though, when he was violently awakened again.

"Who is knocking?" whispered his wife lying beside him on the floor.

"I don't know," he whispered back breathlessly.

The second time the knocking came it was so loud and imperious that the rickety old door could have fallen down.

"Who is knocking?" he asked then, his voice parched and trembling.

"Na tief-man and him people," came the cool reply. "Make you hopen de door." This was followed by the heaviest knocking of all.

Maria was the first to raise the alarm, then he followed and all their children.

"Police-o! Thieves-o! Neighbours-o! Police-o! We are lost! We are dead! Neighbours, are you asleep? Wake up! Police-o!"

This went on for a long time and then stopped suddenly. Perhaps they had scared the thief away. There was total silence. But only for a short while.

"You done finish?" asked the voice outside. "Make we help you small. Oya, everybody!"

"Police-o! Tief-man-o! Neighbours-o! we done loss-o! Police-o! . . ."

There were at least five other voices besides the leader's.

Jonathan and his family were now completely paralysed by

terror. Maria and the children sobbed inaudibly like lost souls. Jonathan groaned continuously.

The silence that followed the thieves' alarm vibrated horribly. Jonathan all but begged their leader to speak again and be done with it.

"My frien," said he at long last, "we don try our best for call dem but I tink say dem all done sleep-o . . . So wetin we go do now? Sometaim you wan call soja? Or you wan make we call dem for you? Soja better pass police. No be so?"

"Na so!" replied his men. Jonathan thought he heard even more voices now than before and groaned heavily. His legs were sagging under him and his throat felt like sand-paper.

"My frien, why you no de talk again. I de ask you say you wan make we call soja?"

"No."

"Awrighto. Now make we talk business. We no be bad tief. We no like for make trouble. Trouble done finish. War done finish and all the katakata wey de for inside. No Civil War again. This time na Civil Peace. No be so?"

"Na so!" answered the horrible chorus.

"What do you want from me? I am a poor man. Everything I had went with this war. Why do you come to me? You know people who have money. We . . ."

"Awright! We know say you no get plenty money. But we sef no get even anini. So derefore make you open dis window and give us one hundred pound and we go commot. Orderwise we de come for inside now to show you guitar-boy like dis . . ."

A volley of automatic fire rang through the sky. Maria and the children began to weep aloud again.

"Ah, missisi de cry again. No need for dat. We done talk say we na good tief. We just take our small money and go nwayorly. No molest. Abi we de molest?"

"At all!" sang the chorus.

"My friends," began Jonathan hoarsely. "I hear what you say and I thank you. If I had one hundred pounds . . ."

"Lookia my frien, no be play we come play for your house.

If we make mistake and step for inside you no go like am-o. So derefore ..."

"To God who made me; if you come inside and find one hundred pounds, take it and shoot me and shoot my wife and children. I swear to God. The only money I have in this life is this twenty-pounds *egg-rasher* they gave me today ..."

"OK. Time de go. Make you open dis window and bring the twenty pound. We go manage am like dat."

There were now loud murmurs of dissent among the chorus: "Na lie de man de lie; e get plenty money ... Make we go inside and search properly well ... Wetin be twenty pound? ..."

"Shurrup!" rang the leader's voice like a lone shot in the sky and silenced the murmuring at once. "Are you dere? Bring the money quick!"

"I am coming," said Jonathan fumbling in the darkness with the key of the small wooden box he kept by his side on the mat.

At the first sign of light as neighbours and others assembled to commiserate with him he was already strapping his five-gallon demijohn to his bicycle carrier and his wife, sweating in the open fire, was turning over akara balls in a wide clay bowl of boiling oil. In the corner his eldest son was rinsing out dregs of yesterday's palm wine from old beer bottles.

"I count it as nothing," he told his sympathisers, his eyes on the rope he was tying. "What is *egg-rasher*? Did I depend on it last week? Or is it greater than other things that went with the war? I say, let *egg-rasher* perish in the flames! Let it go where everything else has gone. Nothing puzzles God."

Bessie Head
(1937–1986)

Although much of her work grows out of her own painful experiences with a separatist society, Bessie Head is regarded as a writer whose work is ultimately inclusive and affirming. Born in South Africa, Head experienced firsthand the rigid classification system of apartheid. She was considered "Coloured" (part black, part white) and was denied full citizenship. Unable to feel that she belonged in South Africa, she immigrated to the neighboring nation of Botswana, which she came to regard as her home. Although her conditions as a refugee in Botswana were difficult, Head found tranquillity there. She once said, "In South Africa, all my life I lived in shattered little bits. All those shattered bits began to grow together here [in Botswana]. . . . I have a peace against which all the turmoil is worked out!"

Head came into her own as a writer in Botswana, drawing increasingly on her own experiences in her fiction. Her three novels present differing perspectives on the theme of exile and identity. Her most overtly autobiographical novel, *A Question of Power* (1973), tells about the desperate struggle of a woman of mixed racial background who does battle with a racist society and sexist culture, as well as with her own private demons.

Head also published short stories and historical chronicles that incorporated regional folklore into their narratives. She once explained, "Every story or book starts with something just for myself. Then from that small me it becomes a panorama—the big view that has something for everyone."

The Prisoner Who Wore Glasses
Bessie Head

S carcely a breath of wind disturbed the stillness of the day, and the long rows of cabbages were bright green in the sunlight. Large white clouds drifted slowly across the deep blue sky. Now and then they obscured the sun and caused a chill on the backs of the prisoners who had to work all day long in the cabbage field. This trick the clouds were playing with the sun eventually caused one of the prisoners who wore glasses to stop work, straighten up and peer short-sightedly at them. He was a thin little fellow with a hollowed-out chest and comic knobbly knees. He also had a lot of fanciful ideas because he smiled at the clouds.

"Perhaps they want me to send a message to the children," he thought tenderly, noting that the clouds were drifting in the direction of his home some hundred miles away. But before he could frame the message, the warder in charge of his work span shouted:

"Hey, what you tink you're doing, Brille?"

The prisoner swung round, blinking rapidly, yet at the same time sizing up the enemy. He was a new warder, named Jacobus Stephanus Hannetjie. His eyes were the color of the sky but they were frightening. A simple, primitive, brutal soul gazed out of them. The prisoner bent down quickly and a message was quietly passed down the line:

"We're in for trouble this time, comrades."

"Why?" rippled back up the line.

"Because he's not human," the reply rippled down, and yet only the crunching of the spades as they turned over the earth disturbed the stillness.

This particular work span was known as Span One. It was

composed of ten men, and they were all political prisoners. They were grouped together for convenience, as it was one of the prison regulations that no black warder should be in charge of a political prisoner lest this prisoner convert him to his views. It never seemed to occur to the authorities that this very reasoning was the strength of Span One and a clue to the strange terror they aroused in the warders. As political prisoners they were unlike the other prisoners in the sense that they felt no guilt nor were they outcasts of society. All guilty men instinctively cower, which was why it was the kind of prison where men got knocked out cold with a blow at the back of the head from an iron bar. Up until the arrival of Warder Hannetjie, no warder had dared beat any member of Span One and no warder had lasted more than a week with them. The battle was entirely psychological. Span One was assertive and it was beyond the scope of white warders to handle assertive black men. Thus, Span One had got out of control. They were the best thieves and liars in the camp. They lived all day on raw cabbages. They chatted and smoked tobacco. And since they moved, thought and acted as one, they had perfected every technique of group concealment.

Trouble began that very day between Span One and Warder Hannetjie. It was because of the shortsightedness of Brille. That was the nickname he was given in prison and is the Afrikaans word for someone who wears glasses. Brille could never judge the approach of the prison gates, and on several previous occasions he had munched on cabbages and dropped them almost at the feet of the warder, and all previous warders had overlooked this. Not so Warder Hannetjie.

"Who dropped that cabbage?" he thundered.

Brille stepped out of line.

"I did," he said meekly.

"All right," said Hannetjie. "The whole span goes three meals off."

"But I told you I did it," Brille protested.

The blood rushed to Warder Hannetjie's face.

"Look 'ere," he said. "I don't take orders from a kaffir. I don't know what kind of kaffir you tink you are. Why don't you say Baas. I'm your Baas. Why don't you say Baas, hey?"

Brille blinked his eyes rapidly but by contrast his voice was strangely calm.

"I'm twenty years older than you," he said. It was the first thing that came to mind, but the comrades seemed to think it a huge joke. A titter swept up the line. The next thing Warder Hannetjie whipped out a knobkerrie and gave Brille several blows about the head. What surprised his comrades was the speed with which Brille had removed his glasses or else they would have been smashed to pieces on the ground.

That evening in the cell Brille was very apologetic.

"I'm sorry, comrades," he said. "I've put you into a mess."

"Never mind, brother," they said. "What happens to one of us, happens to all."

"I'll try to make up for it, comrades," he said. "I'll steal something so that you don't go hungry."

Privately, Brille was very philosophical about his head wounds. It was the first time an act of violence had been perpetrated against him, but he had long been a witness of extreme, almost unbelievable human brutality. He had twelve children and his mind traveled back that evening through the sixteen years of *bedlam* in which he had lived. It had all happened in a small drab little three-bedroomed house in a small drab little street in the Eastern Cape, and the children kept coming year after year because neither he nor Martha managed the contraceptives the right way and a teacher's salary never allowed moving to a bigger house and he was always taking exams to improve this salary only to have it all eaten up by hungry mouths. Everything was pretty horrible, especially the way the children fought. They'd get hold of each other's heads and give them a good bashing against the wall. Martha gave up somewhere along the line, so they worked out a thing between them. The bashings, biting and blood were to operate in full swing until he came home. He was to be the bogeyman, and when it worked he never failed to have a sense of godhead at the way in which his presence could change savages into fairly reasonable human beings.

Yet somehow it was this chaos and mismanagement at the center of his life that drove him into politics. It was really an ordered beautiful world with just a few basic slogans to learn along with the rights of mankind. At one stage, before things became very bad, there were conferences to attend, all very far away from home.

"Let's face it," he thought ruefully. "I'm only learning right now what it means to be a politician. All this while I've been running away from Martha and the kids."

And the pain in his head brought a hard lump to his throat. That was what the children did to each other daily and Martha wasn't managing, and if Warder Hannetjie had not interrupted him that morning, he would have sent the following message:

"Be good comrades, my children. Cooperate, then life will run smoothly."

The next day Warder Hannetjie caught this old man with twelve children stealing grapes from the farm shed. They were an enormous quantity of grapes in a ten-gallon tin, and for this misdeed the old man spent a week in the isolation cell. In fact, Span One as a whole was in constant trouble. Warder Hannetjie seemed to have eyes at the back of his head. He uncovered the trick about the cabbages, how they were split in two with the spade and immediately covered with earth and then unearthed again and eaten with split-second timing. He found out how tobacco smoke was beaten into the ground, and he found out how conversations were whispered down the wind.

For about two weeks Span One lived in acute misery. The cabbages, tobacco and conversations had been the pivot of jail life to them. Then one evening they noticed that their good old comrade who wore the glasses was looking rather pleased with himself. He pulled out a four-ounce packet of tobacco by way of explanation, and the comrades fell upon it with great greed. Brille merely smiled. After all, he was the father of many children. But when the last shred had disappeared, it occurred to the comrades that they ought to be puzzled. Someone said:

"I say, brother. We're watched like hawks these days. Where did you get the tobacco?"

"Hannetjie gave it to me," said Brille.

There was a long silence. Into it dropped a quiet bombshell.

"I saw Hannetjie in the shed today," and the failing eyesight blinked rapidly. "I caught him in the act of stealing five bags of fertilizer, and he bribed me to keep my mouth shut."

There was another long silence.

"Prison is an evil life," Brille continued, apparently discussing some irrelevant matter. "It makes a man contemplate all kinds of evil deeds."

He held out his hand and closed it.

"You know, comrades," he said. "I've got Hannetjie. I'll betray him tomorrow."

Everyone began talking at once.

"Forget it, brother. You'll get shot."

Brille laughed.

"I won't," he said. "That is what I mean about evil. I am a father of children, and I saw today that Hannetjie is just a child and stupidly truthful. I'm going to punish him severely because we need a good warder."

The following day, with Brille as witness, Hannetjie confessed to the theft of the fertilizer and was fined a large sum of money. From then on Span One did very much as they pleased while Warder Hannetjie stood by and said nothing. But it was Brille who carried this to extremes. One day, at the close of work Warder Hannetjie said:

"Brille, pick up my jacket and carry it back to the camp."

"But nothing in the regulations says I'm your servant, Hannetjie," Brille replied coolly.

"I've told you not to call me Hannetjie. You must say Baas," but Warder Hannetjie's voice lacked conviction. In turn, Brille squinted up at him.

"I'll tell you something about this Baas business, Hannetjie," he said. "One of these days we are going to run the country. You are going to clean my car. Now, I have a fifteen-year-old son, and I'd die of shame if you had to tell him that I ever called you Baas."

Warder Hannetjie went red in the face and picked up his coat.

On another occasion Brille was seen to be walking about the prison yard, openly smoking tobacco. On being taken before the prison commander he claimed to have received the tobacco from Warder Hannetjie. All throughout the tirade from his chief, Warder Hannetjie failed to defend himself, but his nerve broke completely. He called Brille to one side.

"Brille," he said. "This thing between you and me must end. You may not know it, but I have a wife and children, and you're driving me to suicide."

"Why don't you like your own medicine, Hannetjie?" Brille asked quietly.

"I can give you anything you want," Warder Hannetjie said in desperation.

"It's not only me but the whole of Span One," said Brille cunningly. "The whole of Span One wants something from you."

Warder Hannetjie brightened with relief.

"I tink I can manage if it's tobacco you want," he said.

Brille looked at him, for the first time struck with pity and guilt. He wondered if he had carried the whole business too far. The man was really a child.

"It's not tobacco we want, but you," he said. "We want you on our side. We want a good warder because without a good warder we won't be able to manage the long stretch ahead."

Warder Hannetjie interpreted this request in his own fashion, and his interpretation of what was good and human often left the prisoners of Span One speechless with surprise. He had a way of slipping off his revolver and picking up a spade and digging alongside Span One. He had a way of producing unheard-of luxuries like boiled eggs from his farm nearby and things like cigarettes, and Span One responded nobly and got the reputation of being the best work span in the camp. And it wasn't only taken from their side. They were awfully good at stealing commodities like fertilizer which were needed on the farm of Warder Hannetjie.

R. K. Narayan
(1906–   )

Rasipuram Krishnaswami Narayan is often considered India's greatest English-language writer. British novelist Graham Greene has commented, "Narayan . . . wakes in me a spring of gratitude, for he has offered me a second home. Without him I could never have known what it is like to be Indian." Narayan's novel *The Guide* (1958) won India's highest literary award, and in 1964 Prime Minister Nehru awarded him the Padma Bhushan for distinguished service.

Born in Madras, India, Narayan was one of nine children in a middle-class family of Brahmins, the highest caste in the Hindu system. Although his first language was Tamil, as an educated Indian he learned English early, and he writes in an English to which he purposely adds an Indian flavor.

Narayan's father, a headmaster in the government's education service, subscribed to British and American news and literary magazines, and as a boy Narayan happily immersed himself in these and in classics of world literature.

Narayan attended Maharajah's College and took a teaching position after graduation, but he soon left teaching to devote himself to writing. Sympathizing with his desire to become a writer, his grandmother chose a day that was astrologically auspicious, and on that day he bought a notebook to begin his first novel. He invented a small Indian town called Malgudi and a boy called Swami, and he faithfully wrote several pages each day. "Each day as I sat down to write," he explains, "I had no notion of what would be coming. All that I could be certain of was the central character. I reread the first draft at night to make out how it was shaping and undertook, until far into the night, corrections, revisions, and tightening up of sentences. I began to notice that the sentences acquired a new strength and finality while being rewritten. . . ." When Narayan was twenty-eight, a friend in England showed Narayan's manuscript to Graham Greene, who took it to his publisher. In 1935, *Swami and Friends* was published in London. The novel sold poorly at first, but reviews were favorable. Narayan's career was launched.

Narayan's works include many other novels set in Malgudi, essays, an autobiography (*My Days*, 1974), and prose adaptations of India's ancient epics, the *Ramayana* and the *Mahabharata*. He has also written over two hundred short stories. "I enjoy writing a short story," he says. "Unlike the novel, the short story can be brought into existence through a mere suggestion of detail, the focus being kept on a central idea or climax. . . . I discover a story when a personality passes through a crisis of spirit or circumstances."

An Astrologer's Day
R. K. Narayan

*The "astrologer" in this story represents a well-known
figure in any Indian marketplace, a fortuneteller who
may read palms, consult charts of constellations and
planets, cast cowrie shells and interpret the way they fall,
or let a customer choose a small scroll of mystical
"palmyra" writing and then interpret its contents.*

Punctually at midday he opened his bag and spread out his
professional equipment, which consisted of a dozen cowrie
shells, a square piece of cloth with obscure mystic charts on it, a
notebook, and a bundle of palmyra writing. His forehead was
resplendent with sacred ash and vermilion, and his eyes sparkled
with a sharp abnormal gleam which was really an outcome of a
continual searching look for customers, but which his simple
clients took to be a prophetic light and felt comforted. The power
of his eyes were considerably enhanced by their position—placed
as they were between the painted forehead and the dark whiskers
which streamed down his cheeks: even a half-wit's eyes would
sparkle in such a setting. To crown the effect he wound a saffron-
colored turban around his head. This color scheme never failed.
People were attracted to him as bees are attracted to cosmos or
dahlia stalks. He sat under the boughs of a spreading tamarind
tree which flanked a path running through the town hall park.
It was a remarkable place in many ways: a surging crowd was
always moving up and down this narrow road morning till night.
A variety of trades and occupations was represented all along its
way: medicine sellers, sellers of stolen hardware and junk, magicians, and, above all, an auctioneer of cheap cloth, who created
enough din all day to attract the whole town. Next to him in

166

vociferousness came a vendor of fried groundnut, who gave his ware a fancy name each day, calling it "Bombay Ice Cream" one day, and on the next "Delhi Almond," and on the third "Raja's Delicacy," and so on and so forth, and people flocked to him. A considerable portion of this crowd dallied before the astrologer too. The astrologer transacted his business by the light of a flare which crackled and smoked up above the groundnut heap nearby. Half the enchantment of the place was due to the fact that it did not have the benefit of municipal lighting. The place was lit up by shop lights. One or two had hissing gaslights, some had naked flares stuck on poles, some were lit up by old cycle lamps, and one or two, like the astrologer's, managed without lights of their own. It was a bewildering crisscross of light rays and moving shadows. This suited the astrologer very well, for the simple reason that he had not in the least intended to be an astrologer when he began life; and he knew no more of what was going to happen to others than he knew what was going to happen to himself next minute. He was as much a stranger to the stars as were his innocent customers. Yet he said things which pleased and astonished everyone: that was more a matter of study, practice, and shrewd guesswork. All the same, it was as much an honest man's labor as any other, and he deserved the wages he carried home at the end of a day.

He had left his village without any previous thought or plan. If he had continued there he would have carried on the work of his forefathers—namely, tilling the land, living, marrying, and ripening in his cornfield and ancestral home. But that was not to be. He had to leave home without telling anyone, and he could not rest till he left it behind a couple of hundred miles. To a villager it is a great deal, as if an ocean flowed between.

He had a working analysis of mankind's troubles: marriage, money, and the tangles of human ties. Long practice had sharpened his perception. Within five minutes he understood what was wrong. He charged three paise per question, never opened his mouth till the other had spoken for at least ten minutes, which provided him enough stuff for a dozen answers and advices. When he told the person before him, gazing at his palm,

"In many ways you are not getting the fullest results for your efforts," nine out of ten were disposed to agree with him. Or he questioned: "Is there any woman in your family, maybe even a distant relative, who is not well disposed towards you?" Or he gave an analysis of character: "Most of your troubles are due to your nature. How can you be otherwise with Saturn where he is? You have an impetuous nature and a rough exterior." This endeared him to their hearts immediately, for even the mildest of us loves to think that he has a forbidding exterior.

The nuts vendor blew out his flare and rose to go home. This was a signal for the astrologer to bundle up too, since it left him in darkness except for a little shaft of green light which strayed in from somewhere and touched the ground before him. He picked up his cowrie shells and paraphernalia and was putting them back into his bag when the green shaft of light was blotted out; he looked up and saw a man standing before him. He sensed a possible client and said, "You look so careworn. It will do you good to sit down for a while and chat with me." The other grumbled some reply vaguely. The astrologer pressed his invitation; whereupon the other thrust his palm under his nose, saying, "You call yourself an astrologer?" The astrologer felt challenged and said, tilting the other's palm towards the green shaft of light, "Yours is a nature . . ." "Oh, stop that," the other said. "Tell me something worthwhile. . . ."

Our friend felt piqued. "I charge only three paise per question, and what you get ought to be good enough for your money. . . ." At this the other withdrew his arm, took out an anna, and flung it out to him, saying, "I have some questions to ask. If I prove you are bluffing, you must return that anna to me with interest."

"If you find my answers satisfactory, will you give me five rupees?"

"No."

"Or will you give me eight annas?"

"All right, provided you give me twice as much if you are wrong," said the stranger. This pact was accepted after a little further argument. The astrologer sent up a prayer to heaven as the other lit a cheroot. The astrologer caught a glimpse of his face by the match light. There was a pause as cars hooted on the road, jutka drivers swore at their horses, and the babble of the crowd agitated the semidarkness of the park. The other sat down, sucking his cheroot, puffing out, sat there ruthlessly. The astrologer felt very uncomfortable. "Here, take your anna back. I am not used to such challenges. It is late for me today. . . ." He made preparations to bundle up. The other held his wrist and said, "You can't get out of it now. You dragged me in while I was passing." The astrologer shivered in his grip; and his voice shook and became faint. "Leave me today. I will speak to you tomorrow." The other thrust his palm in his face and said, "Challenge is challenge. Go on." The astrologer proceeded with his throat drying up, "There is a woman . . ."

"Stop," said the other. "I don't want all that. Shall I succeed in my present search or not? Answer this and go. Otherwise I will not let you go till you disgorge all your coins." The astrologer muttered a few incantations and replied, "All right. I will speak. But will you give me a rupee if what I say is convincing? Otherwise I will not open my mouth, and you may do what you like." After a good deal of haggling the other agreed. The astrologer said, "You were left for dead. Am I right?"

"Ah, tell me more."

"A knife has passed through you once?" said the astrologer.

"Good fellow!" He bared his chest to show the scar. "What else?"

"And then you were pushed into a well nearby in the field. You were left for dead."

"I should have been dead if some passerby had not chanced to peep into the well," exclaimed the other, overwhelmed by enthusiasm. "When shall I get at him?" he asked, clenching his fist.

"In the next world," answered the astrologer. "He died four months ago in a far-off town. You will never see any more of him." The other groaned on hearing it. The astrologer proceeded:

"Guru Nayak—"

"You know my name!" the other said, taken aback.

"As I know all other things. Guru Nayak, listen carefully to what I have to say. Your village is two days' journey due north of this town. Take the next train and begone. I see once again great danger to your life if you go from home." He took out a pinch of sacred ash and held it to him. "Rub it on your forehead and go home. Never travel southward again, and you will live to be a hundred."

"Why should I leave home again?" the other said reflectively. "I was only going away now and then to look for him and to choke out his life if I met him." He shook his head regretfully. "He has escaped my hands. I hope at least he died as he deserved." "Yes," said the astrologer. "He was crushed under a lorry." The other looked gratified to hear it.

The place was deserted by the time the astrologer picked up his articles and put them into his bag. The green shaft was also gone, leaving the place in darkness and silence. The stranger had gone off into the night, after giving the astrologer a handful of coins.

It was nearly midnight when the astrologer reached home. His wife was waiting for him at the door and demanded an explanation. He flung the coins at her and said, "Count them. One man gave all that."

"Twelve and a half annas," she said, counting. She was overjoyed. "I can buy some jaggery and coconut tomorrow. The child has been asking for sweets for so many days now. I will prepare some nice stuff for her."

"The swine has cheated me! He promised me a rupee," said the astrologer. She looked up at him. "You look worried. What is wrong?"

"Nothing."

After dinner, sitting on the pyol, he told her, "Do you know a great load is gone from me today? I thought I had the blood of a man on my hands all these years. That was the reason why I ran away from home, settled here, and married you. He is alive."

She gasped. "You tried to kill!"

"Yes, in our village, when I was a silly youngster. We drank, gambled, and quarreled badly one day—why think of it now? Time to sleep," he said, yawning, and stretched himself on the pyol.

Heberto Padilla
(1932–   )

Heberto Padilla Lorenzo grew up in Pinar del Río, Cuba, under the military regime of strongman Fulgencio Batista. After graduating from the University of Havana, Padilla worked in the United States as a journalist and language teacher. In 1959, Fidel Castro overthrew Batista's corrupt government, and Padilla, at twenty-seven, returned to Cuba, full of hope for the new government and for the freedom it promised.

Castro's government made Padilla the editor of a weekly literary magazine in the official, government-run newspaper, *Revolución*. Padilla was thirty when the first volume of his own poetry, *El justo tiempo humano* (*Just, Human Time*, 1962), appeared, winning acclaim throughout Latin America.

Padilla also worked as a director of Cuba's government cultural agency. As time went on, he began to voice doubts about the Cuban government's control of the press, and he found himself unable to get work.

The crackdown came when Padilla was forty. He was arrested, beaten, and thrown into prison. The Cuban government ignored protests from the world literary community, and Padilla eventually was badgered into appearing before Cuba's state-run Union of Writers and Artists—an organization he had cofounded in 1960—to "repent." He was then released to begin a sentence of forced farm labor. Afterward, still an outcast within Cuba, he was prevented from leaving the country. International political and literary figures worked to obtain Padilla's freedom, and finally, in 1980 (when Padilla was almost fifty), he was allowed to emigrate to the United States.

Today, Padilla continues writing. "I do not admire people who suffer professionally," he has said. "I want to be a new man. I am eager to be alive. My duty is to write."

Landscapes
Heberto Padilla

You can see them everywhere in Cuba.
Green or red or yellow, flaking off from the water
and the sun, true landscapes of these times
of war.
5   The wind tugs at the Coca-Cola signs.
The clocks courtesy of Canada Dry are stopped
at the old time.
The neon signs, broken, crackle and sputter in the rain.
Esso's is something like this
10   S   O   S
and above there are some crude letters
reading   P A T R I A O M U E R T E.

Translated from the Spanish by
Alastair Reid and Andrew Hurley

Julia Alvarez
(1950–   )

When Julia Alvarez graduated from high school, her doting family gave her a typewriter and predicted that one day her name would be known throughout the United States. Alvarez must have laughed to herself; after all, many of her classmates couldn't even pronounce her name. Nevertheless, her family's prediction has come true: Alvarez is an award-winning and best-selling poet and novelist.

Born in New York City, Julia Alvarez spent her childhood in the Dominican Republic, surrounded by "my gang of cousins and the smell of mangoes and the iridescent, vibrating green of hummingbirds." When she was ten years old, her father entered into a secret plot to overthrow Dominican dictator Rafael Trujillo Molina. Just before her father was to be arrested, an American agent tipped the family off, and they escaped to the United States.

Though the young Alvarez had always dreamed of returning to the United States, she felt out of place at first. Later, she realized that, despite the difficulties, her experiences as an immigrant had deepened her perceptions. "We [immigrants] travel on that border between two worlds," she explains, "and we can see both points of view." As a writer, she would find that her ability to shift perspectives was one of her greatest strengths.

After college, Alvarez taught poetry in schools and worked on her own writing. Her first book, a volume of poetry appropriately titled *Homecoming*, appeared in 1984. She went on to win the American Academy of Poetry Prize. Her novels *How the Garcia Girls Lost Their Accents* (1991), *In the Time of the Butterflies* (1994), and *¡Yo!* (1997) focus on the charged and dangerous lives of political dissidents and the small, daily conflicts faced by immigrant families.

Audition
Julia Alvarez

Porfirio drove Mami and me
to Cook's mountain village
to find a new pantry maid.
Cook had given Mami a tip
5   that her home town was girl-heavy,
the men lured away to the cities.
We drove to the interior,
climbing a steep, serpentine,
say-your-last-prayers road.
10 I leaned toward my mother
as if my weight could throw
the car's balance away
from the sheer drop below.
Late morning we entered
15 a dusty village of huts.
Mami rolled down her window
and queried an old woman,
Did she know of any girls
looking for work as maids?
20 Soon we were surrounded
by a dozen señoritas.
Under the thatched cantina
Mami conducted interviews—
a mix of personal questions
25 and Sphinx-like intelligence tests.

Do you have children, a novio?
Would you hit a child who hit you?
If I give you a quarter to buy
guineos at two for a nickel,
30 *how many will you bring back?*
As she interviewed I sat by,
looking the girls over;
one of them would soon
be telling me what to do,
35 reporting my misbehaviors.
Most seemed nice enough,
befriending me with smiles,
exclamations on my good hair,
my being such a darling.
40 Those were the ones I favored.
I'd fool them with sweet looks,
improve my bad reputation.
As we interviewed we heard
by the creek that flowed nearby
45 a high, clear voice singing
a plaintive lullaby . . .
as if the sunlight filling
the cups of the allamandas,
the turquoise sky dappled
50 with angel-feather clouds,
the creek trickling down
the emerald green of the mountain
had found a voice in her voice.
We listened. Mami's hard-line,
55 employer-to-be face
softened with quiet sweetness.
The voice came closer, louder—

a slender girl with a basket
of wrung rags on her head
60   passed by the cantina,
oblivious of our presence.
Who is she? my mother asked.
Gladys, the girls replied.
Gladys! my mother called
65   as she would for months to come.
Gladys, come clear the plates!
Gladys, answer the door!
Gladys! the young girl turned—
Abruptly, her singing stopped.

Edwidge Danticat

(1969–)

Haitian-born Edwidge Danticat has been writing for over half her young life. Her parents moved from Haiti to New York City without her when she was very young; she joined them when she was twelve. Feeling isolated from her American classmates because of the way she spoke and dressed, Danticat began to write about Haiti as a kind of solace. After graduation from Barnard College, she published several collections of stories and (so far) two novels, *Breath, Eyes, Memory* (1994) and *The Farming of Bones* (1998). She currently makes her home in Brooklyn, New York.

Danticat has already attracted many admirers for her powerful and imaginative writing. She won the Pushcart Short Story Prize in 1995 and has been given awards from *The Caribbean Writer, Seventeen,* and *Essence* magazines. Her first novel was a finalist for the National Book Award. The tales in Danticat's short-story collection *Krik? Krak!* (1995) have been described as "spare, luminous stories that read like poems."

Danticat has mixed feelings about her role as a Haitian-American writer. She would prefer not to be hailed as "the voice" speaking for Haitian-Americans. "I don't really see myself as the voice for the Haitian-American experience," she says. "There are many. I'm just one."

The Book of the Dead
Edwidge Danticat

My father is gone. I am slouched in a cast-aluminum chair across from two men, one the manager of the hotel where we're staying and the other a policeman. They are waiting for me to explain what has become of him, my father.

The manager—"Mr. Flavio Salinas," the plaque on his office door reads—has the most striking pair of chartreuse eyes I have ever seen on a man with an island-Spanish lilt to his voice.

The officer is a baby-faced, short white Floridian with a pot belly.

"Where are you and your daddy from, Ms. Bienaimé?" he asks.

I answer "Haiti," even though I was born and raised in East Flatbush, Brooklyn, and have never visited my parents' birthplace. I do this because it is one more thing I have longed to have in common with my parents.

The officer plows forward. "You down here in Lakeland from Haiti?"

"We live in New York. We were on our way to Tampa."

I find Manager Salinas's office gaudy. The walls are covered with orange-and-green wallpaper, briefly interrupted by a giant gold-leaf-bordered print of a Victorian cottage that somehow resembles the building we're in. Patting his light-green tie, he whispers reassuringly, "Officer Bo and I will do the best we can to help you find your father."

We start out with a brief description: "Sixty-four, five feet eight inches, two hundred and twenty pounds, moon-faced, with thinning salt-and-pepper hair. Velvet-brown eyes—"

"Velvet-brown?" says Officer Bo.

"Deep brown—same color as his complexion."

My father has had partial frontal dentures for ten years, since he fell off his and my mother's bed when his prison nightmares began. I mention that, too. Just the dentures, not the nightmares. I also bring up the claw-shaped marks that run from his left ear down along his cheek to the corner of his mouth—the only visible reminder of the year he spent at Fort Dimanche, the Port-au-Prince prison ironically named after the Lord's Day.

"Does your daddy have any kind of mental illness, senility?" asks Officer Bo.

"No."

"Do you have any pictures of your daddy?"

I feel like less of a daughter because I'm not carrying a photograph in my wallet. I had hoped to take some pictures of him on our trip. At one of the rest stops I bought a disposable camera and pointed it at my father. No, no, he had protested, covering his face with both hands like a little boy protecting his cheeks from a slap. He did not want any more pictures taken of him for the rest of his life. He was feeling too ugly.

"That's too bad," says Officer Bo. "Does he speak English, your daddy? He can ask for directions, et cetera?"

"Yes."

"Is there anything that might make your father run away from you—particularly here in Lakeland?" Manager Salinas interjects. "Did you two have a fight?"

I had never tried to tell my father's story in words before now, but my first sculpture of him was the reason for our trip: a two-foot-high mahogany figure of my father, naked, crouching on the floor, his back arched like the curve of a crescent moon, his downcast eyes fixed on his short stubby fingers and the wide palms of his hands. It was hardly revolutionary, minimalist at best, but it was my favorite of all my attempted representations of him. It was the way I had imagined him in prison.

The last time I had seen my father? The previous night, before falling asleep. When we pulled into the pebbled driveway, densely lined with palm and banana trees, it was almost midnight. All the restaurants in the area were closed. There was nothing to do but shower and go to bed.

"It is like a paradise here," my father said when he saw the room. It had the same orange-and-green wallpaper as Salinas's office, and the plush green carpet matched the walls. "Look, Annie," he said, "it is like grass under our feet." He was always searching for a glimpse of paradise, my father.

He picked the bed closest to the bathroom, removed the top of his gray jogging suit, and unpacked his toiletries. Soon after, I heard him humming, as he always did, in the shower.

After he got into bed, I took a bath, pulled my hair back in a ponytail, and checked on the sculpture—just felt it a little bit through the bubble padding and carton wrapping to make sure it wasn't broken. Then I slipped under the covers, closed my eyes, and tried to sleep.

I pictured the client to whom I was delivering the sculpture: Gabrielle Fonteneau, a young woman about my age, an actress on a nationally syndicated television series. My friend Jonas, the principal at the East Flatbush elementary school where I teach drawing to fifth graders, had shown her a picture of my "Father" sculpture, and, the way Jonas told it, Gabrielle Fonteneau had fallen in love with it and wished to offer it as a gift to her father on his birthday.

Since this was my first big sale, I wanted to make sure that the piece got there safely. Besides, I needed a weekend away, and both my mother and I figured that my father, who watched a lot of television, both in his barbershop and at home, would enjoy meeting Gabrielle, too. But when I woke up the next morning my father was gone.

I showered, put on my driving jeans and a T-shirt, and waited. I watched a half hour of midmorning local news, smoked three mentholated cigarettes even though we were in a nonsmoking room, and waited some more. By noon, four hours had gone by. And it was only then that I noticed that the car was still there but the sculpture was gone.

I decided to start looking for my father: in the east garden, the west garden, the dining room, the exercise room, and in the few guest rooms cracked open while the maid changed the sheets; in the little convenience store at the Amoco gas station nearby; even in the Salvation Army thrift shop that from a distance seemed to blend into the interstate. All that waiting and looking actually took six hours, and I felt guilty for having held back so long before going to the front desk to ask, "Have you seen my father?"

I feel Officer Bo's fingers gently stroking my wrist. Up close he smells like fried eggs and gasoline, like breakfast at the Amoco. "I'll put the word out with the other boys," he says. "Salinas here will be in his office. Why don't you go back to your room in case he shows up there?"

I return to the room and lie in the unmade bed, jumping up when I hear the click from the electronic key in the door. It's only the housekeeper. I turn down the late-afternoon cleaning and call my mother at the beauty salon where she perms, presses, and braids hair, next door to my father's barbershop. But she isn't there. So I call my parents' house and leave the hotel number on their machine. "Please call me as soon as you can, Manman. It's about Papi."

Once, when I was twelve, I overheard my mother telling a young woman who was about to get married how she and my father had first met on the sidewalk in front of Fort Dimanche the evening that my father was released from jail. (At a dance, my father had fought with a soldier out of uniform who had him arrested and thrown in prison for a year.) That night, my mother was returning home from a sewing class when he stumbled out of the prison gates and collapsed into her arms, his face still bleeding from his last beating. They married and left for New York a year later. "We were like two seeds planted in a rock," my mother had told the young woman, "but somehow when our daughter, Annie, came we took root."

My mother soon calls me back, her voice staccato with worry.

"Where is Papi?"

"I lost him."

"How you lost him?"

"He got up before I did and disappeared."

"How long he been gone?"

"Eight hours," I say, almost not believing myself that it's been that long.

My mother is clicking her tongue and humming. I can see her sitting at the kitchen table, her eyes closed, her fingers sliding up and down her flesh-colored stockinged legs.

"You call police?"

"Yes."

"What they say?"

"To wait, that he'll come back."

My mother is thumping her fingers against the phone's mouthpiece, which is giving me a slight ache in my right ear.

"Tell me where you are," she says. "Two more hours and he's not there, call me, I come."

I dial Gabrielle Fonteneau's cellular-phone number. When she answers, her voice sounds just as it does on television, but more silken and seductive without the sitcom laugh track.

"To think," my father once said while watching her show, "Haitian-born actresses on American television."

"And one of them wants to buy my stuff," I'd added.

When she speaks, Gabrielle Fonteneau sounds as if she's in a place with cicadas, waterfalls, palm trees, and citronella candles to keep the mosquitoes away. I realize that I, too, am in such a place, but I can't appreciate it.

"So nice of you to come all this way to deliver the sculpture," she says. "Jonas tell you why I like it so much? My papa was a journalist in Port-au-Prince. In 1975, he wrote a story criticizing the dictatorship, and he was arrested and put in jail."

"Fort Dimanche?"

"No, another one," she says. "Caserne. Papa kept track of days there by scraping lines with his fingernails on the walls of his cell. One of the guards didn't like this, so he pulled out all his fingernails with pliers."

I think of the photo spread I saw in the *Haitian Times* of Gabrielle Fonteneau and her parents in their living room in Tampa. Her father was described as a lawyer, his daughter's manager; her mother a court stenographer. There was no hint in that photograph of what had once happened to the father. Perhaps people don't see anything in my father's face, either, in spite of his scars.

"We celebrate his birthday on the day he was released from prison," she says. "It's the hands I love so much in your sculpture. They're so strong."

I am drifting away from Gabrielle Fonteneau when I hear her say, "So when will you get here? You have instructions from Jonas, right? Maybe we can make you lunch. My mother makes great *lanbi*."

"I'll be there at twelve tomorrow," I say. "My father is with me. We are making a little weekend vacation of this."

My father loves museums. When he isn't working in his barbershop, he's often at the Brooklyn Museum. The ancient Egyptian rooms are his favorites.

"The Egyptians, they was like us," he likes to say. The Egyptians worshipped their gods in many forms and were often ruled by foreigners. The pharaohs were like the dictators he had fled. But what he admires most about the Egyptians is the way they mourned.

"Yes, they grieve," he'll say. He marvels at the mummification that went on for weeks, resulting in bodies that survived thousands of years.

My whole adult life, I have struggled to find the proper manner of sculpting my father, a man who learned about art by standing with me most of the Saturday mornings of my childhood, mesmerized by the golden masks, the shawabtis, and Osiris, ruler of the underworld.

When my father finally appears in the hotel-room doorway, I am awed by him. Smiling, he looks like a much younger man, further bronzed after a long day at the beach.

"Annie, let your father talk to you." He walks over to my bed, bends down to unlace his sneakers. "*On ti koze*, a little chat."

"Where were you? Where is the sculpture, Papi?" I feel my

eyes twitching, a nervous reaction I inherited from my mother.

"That's why we need to chat," he says. "I have objections with your statue."

He pulls off his sneakers and rubs his feet with both hands.

"I don't want you to sell that statue," he says. Then he picks up the phone and calls my mother.

"I know she called you," he says to her in Creole. "Her head is so hot. She panics so easily. I was just out walking, thinking."

I hear my mother lovingly scolding him and telling him not to leave me again. When he hangs up the phone, he picks up his sneakers and puts them back on.

"Where is the sculpture?" My eyes are twitching so hard now that I can barely see.

"Let us go," he says. "I will take you to it."

As my father maneuvers the car out of the parking lot, I tell myself he might be ill, mentally ill, even though I have never detected anything wrong beyond his prison night-mares. I am trying to piece it together, this sudden yet fa-miliar picture of a parent's vulnerability. When I was ten years old and my father had the chicken pox, I overheard him say to a friend on the phone, "The doctor tells me that at my age chicken pox can kill a man." This was the first time I realized that my father could die. I looked up the word "kill" in every dictionary and encyclopedia at school, trying to comprehend what it meant, that my father could be eradicated from my life.

My father stops the car on the side of the highway near a man-made lake, one of those artificial creations of the modern tropical city, with curved stone benches surrounding stagnant water. There is little light to see by except a half-moon. He heads toward one of the benches, and I sit down next to him, letting my hands dangle between my legs.

"Is this where the sculpture is?" I ask.

"In the water," he says.

"O.K.," I say. "But please know this about yourself. You are an especially harsh critic."

My father tries to smother a smile.

"Why?" I ask.

He scratches his chin. Anger is a wasted emotion, I've always thought. My parents got angry at unfair politics in New York or Port-au-Prince, but they never got angry at my grades—at all the B's I got in everything but art classes—or at my not eating vegetables or occasionally vomiting my daily spoonful of cod-liver oil. Ordinary anger, I thought, was a weakness. But now I am angry. I want to hit my father, beat the craziness out of his head.

"Annie," he says. "When I first saw your statue, I wanted to be buried with it, to take it with me into the other world."

"Like the ancient Egyptians," I say.

He smiles, grateful, I think, that I still recall his passions.

"Annie," he asks, "do you remember when I read to you from 'The Book of the Dead'?"

"Are you dying?" I say to my father. "Because I can only forgive you for this if you are. You can't take this back."

He is silent for a moment too long.

I think I hear crickets, though I cannot imagine where they might be. There is the highway, the cars racing by, the half-moon, the lake dug up from the depths of the ground, the allée of royal palms beyond. And there is me and my father.

"You remember the judgment of the dead," my father says, "when the heart of a person is put on a scale. If it is heavy, then this person cannot enter the other world."

It is a testament to my upbringing that I am not yelling at him.

"I don't deserve a statue," he says, even while looking like one: the Madonna of Humility, for example, contemplating her losses in the dust.

"Annie, your father was the hunter," he says. "He was not the prey."

"What are you saying?" I ask.

"We have a proverb," he says. " 'One day for the hunter, one day for the prey.' Your father was the hunter. He was not the prey." Each word is hard-won as it leaves my father's mouth, balanced like those hearts on the Egyptian scale.

"Annie, when I saw your mother the first time, I was not just out of prison. I was a guard in the prison. One of the prisoners I was questioning had scratched me with a piece of tin. I went out to the street in a rage, blood all over my face. I was about to go back and do something bad, very bad. But instead comes your mother. I smash into her, and she asks me what I am doing there. I told her I was just let go from prison and she held my face and cried in my hair."

"And the nightmares, what are they?"

"Of what I, your father, did to others."

"Does Manman know?"

"I told her, Annie, before we married."

I am the one who drives back to the hotel. In the car, he says, "Annie, I am still your father, still your mother's husband. I would not do these things now."

When we get back to the hotel room, I leave a message for Officer Bo, and another for Manager Salinas, telling them that I have found my father. He has slipped into the bathroom, and now he runs the shower at full force. When it seems that he is never coming out, I call my mother at home in Brooklyn.

"How do you love him?" I whisper into the phone.

My mother is tapping her fingers against the mouthpiece.

"I don't know, Annie," she whispers back, as though there is a chance that she might also be overheard by him. "I feel only that you and me, we saved him. When I met him, it made him stop hurting the people. This is how I see it. He was a seed thrown into a rock, and you and me, Annie, we helped push a flower out of the rock."

When I get up the next morning, my father is already dressed. He is sitting on the edge of his bed with his back to me, his head bowed, his face buried in his hands. If I were sculpting him, I would make him a praying mantis, crouching motionless, seeming to pray while waiting to strike.

With his back still turned, my father says, "Will you call those people and tell them you have it no more, the statue?"

"We were invited to lunch there. I believe we should go."
He raises his shoulders and shrugs. It is up to me.

The drive to Gabrielle Fonteneau's house seems longer than the
twenty-four hours it took to drive from New York: the ocean, the
palms along the road, the highway so imposingly neat. My father fills in the silence in the car by saying, "So now you know,
Annie, why your mother and me, we have never returned home."

The Fonteneaus' house is made of bricks of white coral, on
a cul-de-sac with a row of banyans separating the two sides of
the street.

Silently, we get out of the car and follow a concrete path to
the front door. Before we can knock, an older woman walks out.
Like Gabrielle, she has stunning midnight-black eyes and skin
the color of sorrel, with spiralling curls brushing the sides of her
face. When Gabrielle's father joins her, I realize where Gabrielle
Fonteneau gets her height. He is more than six feet tall.

Mr. Fonteneau extends his hands, first to my father and then
to me. They're large, twice the size of my father's. The fingernails have grown back, thick, densely dark, as though the past
had nestled itself there in black ink.

We move slowly through the living room, which has a cathe-
dral ceiling and walls covered with Haitian paintings—Obin,
Hyppolite, Tiga, Duval-Carrié. Out on the back terrace, which
towers over a nursery of orchids and red dracaenas, a table is
set for lunch.

Mr. Fonteneau asks my father where his family is from in
Haiti, and my father lies. In the past, I thought he always said
a different province because he had lived in all those places,
but I realize now that he says this to keep anyone from trac-
ing him, even though twenty-six years and eighty more pounds
shield him from the threat of immediate recognition.

When Gabrielle Fonteneau makes her entrance, in an off-the-
shoulder ruby dress, my father and I stand up.

"Gabrielle," she says, when she shakes hands with my father,
who blurts out spontaneously, "You are one of the flowers of
Haiti."

Gabrielle Fonteneau tilts her head coyly.

"We eat now," Mrs. Fonteneau announces, leading me and my father to a bathroom to wash up before the meal. Standing before a pink seashell-shaped sink, my father and I dip our hands under the faucet flow.

"Annie," my father says, "we always thought, your mother and me, that children could raise their parents higher. Look at what this girl has done for her parents."

During the meal of conch, plantains, and mushroom rice, Mr. Fonteneau tries to draw my father into conversation. He asks when my father was last in Haiti.

"Twenty-six years," my father replies.

"No going back for you?" asks Mrs. Fonteneau.

"I have not had the opportunity," my father says.

"We go back every year to a beautiful place overlooking the ocean in the mountains in Jacmel," says Mrs. Fonteneau.

"Have you ever been to Jacmel?" Gabrielle Fonteneau asks me.

I shake my head no.

"We are fortunate," Mrs. Fonteneau says, "that we have another place to go where we can say our rain is sweeter, our dust is lighter, our beach is prettier."

"So now we are tasting rain and weighing dust," Mr. Fonteneau says, and laughs.

"There is nothing like drinking the sweet juice from a green coconut you fetched yourself from your own tree, or sinking your hand in sand from the beach in your own country," Mrs. Fonteneau says.

"When did you ever climb a coconut tree?" Mr. Fonteneau says, teasing his wife.

I am imagining what my father's nightmares might be. Maybe he dreams of dipping his hands in the sand on a beach in his own country and finds that what he comes up with is a fist full of blood.

After lunch, my father asks if he can have a closer look at the Fonteneaus' back-yard garden. While he's taking the tour, I confess to Gabrielle Fonteneau that I don't have the sculpture.

"My father threw it away," I say.

Gabrielle Fonteneau frowns.

"I don't know," she says. "Was there even a sculpture at all? I trust Jonas, but maybe you fooled him, too. Is this some scam, to get into our home?"

"There was a sculpture," I say. "Jonas will tell you that. My father just didn't like it, so he threw it away."

She raises her perfectly arched eyebrows, perhaps out of concern for my father's sanity or my own.

"I'm really disappointed," she says. "I wanted it for a reason. My father goes home when he looks at a piece of art. He goes home deep inside himself. For a long time, he used to hide his fingers from people. It's like he was making a fist all the time. I wanted to give him this thing so that he knows we understand what happened to him."

"I am truly sorry," I say.

Over her shoulders, I see her parents guiding my father through rows of lemongrass. I want to promise her that I will make her another sculpture, one especially modelled on her father. But I don't know when I will be able to work on anything again. I have lost my subject, the father I loved as well as pitied.

In the garden, I watch my father snap a white orchid from its stem and hold it out toward Mrs. Fonteneau, who accepts it with a nod of thanks.

"I don't understand," Gabrielle Fonteneau says. "You did all this for nothing."

I wave to my father to signal that we should perhaps leave now, and he comes toward me, the Fonteneaus trailing slowly behind him.

With each step he rubs the scars on the side of his face.

Perhaps the last person my father harmed had dreamed this moment into my father's future—his daughter seeing those marks, like chunks of warm plaster still clinging to a cast, and questioning him about them, giving him a chance to either lie or tell the truth. After all, we have the proverb, as my father would say: "Those who give the blows may try to forget, but those who carry the scars must remember."

THE POWER
OF
LOVE

Pablo Neruda
(1904–1973)

Like many other Latin American and European writers, Pablo Neruda did not distinguish between poetry and politics. He once said that he had lived "singing and defending the Chilean people."

Born in a frontier town in Chile, Neruda was given the name Neftalí Ricardo Reyes Basoalto. He assumed his new name at the outset of his writing career to avoid upsetting his father, a railway worker. When his friend Federico García Lorca, the great Spanish poet, was murdered by fascists in 1939, during the Spanish Civil War, Neruda began attacking his own country's repressive and corrupt right-wing government. In 1945, he became a senator, but he was declared a traitor and forced into hiding. He went into exile from 1948 to 1952, when the government withdrew the order for his arrest and he returned to Chile. In 1970, he supported his friend Salvador Allende Gossens in his successful run for the presidency of Chile. Allende, however, was ousted and died in a violent coup in 1973, the same year that Neruda himself died.

Despite his fervent political convictions, Neruda is best known today for his love poems. He won the Nobel Prize in literature in 1971. Neruda said that his primary poetic "creditor" was Walt Whitman, the American poet, in whose poetry "the ignorant are never ignored and the human condition is never mocked." Like Whitman, Neruda believed that the personal and the political are two sides of the same coin. Love is at the heart of the political justice that both writers envisioned in their poetry.

Love
Pablo Neruda

So many days, oh so many days
seeing you so tangible and so close,
how do I pay, with what do I pay?

The bloodthirsty spring
5 has awakened in the woods.
The foxes start from their earths,
the serpents drink the dew,
and I go with you in the leaves
10 between the pines and the silence,
asking myself how and when
I will have to pay for my luck.

Of everything I have seen,
it's you I want to go on seeing;
of everything I've touched,
15 it's your flesh I want to go on touching.
I love your orange laughter.
I am moved by the sight of you sleeping.

What am I to do, love, loved one?
20 I don't know how others love
or how people loved in the past.
I live, watching you, loving you.
Being in love is my nature.

You please me more each afternoon.

Where is she? I keep on asking
25 if your eyes disappear.
How long she's taking! I think, and I'm hurt.
I feel poor, foolish and sad,
and you arrive and you are lightning
glancing off the peach trees.

30 That's why I love you and yet not why.
There are so many reasons, and yet so few,
for love has to be so,
involving and general,
particular and terrifying,
35 honoured and yet in mourning,
flowering like the stars,
and measureless as a kiss.

Translated from the Spanish by Alastair Reid

The Book of Ruth

The story of Ruth is set about 1100 B.C., *but it was probably written nearly seven hundred years later. At that time, the Hebrew leaders were concerned that marriage with foreigners was threatening the identity of the Jewish people.*

In the story, Ruth is a woman from Moab (mō′ab′), *a kingdom east of the Dead Sea. The religion of Moab involves the use of idols—a practice that the Hebrews condemn. As we learn in the story, Ruth marries a Jewish man from a family that came to Moab from Judah, but she is soon left widowed and childless.*

When Ruth's mother-in-law, Naomi, decides to return to Judah, Ruth loyally stays with her, adopts the Jewish religion, and ultimately marries Boaz (bō′az′), *a relative of her deceased husband. By the end of the story, we learn that Ruth, the outsider, is the ancestor of the great King David. The story can be viewed, then, as a lesson about compassion and tolerance.*

Chapter 1

Now it came to pass in the days when the judges ruled, that there was a famine in the land. And a certain man of Bethlehem-Judah went to sojourn in the country of Moab, he, and his wife, and his two sons.

And the name of the man was Elimelech, and the name of his wife Naomi, and the name of his two sons Mahlon and Chilion, Ephrathites of Bethlehem-Judah. And they came into the country of Moab, and continued there.

And Elimelech Naomi's husband died; and she was left, and her two sons.

And they took them wives of the women of Moab; the name of the one was Orpah, and the name of the other Ruth: and they dwelled there about ten years.

And Mahlon and Chilion died also both of them; and the woman was left of her two sons and her husband.

Then she arose with her daughters in law, that she might return from the country of Moab: for she had heard in the country of Moab how that the Lord had visited his people in giving them bread.

Wherefore she went forth out of the place where she was, and her two daughters in law with her; and they went on the way to return unto the land of Judah.

And Naomi said unto her two daughters in law, "Go, return each to her mother's house: the Lord deal kindly with you, as ye have dealt with the dead, and with me.

"The Lord grant you that ye may find rest, each of you in the house of her husband." Then she kissed them; and they lifted up their voice, and wept.

And they said unto her, "Surely we will return with thee unto thy people."

And Naomi said, "Turn again, my daughters: why will ye go with me? Are there yet any more sons in my womb, that they may be your husbands?

"Turn again, my daughters, go your way; for I am too old to have an husband. If I should say, 'I have hope,' if I should have an husband also tonight, and should also bear sons;

"Would ye tarry for them till they were grown? Would ye stay for them from having husbands? Nay, my daughters; for it grieveth me much for your sakes that the hand of the Lord is gone out against me."

And they lifted up their voice, and wept again: and Orpah kissed her mother in law; but Ruth clave unto her.

And she said, "Behold, thy sister in law is gone back unto

her people, and unto her gods: return thou after thy sister in law."

And Ruth said, "Intreat me not to leave thee, or to return from following after thee: for whither thou goest, I will go; and where thou lodgest, I will lodge: thy people shall be my people, and thy God my God:

"Where thou diest, will I die, and there will I be buried: the Lord do so to me, and more also, if ought but death part thee and me."

When she saw that she was stedfastly minded to go with her, then she left speaking unto her.

So they two went until they came to Bethlehem. And it came to pass, when they were come to Bethlehem, that all the city was moved about them, and they said, "Is this Naomi?"

And she said unto them, "Call me not Naomi, call me Mara:[1] for the Almighty hath dealt very bitterly with me.

"I went out full, and the Lord hath brought me home again empty: why then call ye me Naomi, seeing the Lord hath testified against me, and the Almighty hath afflicted me?"

So Naomi returned, and Ruth the Moabitess, her daughter in law, with her, which returned out of the country of Moab: and they came to Bethlehem in the beginning of barley harvest.

Chapter 2

And Naomi had a kinsman of her husband's, a mighty man of wealth, of the family of Elimelech; and his name was Boaz.

And Ruth the Moabitess said unto Naomi, "Let me now go to the field, and glean ears of corn[2] after him in whose sight I shall find grace." And she said unto her, "Go, my daughter."

And she went, and came, and gleaned in the field after the reapers: and her hap was to light on a part of the field be-

---

1. Naomi . . . Mara: Naomi means "sweet" in Hebrew; Mara means "bitter."
2. glean: According to Biblical law, the poor were entitled to glean in the fields—that is, to gather the bits of grain left or dropped by the reapers; **corn:** here, grain.

longing unto Boaz, who was of the kindred of Elimelech.

And, behold, Boaz came from Bethlehem, and said unto the reapers, "The Lord be with you." And they answered him, "The Lord bless thee."

Then said Boaz unto his servant that was set over the reapers, "Whose damsel is this?"

And the servant that was set over the reapers answered and said, "It is the Moabitish damsel that came back with Naomi out of the country of Moab:

"And she said, 'I pray you, let me glean and gather after the reapers among the sheaves': so she came, and hath continued even from the morning until now, that she tarried a little in the house."

Then said Boaz unto Ruth, "Hearest thou not, my daughter? Go not to glean in another field, neither go from hence, but abide here fast by my maidens:

"Let thine eyes be on the field that they do reap, and go thou after them: have I not charged the young men that they shall not touch thee? And when thou art athirst, go unto the vessels, and drink of that which the young men have drawn."

Then she fell on her face, and bowed herself to the ground, and said unto him, "Why have I found grace in thine eyes, that thou shouldest take knowledge of me, seeing I am a stranger?"

And Boaz answered and said unto her, "It hath fully been shewed me, all that thou hast done unto thy mother in law since the death of thine husband: and how thou hast left thy father and thy mother, and the land of thy nativity, and art come unto a people which thou knewest not heretofore.

"The Lord recompense thy work, and a full reward be given thee of the Lord God of Israel, under whose wings thou art come to trust."

Then she said, "Let me find favour in thy sight, my lord; for that thou hast comforted me, and for that thou hast spoken friendly unto thine handmaid, though I be not like unto one of thine handmaidens."

And Boaz said unto her, "At mealtime come thou hither, and

eat of the bread, and dip thy morsel in the vinegar." And she sat beside the reapers: and he reached her parched corn, and she did eat, and was sufficed, and left.

And when she was risen up to glean, Boaz commanded his young men, saying, "Let her glean even among the sheaves, and reproach her not:

"And let fall also some of the handfuls of purpose for her, and leave them, that she may glean them, and rebuke her not."

So she gleaned in the field until even, and beat out that she had gleaned: and it was about an ephah of barley.

And she took it up, and went into the city: and her mother in law saw what she had gleaned: and she brought forth, and gave to her that she had reserved after she was sufficed.

And her mother in law said unto her, "Where hast thou gleaned today? And where wroughtest thou? Blessed be he that did take knowledge of thee." And she shewed her mother in law with whom she had wrought, and said, "The man's name with whom I wrought today is Boaz."

And Naomi said unto her daughter in law, "Blessed be he of the Lord, who hath not left off his kindness to the living and to the dead." And Naomi said unto her, "The man is near of kin unto us, one of our next kinsmen."

And Ruth the Moabitess said, "He said unto me also, 'Thou shalt keep fast by my young men, until they have ended all my harvest.'"

And Naomi said unto Ruth her daughter in law, "It is good, my daughter, that thou go out with his maidens, that they meet thee not in any other field."

So she kept fast by the maidens of Boaz to glean unto the end of barley harvest and of wheat harvest; and dwelt with her mother in law.

Chapter 3

Then Naomi her mother in law said unto her, "My daughter, shall I not seek rest for thee, that it may be well with thee?

"And now is not Boaz of our kindred, with whose maidens

thou wast? Behold, he winnoweth barley tonight in the threshing floor.

"Wash thyself therefore, and anoint thee, and put thy raiment upon thee, and get thee down to the floor: but make not thyself known unto the man, until he shall have done eating and drinking.

"And it shall be, when he lieth down, that thou shalt mark the place where he shall lie, and thou shalt go in, and uncover his feet, and lay thee down; and he will tell thee what thou shalt do."

And she said unto her, "All that thou sayest unto me I will do."

And she went down unto the floor, and did according to all that her mother in law bade her.

And when Boaz had eaten and drunk, and his heart was merry, he went to lie down at the end of the heap of corn: and she came softly, and uncovered his feet, and laid her down.

And it came to pass at midnight, that the man was afraid, and turned himself: and, behold, a woman lay at his feet.

And he said, "Who art thou?" And she answered, "I am Ruth thine handmaid: spread therefore thy skirt over thine handmaid; for thou art a near kinsman."[3]

And he said, "Blessed be thou of the Lord, my daughter: for thou hast shewed more kindness in the latter end than at the beginning, inasmuch as thou followedst not young men, whether poor or rich.

"And now, my daughter, fear not; I will do to thee all that thou requirest: for all the city of my people doth know that thou art a virtuous woman.

"And now it is true that I am thy near kinsman: howbeit there is a kinsman nearer than I.

"Tarry this night, and it shall be in the morning, that if he

---

3. **near kinsman:** The ancient Hebrews practiced a custom called *levirate* (lev′ə·rit) marriage. According to this custom, a close male relative of the dead husband, such as a brother, was obliged to marry the widow if the husband had left no son. The firstborn son of this marriage would be raised in the name of the dead husband and would be considered his legal heir.

will perform unto thee the part of a kinsman, well; let him do the kinsman's part: but if he will not do the part of a kinsman to thee, then will I do the part of a kinsman to thee, as the Lord liveth: lie down until the morning."

And she lay at his feet until the morning: and she rose up before one could know another. And he said, "Let it not be known that a woman came into the floor."

Also he said, "Bring the vail that thou hast upon thee, and hold it." And when she held it, he measured six measures of barley, and laid it on her: and she went into the city.

And when she came to her mother in law, she said, "Who art thou, my daughter?" And she told her all that the man had done to her.

And she said, "These six measures of barley gave he me; for he said to me, 'Go not empty unto thy mother in law.'"

Then said she, "Sit still, my daughter, until thou know how the matter will fall: for the man will not be in rest, until he have finished the thing this day."

Chapter 4

Then went Boaz up to the gate, and sat him down there: and, behold, the kinsman of whom Boaz spake came by; unto whom he said, "Ho, such a one! Turn aside, sit down here." And he turned aside, and sat down.

And he took ten men of the elders of the city, and said, "Sit ye down here." And they sat down.

And he said unto the kinsman, "Naomi, that is come again out of the country of Moab, selleth a parcel of land, which was our brother Elimelech's:

"And I thought to advertise thee, saying, 'Buy it before the inhabitants, and before the elders of my people. If thou wilt redeem it, redeem it: but if thou wilt not redeem it, then tell me, that I may know: for there is none to redeem it beside thee; and I am after thee.'" And he said, "I will redeem it."

Then said Boaz, "What day thou buyest the field of the hand of Naomi, thou must buy it also of Ruth the Moabitess, the wife of the dead, to raise up the name of the dead upon his inheritance."

And the kinsman said, "I cannot redeem it for myself, lest I mar mine own inheritance: redeem thou my right to thyself; for I cannot redeem it."

Now this was the manner in former time in Israel concerning redeeming and concerning changing, for to confirm all things; a man plucked off his shoe, and gave it to his neighbour: and this was a testimony in Israel.

Therefore the kinsman said unto Boaz, "Buy it for thee." So he drew off his shoe.

And Boaz said unto the elders, and unto all the people, "Ye are witnesses this day, that I have bought all that was Elimelech's, and all that was Chilion's and Mahlon's, of the hand of Naomi.

"Moreover Ruth the Moabitess, the wife of Mahlon, have I purchased to be my wife, to raise up the name of the dead upon his inheritance, that the name of the dead be not cut off from among his brethren, and from the gate of his place: ye are witnesses this day."

And all the people that were in the gate, and the elders, said, "We are witnesses. The Lord make the woman that is come into thine house like Rachel and like Leah,[4] which two did build the house of Israel: and do thou worthily in Ephratah, and be famous in Bethlehem:

"And let thy house be like the house of Pharez, whom Tamar bare unto Judah,[5] of the seed which the Lord shall give thee of this young woman."

So Boaz took Ruth, and she was his wife: and when he went in unto her, the Lord gave her conception, and she bare a son.

And the women said unto Naomi, "Blessed be the Lord, which hath not left thee this day without a kinsman, that his name may be famous in Israel.

---

4. **Rachel . . . Leah:** the wives of Jacob and ancestors of most of the twelve tribes of Israel.
5. **Tamar:** like Ruth, a childless widow; **Judah:** her father-in-law.

"And he shall be unto thee a restorer of thy life, and a nourisher of thine old age: for thy daughter in law, which loveth thee, which is better to thee than seven sons, hath born him."

And Naomi took the child, and laid it in her bosom, and became nurse unto it.

And the women her neighbours gave it a name, saying, "There is a son born to Naomi"; and they called his name Obed: he is the father of Jesse, the father of David.

Now these are the generations of Pharez: Pharez begat Hezron. And Hezron begat Ram, and Ram begat Amminadab. And Ammindab begat Nahshon, and Nahshon begat Salmon. And Salmon begat Boaz, and Boaz begat Obed. And Obed begat Jesse, and Jesse begat David.

Translated from the Hebrew in the King James Bible

Haiku Poets

Matsuo Bashō
(1644–1694)

In his own day, Bashō was revered in Japan as the greatest master of haiku. Bashō took his name from the name of a tree, which a disciple planted in the garden of a desolate hut to which the poet had retreated. The poet associated himself with that tree, with its delicate leaves easily torn by the wind.

Taniguchi Buson
(1716–1783)

Little information survives about the life of Buson, who was a painter as well as a poet. Like all haiku poets, he was deeply influenced by Bashō. Although Buson lived during difficult times, he removed his poetry from all worldly concerns.

Kobayashi Issa
(1762–1826)

Issa lived in poverty most of his life, enduring the deaths of his wife and five children and eking out an existence studying under Chikua, one of the leading haiku poets of the period. Somehow transcending the sadness and disappointments of his life, Issa wrote extraordinarily simple poems full of wry humor and tenderness, especially for small, weak animals.

Masaoka Shiki
(1867–1902)

Shiki helped to resurrect the haiku after several decades of decline that began with the death of Issa. Shiki established a basis for a new school of haiku, urging poets to be natural, to write to please themselves, to say only what is necessary, and to realize that haiku are not logical, but evocative.

Haiku

Probably no two practitioners would agree on exactly what a haiku is. In general, a Japanese haiku has a classical form: seventeen syllables, five in lines 1 and 3 and seven in line 2. A haiku presents images from everyday life—often contrasting images—and usually contains a seasonal word or symbol called a kigo. *Many haiku, influenced by Zen Buddhism, invite readers to experience a moment of discovery or enlightenment—*satori.

On a Journey

Wake up! Wake up! It's I,
   who want you for companion,
   sleeping butterfly!

BASHŌ

An Invitation to Etsujin

Snow that we two
   looked at together—this year
   has it fallen anew?

BASHŌ

Symphony in White

Blossoms on the pear—
   and a woman in the moonlight
   reads a letter there.

BUSON

.*The Lover*

What utter delight
    to the eye—my dearest one's fan,
      so perfectly white!
                    BUSON

Parting

For me who go,
    for you who stay—
      two autumns.
             BUSON

The Sudden Chillness

The piercing chill I feel:
    my dead wife's comb, in our bedroom,
      under my heel . . .
                BUSON

A Wish

My grumbling wife—
    if only she were here!
      This moon tonight . . .
             ISSA

Spring Road

Backward I gaze;
    one whom I had chanced to meet
      is lost in haze.

                    SHIKI

The Flower Wreath

Butterflies
    love and follow this flower wreath—
      that on the coffin lies.

                    SHIKI

The Parasol

Dear, your parasol,
    in all this blazing sunshine—
      is so very small!

                    SHIKI

Translated from the Japanese by Harold G. Henderson

Anton Chekhov
(1860–1904)

Anton Pavlovich Chekhov, the grandson of a serf who had bought his family's freedom, was born in Taganrog, Russia, a small town near the Black Sea. When Anton was a teenager, his father's general store went bankrupt, and the family fled to Moscow. However, the father's creditor demanded that Anton remain in Taganrog as a sort of hostage to tutor the creditor's son at a cheap rate.

Three years later, Anton himself was able to move to Moscow. There he rescued his family from debt, helped educate his brothers and sisters, and enrolled at the medical school at Moscow University. The financial problems that had rocked his family continued, however, and Chekhov began writing comic sketches and light short stories to earn money. These early stories had scant literary merit and are rarely read today, but they helped Chekhov develop the concise, efficient prose that characterizes his later work.

Although Chekhov finished his medical degree and practiced as a doctor, he never completely devoted himself to medicine. Literature had become a more profitable career. In the mid-1880s, he began writing the carefully crafted stories that earned him the reputation as one of the best young Russian writers. Chekhov used his medical knowledge in his stories: His characters are often motivated by psychosomatic illnesses or by the psychological effects caused by physical disease.

Like Maupassant, by whom he was influenced, Chekhov played a considerable part in the development of the short story. His principal contribution was the subtle and precise exploration of a mood or of a psychological state. It has been said that the words of critic Anatole France apply to Chekhov's writings better than to those of anyone else: "Russian fiction is largely the account of the undoing of human life, rather than of its shaping."

In his twenties, Chekhov began writing one-act farces like *A Marriage Proposal*. His first important play, *The Seagull* (1895), is a satire about a group of bohemian artists and a doctor, who is their detached observer. The play opened in St. Petersburg, where it set off a riot. The jeers from the audience sent an appalled Chekhov out of the theater, vowing never again to write another play. Fortunately, that vow was forgotten, and Chekhov went on to write some of the great plays in world literature: *Uncle Vanya*, *The Three Sisters*, and *The Cherry Orchard*—plays still staged today all over the world.

Chekhov had discovered signs of tuberculosis in his body when he was only twenty-four years old. In March 1897, as he was having dinner at the Hermitage, an art museum in St. Petersburg, blood started flowing from his mouth. As the disease wasted him, Chekhov traveled from one warm spa to another seeking a cure. He continued working, however, and in the last months of his life, he wrote furiously. He had long been dissatisfied with the productions of his plays, and he was determined to see *The Cherry Orchard*, his final play, produced as he wished it. He rewrote and revised as rehearsals continued. *The Cherry Orchard*, Chekhov's farewell to Russia and to his own life, premiered on January 17, 1904. Chekhov was taken from his bed to see the end of the third act. Six months later, he was dead.

A Marriage Proposal
Anton Chekhov

Characters

Stepan Stepanovitch Tschubukov (ste·pän′ ste·pä′nô·vich chŏŏ·bŏŏ′kôf), a country farmer

Natalia Stepanovna (nä·täl′yä ste·pä′nôv·nä), his daughter, age twenty-five

Ivan Vassiliyitch Lomov (i·vän′ vä·sil′ē·yich lô′môf), Tschubukov's neighbor

SCENE: *Reception room in* TSCHUBUKOV's *country home in Russia.* TSCHUBUKOV *is seen as the curtain rises.* LOMOV *enters, wearing a dress suit.*

Tschubukov (*going toward him and greeting him*). Who is this I see? My dear fellow! Ivan Vassiliyitch! I'm so glad to see you! (*Shakes hands*) But this is a surprise! How are you?

Lomov. Thank you! And how are you?

Tschubukov. Oh, so-so, my friend. Please sit down. It isn't right to forget one's neighbor. But tell me, why all this ceremony? Dress clothes, white gloves and all? Are you on your way to some engagement, my good fellow?

Lomov. No, I have no engagement except with you, Stepan Stepanovitch.

Tschubukov. But why in evening clothes, my friend? This isn't New Year's!

Lomov. You see, it's simply this, that—(*composing himself*)—I have come to you, Stepan Stepanovitch, to trouble you with a request. It is not the first time I have had the honor of turning to you for assistance, and you have always, that is—I beg your pardon, I am a bit excited! I'll take a drink of water first, dear Stepan Stepanovitch. (*He drinks.*)

Tschubukov (*aside*). He's come to borrow money! I won't give him any! (*To* LOMOV) What is it, then, dear Lomov?

Lomov. You see—dear—Stepanovitch, pardon me, Stepan—Stepan—dearvitch—I mean—I am terribly nervous, as you will be so good as to see—! What I mean to say—you are the only one who can help me, though I don't deserve it, and—and I have no right whatever to make this request of you.

Tschubukov. Oh, don't beat about the bush, my dear fellow. Tell me!

Lomov. Immediately—in a moment. Here it is, then: I have come to ask for the hand of your daughter, Natalia Stepanovna.

Tschubukov (*joyfully*). Angel! Ivan Vassiliyitch! Say that once again! I didn't quite hear it!

Lomov. I have the honor to beg——

Tschubukov (*interrupting*). My dear, dear man! I am so happy that everything is so—everything! (*Embraces and kisses him*) I have wanted this to happen for so long. It has been my dearest wish! (*He represses a tear.*) And I have always loved you, my dear fellow, as my own son! May God give you His blessings and His grace and—I always wanted it to happen. But why am I standing here like a blockhead? I am completely dumbfounded with pleasure, completely dumbfounded. My whole being—I'll call Natalia——

Lomov. Dear Stepan Stepanovitch, what do you think? May I hope for Natalia Stepanovna's acceptance?

Tschubukov. Really! A fine boy like you—and you think she won't accept on the minute? Lovesick as a cat and all that—! (*He goes out at right.*)

Lomov. I'm cold. My whole body is trembling as though I was going to take my examination! But the chief thing is to settle matters! If a person meditates too much, or hesitates, or talks about it, waits for an ideal or for true love, he never gets it. Brrr! It's cold! Natalia is an excellent housekeeper, not at all bad-looking, well educated—what more could I ask? I'm so excited my ears are roaring! (*He drinks water.*) And not to marry, that won't do! In the first place, I'm thirty-five—a critical age, you might say. In the second place, I must live a well-regulated life. I have a weak heart, continual palpitation, and I am very sensitive and always getting excited. My lips begin to tremble and the pulse in my right temple throbs terribly. But the worst of all is sleep! I hardly lie down and begin to doze before something in my left side begins to pull and tug, and something begins to hammer in my left should—and in my head, too! I jump up like a madman, walk about a little, lie down again, but the moment I fall asleep I have a terrible cramp in the side. And so it is all night long!

[NATALIA STEPANOVNA *enters.*]

Natalia. Ah! It's you. Papa said to go in—there was a dealer in there who'd come to buy something. Good afternoon, Ivan Vassiliyitch.

Lomov. Good day, my dear Natalia Stepanovna.

Natalia. You must pardon me for wearing my apron and this old dress. We are working today. Why haven't you come to see us oftener? You've not been here for so long! Sit down. (*They sit down.*) Won't you have something to eat?

Lomov. Thank you, I have just had lunch.

Natalia. Smoke, do, there are the matches. Today it is beautiful and only yesterday it rained so hard that the workmen couldn't do a stroke of work. How many bricks have you cut? Think of it! I was so anxious that I had the whole field mowed, and now I'm sorry I did it, because I'm afraid the hay will rot. It would have been better if I had waited. But what on earth is this? You are in evening clothes! The latest cut! Are you on your way to a ball? And you seem to be looking better, too— really. Why are you dressed up so gorgeously?

Lomov (*excited*). You see, my dear Natalia Stepanovna—it's simply this: I have decided to ask you to listen to me—of course it will be a surprise, and indeed you'll be angry, but I—— (*Aside*) How fearfully cold it is!

Natalia. What is it? (*A pause*) Well?

Lomov. I'll try to be brief. My dear Natalia Stepanovna, as you know, for many years, since my childhood, I have had the honor to know your family. My poor aunt and her husband, from whom, as you know, I inherited the estate, always had the greatest respect for your father and your poor mother. The Lomovs and the Tschubukovs have been for decades on the friendliest, indeed the closest, terms with each other, and furthermore my property, as you know, adjoins your own. If you will be so good as to remember, my meadows touch your birchwoods.

Natalia. Pardon the interruption. You said "my meadows"— but are they yours?

Lomov. Yes, they belong to me.

Natalia. What nonsense! The meadows belong to us—not to you!

Lomov. No, to me! Now, my dear Natalia Stepanovna!

Natalia. Well, that is certainly news to me. How do they belong to you?

Lomov. How? I am speaking of the meadows lying between your birchwoods and my brick earth.

Natalia. Yes, exactly, They belong to us.

Lomov. No, you are mistaken, my dear Natalia Stepanovna, they belong to me.

Natalia. Try to remember exactly, Ivan Vassiliyitch. Is it so long ago that you inherited them?

Lomov. Long ago! As far back as I can remember they have always belonged to us.

Natalia. But that isn't true! You'll pardon my saying so.

Lomov. It is all a matter of record, my dear Natalia Stepanovna. It is true that at one time the title to the meadows was disputed, but now everyone knows they belong to me. There is no room for discussion. Be so good as to listen: my aunt's grandmother put these meadows, free from all costs, into the hands of your father's grandfather's peasants for a certain time while they were making bricks for my grandmother. These people used the meadows free of cost for about forty years, living there as they would on their own property. Later, however, when——

Natalia. There's not a word of truth in that! My grandfather, and my great-grandfather, too, knew that their estate reached back to the swamp, so that the meadows belong to us. What further discussion can there be? I can't understand it. It is really most annoying.

Lomov. I'll show you the papers, Natalia Stepanovna.

Natalia. No, either you are joking, or trying to lead me into a discussion. That's not at all nice! We have owned this property for nearly three hundred years, and now all at once we hear that it doesn't belong to us. Ivan Vassiliyitch, you will pardon me, but I really can't believe my ears. So far as I am concerned, the meadows are worth very little. In all they don't contain more than five acres and they are worth only a few hundred rubles, say three hundred, but the injustice of the thing is what affects me. Say what you will, I can't bear injustice.

Lomov. Only listen until I have finished, please! The peasants of your respected father's grandfather, as I have already had the honor to tell you, baked bricks for my grandmother. My aunt's grandmother wished to do them a favor——

Natalia. Grandfather! Grandmother! Aunt! I know nothing about them. All I know is that the meadows belong to us, and that ends the matter.

Lomov. No, they belong to me!

Natalia. And if you keep on explaining it for two days, and put on five suits of evening clothes, the meadows are still ours, ours, ours! I don't want to take your property, but I refuse to give up what belongs to us!

Lomov. Natalia Stepanovna, I don't need the meadows, I am only concerned with the principle. If you are agreeable, I beg of you, accept them as a gift from me!

Natalia. But I can give them to you, because they belong to me! That is very peculiar, Ivan Vassiliyitch! Until now we have considered you as a good neighbor and a good friend; only last year we lent you our threshing machine, so that we couldn't thresh until November, and now you treat us like thieves! You offer to give me my own land. Excuse me, but neighbors don't treat each other that way. In my opinion, it's a very low trick—to speak frankly——

Lomov. According to you I'm a usurper, then, am I? My dear lady, I have never appropriated other people's property, and I shall permit no one to accuse me of such a thing! (*He goes quickly to the bottle and drinks water.*) The meadows are mine!

Natalia. That's not the truth! They are mine!

Lomov. Mine!

Natalia. Eh? I'll prove it to you! This afternoon I'll send my reapers into the meadows.

Lomov. W—h—a—t?

Natalia. My reapers will be there today!

Lomov. And I'll chase them off!

Natalia. If you dare!

Lomov. The meadows are mine, you understand? Mine!

Natalia. Really, you needn't scream so! If you want to scream and snort and rage you may do it at home, but here please keep yourself within the limits of common decency.

Lomov. My dear lady, if it weren't that I were suffering from palpitation of the heart and hammering of the arteries in my temples, I would deal with you very differently! (*In a loud voice*) The meadows belong to me!

Natalia. Us!

Lomov. Me!

[TSCHUBUKOV *enters at right.*]

Tschubukov. What's going on here? What is he yelling about?

Natalia. Papa, please tell this gentleman to whom the meadows belong, to us or to him?

Tschubukov (*to* LOMOV). My dear fellow, the meadows are ours.

Lomov. But, merciful heavens, Stepan Stepanovitch, how do you make that out? You at least might be reasonable. My aunt's grandmother gave the use of the meadows free of cost to your grandfather's peasants; the peasants lived on the land for forty years and used it as their own, but later when——

Tschubukov. Permit me, my dear friend. You forget that your grandmother's peasants never paid, because there had been a lawsuit over the meadows, and everyone knows that the meadows belong to us. You haven't looked at the map.

Lomov. I'll prove to you that they belong to me!

Tschubukov. Don't try to prove it, my dear fellow.

Lomov. I will!

Tschubukov. My good fellow, what are you shrieking about? You can't prove anything by yelling, you know. I don't ask for anything that belongs to you, nor do I intend to give up anything of my own. Why should I? If it has gone so far, my dear man, that you really intend to claim the meadows, I'd rather give them to the peasants than you, and I certainly shall!

Lomov. I can't believe it! By what right can you give away property that doesn't belong to you?

Tschubukov. Really, you must allow me to decide what I am to do with my own land! I'm not accustomed, young man, to have people address me in that tone of voice. I, young man, am twice your age, and I beg you to address me respectfully.

Lomov. No! No! You think I'm a fool! You're making fun of me! You call my property yours and then expect me to stand quietly by and talk to you like a human being. That isn't the way a good neighbor behaves, Stepan Stepanovitch! You are no neighbor, you're no better than a land-grabber. That's what you are!

Tschubukov. Wh—at? What did he say?

Natalia. Papa, send the reapers into the meadows this minute!

Tschubukov (*to* LOMOV). What was that you said, sir?

Natalia. The meadows belong to us and I won't give them up! I won't give them up! I won't give them up!

Lomov. We'll see about that! I'll prove in court that they belong to me.

Tschubukov. In court! You may sue in court, sir, if you like! Oh, I know you, you are only waiting to find an excuse to go to law! You're an intriguer, that's what you are! Your whole family were always looking for quarrels. The whole lot!

Lomov. Kindly refrain from insulting my family. The entire race of Lomov has always been honorable! And never has one been brought to trial for embezzlement, as your dear uncle was!

Tschubukov. And the whole Lomov family were insane!

Natalia. Every one of them!

Tschubukov. Your grandmother was a dipsomaniac, and the younger aunt, Nastasia Michailovna, ran off with an architect.

Lomov. And your mother limped. (*He puts his hand over his heart.*) Oh, my side pains! My temples are bursting! Water!

Tschubukov. And your dear father was a gambler—and a glutton!

Natalia. And your aunt was a gossip like few others!

Lomov. And you are an intriguer. Oh, my heart! And it's an open secret that you cheated at the elections—my eyes are blurred! Where is my hat?

Natalia. Oh, how low! Liar! Disgusting thing!

Lomov. Where's the hat—? My heart! Where shall I go? Where is the door—? Oh—it seems—as though I were dying! I can't— my legs won't hold me——— (*Goes to the door*)

Tschubukov (*following him*). May you never darken my door again!

Natalia. Bring your suit to court! We'll see!

[LOMOV *staggers out at center.*]

Tschubukov (*angrily*). The devil!

Natalia. Such a good-for-nothing! And then they talk about being good neighbors!

Tschubukov. Loafer! Scarecrow! Monster!

Natalia. A swindler like that takes over a piece of property that doesn't belong to him and then dares to argue about it!

Tschubukov. And to think that this fool dares to make a proposal of marriage!

Natalia. What? A proposal of marriage?

Tschubukov. Why, yes! He came here to make you a proposal of marriage.

Natalia. Why didn't you tell me that before?

Tschubukov. That's why he had on his evening clothes! The poor fool!

Natalia. Proposal for me? Oh! (*Falls into an armchair and groans*) Bring him back! Bring him back!

Tschubukov. Bring whom back?

Natalia. Faster, faster, I'm sinking! Bring him back! (*She becomes hysterical.*)

Tschubukov. What is it? What's wrong with you? (*His hands to his head*) I'm cursed with bad luck! I'll shoot myself! I'll hang myself!

Natalia. I'm dying! Bring him back!

Tschubukov. Bah! In a minute! Don't bawl! (*He rushes out at center.*)

Natalia (*groaning*). What have they done to me? Bring him back! Bring him back!

Tschubukov (*comes running in*). He's coming at once! The devil take him! Ugh! Talk to him yourself, I can't.

Natalia (*groaning*). Bring him back!

Tschubukov. He's coming, I tell you! What a task it is to be the father of a grown daughter! I'll cut my throat! I really will cut my throat! We've argued with the fellow, insulted him, and now we've thrown him out!—and you did it all, you!

Natalia. No, you! You haven't any manners, you are brutal! If it weren't for you, he wouldn't have gone!

Tschubukov. Oh, yes, I'm to blame! If I shoot or hang myself, remember *you'll* be to blame. You forced me to it! You!

[LOMOV *appears in the doorway.*]

There, talk to him yourself! (*He goes out.*)

Lomov. Terrible palpitation!—My leg is lamed! My side hurts me——

Natalia. Pardon us, we were angry, Ivan Vassiliyitch. I remember now—the meadows really belong to you.

Lomov. My heart is beating terribly! My meadows—my eyelids tremble—— (*They sit down.*) We were wrong. It was only the principle of the thing—the property isn't worth much to me, but the principle is worth a great deal.

Natalia. Exactly, the principle! Let us talk about something else.

Lomov. Because I have proofs that my aunt's grandmother had, with the peasants of your good father——

Natalia. Enough, enough. (*Aside*) I don't know how to begin. (*To* LOMOV) Are you going hunting soon?

Lomov. Yes, heath-cock shooting, respected Natalia Stepanovna. I expect to begin after the harvest. Oh, did you hear? My dog, Ugadi, you know him—limps!

Natalia. What a shame! How did that happen?

Lomov. I don't know. Perhaps it's a dislocation, or maybe he was bitten by some other dog. (*He sighs.*) The best dog I ever had—to say nothing of his price! I paid Mironov a hundred and twenty-five rubles for him.

Natalia. That was too much to pay, Ivan Vassiliyitch.

Lomov. In my opinion it was very cheap. A wonderful dog!

Natalia. Papa paid eighty-five rubles for his Otkatai, and Otkatai is much better than your Ugadi.

Lomov. Really? Otkatai is better than Ugadi? What an idea! (*He laughs.*) Otkatai better than Ugadi!

Natalia. Of course he is better. It is true Otkatai is still young; he isn't full-grown yet, but in the pack or on the leash with two or three, there is no better than he, even——

Lomov. I really beg your pardon, Natalia Stepanovna, but you quite overlooked the fact that he has a short lower jaw, and a dog with a short lower jaw can't snap.

Natalia. Short lower jaw? That's the first time I ever heard that!

Lomov. I assure you, his lower jaw is shorter than the upper.

Natalia. Have you measured it?

Lomov. I have measured it. He is good at running, though.

Natalia. In the first place, our Otkatai is a purebred, a full-blooded son of Sapragavas and Stameskis, and as for your mongrel, nobody could even figure out his pedigree; he's old and ugly, and as skinny as an old hag.

Lomov. Old, certainly! I wouldn't take five of your Otkatais for him! Ugadi is a dog and Otkatai is—it is laughable to argue about it! Dogs like your Otkatai can be found by the dozens at any dog dealer's, a whole poundful!

Natalia. Ivan Vassiliyitch, you are very contrary today. First our meadows belong to you and then Ugadi is better than Otkatai. I don't like it when a person doesn't say what he really thinks. You know perfectly well that Otkatai is a hundred times better than your silly Ugadi. What makes you keep on saying he isn't?

Lomov. I can see, Natalia Stepanovna, that you consider me either a blind man or a fool. But at least you may as well admit that Otkatai has a short lower jaw!

Natalia. It isn't so!

Lomov. Yes, a short lower jaw!

Natalia (*loudly*). It's not so!

Lomov. What makes you scream, my dear lady?

Natalia. What makes you talk such nonsense? It's disgusting! It is high time that Ugadi was shot, and yet you compare him with Otkatai!

Lomov. Pardon me, but I can't carry on this argument any longer. I have palpitation of the heart!

Natalia. I have always noticed that the hunters who do the most talking know the least about hunting.

Lomov. My dear lady, I beg of you to be still. My heart is bursting! (*He shouts.*) Be still!

Natalia. I won't be still until you admit that Otkatai is better!

[TSCHUBUKOV *enters.*]

Tschubukov. Well, has it begun again?

Natalia. Papa, say frankly, on your honor, which dog is better: Otkatai or Ugadi?

Lomov. Stepan Stepanovitch, I beg of you, just answer this: has your dog a short lower jaw or not? Yes or no?

Tschubukov. And what if he has? Is it of such importance? There is no better dog in the whole country.

Lomov. My Ugadi is better. Tell the truth, now!

Tschubukov. Don't get so excited, my dear fellow! Permit me. Your Ugadi certainly has his good points. He is from a good breed, has a good stride, strong haunches, and so forth. But the dog, if you really want to know it, has two faults; he is old and he has a short lower jaw.

Lomov. Pardon me, I have palpitation of the heart!—Let us keep to facts—just remember in Maruskins' meadows, my Ugadi kept ear to ear with the Count Rasvachai and your dog.

Tschubukov. He was behind, because the Count struck him with his whip.

Lomov. Quite right. All the other dogs were on the fox's scent, but Otkatai found it necessary to bite a sheep.

Tschubukov. That isn't so!—I am sensitive about that and beg you to stop this argument. He struck him because everybody looks on a strange dog of good blood with envy. Even you, sir, aren't free from the sin. No sooner do you find a dog better than Ugadi than you begin to—this, that—his, mine—and so forth! I remember distinctly.

Lomov. I remember something, too!

Tschubukov (*mimicking him*). I remember something, too! What do you remember?

Lomov. Palpitation! My leg is lame—I can't——

Natalia. Palpitation! What kind of hunter are you? You ought to stay in the kitchen by the stove and wrestle with the potato peelings, and not go fox-hunting! Palpitation!

Tschubukov. And what kind of hunter are you? A man with your diseases ought to stay at home and not jolt around in the saddle. If you were a hunter—! But you only ride around in order to find out about other people's dogs, and make trouble for everyone. I am sensitive! Let's drop the subject. Besides, you're no hunter.

Lomov. You only ride around to flatter the Count!—My heart! You intriguer! Swindler!

Tschubukov. And what of it? (*Shouting*) Be still!

Lomov. Intriguer!

Tschubukov. Baby! Puppy! Walking drugstore!

Lomov. Old rat! Oh, I know you!

Tschubukov. Be still! Or I'll shoot you—with my worst gun, like a partridge! Fool! Loafer!

Lomov. Everyone knows that—oh, my heart!—that your poor

late wife beat you. My leg—my temples—Heavens—I'm dying—I——

Tschubukov. And your housekeeper wears the trousers in your house!

Lomov. Here—here—there—there—my heart has burst! My shoulder is torn apart. Where is my shoulder? I'm dying! (*He falls into a chair.*) The doctor! (*Faints*)

Tschubukov. Baby! Half-baked clam! Fool!

Natalia. Nice sort of hunter you are! You can't even sit on a horse. (*To* TSCHUBUKOV) Papa, what's the matter with him? (*She screams.*) Ivan Vassiliyitch! He is dead!

Lomov. I'm ill! I can't breathe! Air!

Natalia. He is dead! (*She shakes* LOMOV *in the chair.*) Ivan Vassiliyitch! What have we done! He is dead! (*She sinks into a chair.*) The doctor—doctor! (*She goes into hysterics.*)

Tschubukov. Ahh! What is it? What's the matter with you?

Natalia (*groaning*). He's dead!—Dead!

Tschubukov. Who is dead? Who? (*Looking at* LOMOV) Yes, he is dead! Water! The doctor! (*Holding the glass to* LOMOV's *lips*) Drink! No, he won't drink! He's dead! What a terrible situation! Why didn't I shoot myself? Why have I never cut my throat? What am I waiting for now? Only give me a knife! Give me a pistol!

[LOMOV *moves.*]

He's coming to! Drink some water—there!

Lomov. Sparks! Mists! Where am I?

Tschubukov. Get married! Quick, and then go to the devil! She's willing! (*He joins the hands of* LOMOV *and* NATALIA.) She's agreed! Only leave me in peace!

Lomov. Wh—what? (*Getting up*) Whom?

Tschubukov. She's willing! Well? Kiss each other and—the devil take you both!

Natalia (*groans*). He lives! Yes, yes, I'm willing!

Tschubukov. Kiss each other!

Lomov. Eh? Whom? (NATALIA *and* LOMOV *kiss.*) Very nice—!

Pardon me, but what is this for? Oh, yes, I understand! My heart—sparks—I am happy, Natalia Stepanovna. (*He kisses her hand.*) My leg is lame!

Natalia. I'm happy, too!

Tschubukov. Ahh! A load off my shoulders! Ahh!

Natalia. And now at least you'll admit that Ugadi is worse than Otkatai!

Lomov. Better!

Natalia. Worse!

Tschubukov. Now the domestic joys have begun.— Champagne!

Lomov. Better!

Natalia. Worse, worse, worse!

Tschubukov (*trying to drown them out*). Champagne, champagne!

CURTAIN

Translated from the Russian by
Hilmar Baukhage and Barrett H. Clark

Isaac Bashevis Singer
(1904–1991)

"I never sit down to write a novel to make a better world or to create good feelings toward the Jews or for any other purpose," Isaac Bashevis Singer once said in an interview. "I knew this from the very beginning, that writing fiction has no other purpose than to give enjoyment to a reader. . . . I consider myself an entertainer. . . . I mean an entertainer of good people, of intellectual people who cannot be entertained by cheap stuff. And I think this is true about fiction in all times."

Singer was born Icek-Hersz Zynger in a village near Warsaw, Poland. His father and both grandfathers were rabbis, and they expected Isaac to continue the tradition. However, a strong influence pulled him in another direction: His older brother, Israel Joshua, was a novelist who wrote on secular topics. Singer was torn by this conflict between the secular and the spiritual, a conflict that was to appear later in various forms in his stories. When he was nineteen, Singer made the move to Warsaw, where he worked as a journalist and occasionally published short stories. He wrote in Hebrew at first, then switched to Yiddish, a language he was to write in for the remainder of his life.

Alarmed at the rise of anti-Semitism in Europe, Singer and his brother decided to immigrate to the United States. Isaac arrived in New York City in 1935. There he earned a living as a freelance writer for the *Jewish Daily Forward*. In 1943, he began to publish stories and novels. Singer lived on the Upper West Side of Manhattan for the rest of his life.

Early in his career, Singer depended upon others to translate his work. Later, as his English improved, he made the translations himself, although even then he required help. "I used to play with the idea [of writing in English]," Singer once said in an interview, "but never seriously. Never. I always knew that a writer has to write in his own language or not at all."

The setting of "The Son from America" is characteristic of Singer's writing—an Eastern European village like the one he grew up in. Singer was sometimes criticized for placing so many of his stories in this setting. "I prefer to write about the world which I knew, which I know, best," Singer responded. "This is Bilgoray, Lublin, the Jews of Kreshev. This is enough for me. I can get from these people art. I don't need to go to the North Pole and write a novel about the Eskimos who live in that neighborhood. I write about the things where I grew up, and where I feel completely at home."

Singer became a master of the short story. In fact, it was his short story "Gimpel the Fool" that first earned him widespread recognition in the United States. Like "Gimpel the Fool," "The Son from America" is told simply, like a spoken tale. Singer allows his meaning to emerge slowly, as in a parable. "When I tell a story, I tell a story," he explains. "I don't try to discuss, criticize, or analyze my characters."

Though Singer was slow to earn recognition in the United States, he eventually won the National Book Award in 1970 for his autobiographical *A Day of Pleasure*, the Nobel Prize in literature in 1978, and three Newbery Honor Book Awards. He once said he never expected to make a living from writing—he was surprised every time he got a check for a story.

The Son from America
Isaac Bashevis Singer

The village of Lentshin was tiny—a sandy marketplace where the peasants of the area met once a week. It was surrounded by little huts with thatched roofs or shingles green with moss. The chimneys looked like pots. Between the huts there were fields, where the owners planted vegetables or pastured their goats.

In the smallest of these huts lived old Berl, a man in his eighties, and his wife, who was called Berlcha (wife of Berl). Old Berl was one of the Jews who had been driven from their villages in Russia and had settled in Poland. In Lentshin, they mocked the mistakes he made while praying aloud. He spoke with a sharp "r." He was short, broad-shouldered, and had a small white beard, and summer and winter he wore a sheepskin hat, a padded cotton jacket, and stout boots. He walked slowly, shuffling his feet. He had a half acre of field, a cow, a goat, and chickens.

The couple had a son, Samuel, who had gone to America forty years ago. It was said in Lentshin that he became a millionaire there. Every month, the Lentshin letter carrier brought old Berl a money order and a letter that no one could read because many of the words were English. How much money Samuel sent his parents remained a secret. Three times a year, Berl and his wife went on foot to Zakroczym and cashed the money orders there. But they never seemed to use the money. What for? The garden, the cow, and the goat provided most of their needs. Besides, Berlcha sold chickens and eggs, and from these there was enough to buy flour for bread.

No one cared to know where Berl kept the money that his son sent him. There were no thieves in Lentshin. The hut consisted of one room, which contained all their belongings: the

228

table, the shelf for meat, the shelf for milk foods, the two beds, and the clay oven. Sometimes the chickens roosted in the woodshed and sometimes, when it was cold, in a coop near the oven. The goat, too, found shelter inside when the weather was bad. The more prosperous villagers had kerosene lamps, but Berl and his wife did not believe in newfangled gadgets. What was wrong with a wick in a dish of oil? Only for the Sabbath would Berlcha buy three tallow candles at the store. In summer, the couple got up at sunrise and retired with the chickens. In the long winter evenings, Berlcha spun flax at her spinning wheel and Berl sat beside her in the silence of those who enjoy their rest.

Once in a while when Berl came home from the synagogue after evening prayers, he brought news to his wife. In Warsaw there were strikers who demanded that the czar abdicate. A heretic by the name of Dr. Herzl had come up with the idea that Jews should settle again in Palestine. Berlcha listened and shook her bonneted head. Her face was yellowish and wrinkled like a cabbage leaf. There were bluish sacks under her eyes. She was half deaf. Berl had to repeat each word he said to her. She would say, "The things that happen in the big cities!"

Here in Lentshin nothing happened except usual events: a cow gave birth to a calf, a young couple had a circumcision party, or a girl was born and there was no party. Occasionally, someone died. Lentshin had no cemetery, and the corpse had to be taken to Zakroczym. Actually, Lentshin had become a village with few young people. The young men left for Zakroczym, for Nowy Dwor, for Warsaw, and sometimes for the United States. Like Samuel's, their letters were illegible, the Yiddish mixed with the languages of the countries where they were now living. They sent photographs in which the men wore top hats and the women fancy dresses like squiresses.

Berl and Berlcha also received such photographs. But their eyes were failing and neither he nor she had glasses. They could barely make out the pictures. Samuel had sons and daughters with Gentile names—and grandchildren who had married and had their own offspring. Their names were so strange that Berl and Berlcha could never remember them. But what difference do names make? America was far, far away on the other side of the ocean, at the edge of the world. A Talmud teacher who came to Lentshin had said that Americans walked with their heads down and their feet up. Berl and Berlcha could not grasp this. How was it possible? But since the teacher said so it must be true. Berlcha pondered for some time and then she said, "One can get accustomed to everything."

And so it remained. From too much thinking—God forbid—one may lose one's wits.

One Friday morning, when Berlcha was kneading the dough for the Sabbath loaves, the door opened and a nobleman entered. He was so tall that he had to bend down to get through the door. He wore a beaver hat and a cloak bordered with fur. He was followed by Chazkel, the coachman from Zakroczym, who carried two leather valises with brass locks. In astonishment Berlcha raised her eyes.

The nobleman looked around and said to the coachman in Yiddish, "Here it is." He took out a silver ruble and paid him. The coachman tried to hand him change but he said, "You can go now."

When the coachman closed the door, the nobleman said, "Mother, it's me, your son Samuel—Sam."

Berlcha heard the words and her legs grew numb. Her hands, to which pieces of dough were sticking, lost their power. The nobleman hugged her, kissed her forehead, both her cheeks. Berlcha began to cackle like a hen, "My son!" At that moment Berl came in from the woodshed his arms piled with logs. The goat followed him. When he saw a nobleman kissing his wife, Berl dropped the wood and exclaimed, "What is this?"

The nobleman let go of Berlcha and embraced Berl. "Father!"

For a long time Berl was unable to utter a sound. He wanted to recite holy words that he had read in the Yiddish Bible, but he could remember nothing. Then he asked, "Are you Samuel?"

"Yes, Father, I am Samuel."

"Well, peace be with you." Berl grasped his son's hand. He

was still not sure that he was not being fooled. Samuel wasn't as tall and heavy as this man, but then Berl reminded himself that Samuel was only fifteen years old when he had left home. He must have grown in that far-away country. Berl asked, "Why didn't you let us know that you were coming?"

"Didn't you receive my cable?" Samuel asked.

Berl did not know what a cable was.

Berlcha had scraped the dough from her hands and enfolded her son. He kissed her again and asked, "Mother, didn't you receive a cable?"

"What? If I lived to see this, I am happy to die," Berlcha said, amazed by her own words. Berl, too, was amazed. These were just the words he would have said earlier if he had been able to remember. After a while Berl came to himself and said, "Pescha, you will have to make a double Sabbath pudding in addition to the stew."

It was years since Berl had called Berlcha by her given name. When he wanted to address her, he would say, "Listen," or "Say." It is the young or those from the big cities who call a wife by her name. Only now did Berlcha begin to cry. Yellow tears ran from her eyes, and everything became dim. Then she called out, "It's Friday—I have to prepare for the Sabbath." Yes, she had to knead the dough and braid the loaves. With such a guest, she had to make a larger Sabbath stew. The winter day is short and she must hurry.

Her son understood what was worrying her, because he said, "Mother, I will help you."

Berlcha wanted to laugh, but a choked sob came out. "What are you saying? God forbid."

The nobleman took off his cloak and jacket and remained in his vest, on which hung a solid-gold watch chain. He rolled up his sleeves and came to the trough. "Mother, I was a baker for many years in New York," he said, and he began to knead the dough.

"What! You are my darling son who will say Kaddish for me." She wept raspingly. Her strength left her, and she slumped onto the bed.

Berl said, "Women will always be women." And he went to the shed to get more wood. The goat sat down near the oven; she gazed with surprise at this strange man—his height and his bizarre clothes.

The neighbors had heard the good news that Berl's son had arrived from America and they came to greet him. The women began to help Berlcha prepare for the Sabbath. Some laughed, some cried. The room was full of people, as at a wedding. They asked Berl's son, "What is new in America?" And Berl's son answered, "America is all right."

"Do Jews make a living?"

"One eats white bread there on weekdays."

"Do they remain Jews?"

"I am not a Gentile."

After Berlcha blessed the candles, father and son went to the little synagogue across the street. A new snow had fallen. The son took large steps, but Berl warned him, "Slow down."

In the synagogue the Jews recited "Let Us Exult" and "Come, My Groom." All the time, the snow outside kept falling. After prayers, when Berl and Samuel left the Holy Place, the village was unrecognizable. Everything was covered in snow. One could see only the contours of the roofs and the candles in the windows. Samuel said, "Nothing has changed here."

Berlcha had prepared gefilte fish, chicken soup with rice, meat, carrot stew. Berl recited the benediction over a glass of ritual wine. The family ate and drank, and when it grew quiet for a while one could her the chirping of the house cricket. The son talked a lot, but Berl and Berlcha understood little. His Yiddish was different and contained foreign words.

After the final blessing Samuel asked, "Father, what did you do with all the money I sent you?"

Berl raised his white brows. "It's here."

"Didn't you put it in a bank?"

"There is no bank in Lentshin."

"Where do you keep it?"

Berl hesitated. "One is not allowed to touch money on the Sabbath, but I will show you." He crouched beside the bed and began to shove something heavy. A boot appeared. Its top was stuffed with straw. Berl removed the straw and the son saw that the boot was full of gold coins. He lifted it.

"Father, this is a treasure!" he called out.

"Well."

"Why didn't you spend it?"

"On what? Thank God, we have everything."

"Why didn't you travel somewhere?"

"Where to? This is our home."

The son asked one question after the other, but Berl's answer was always the same: they wanted for nothing. The garden, the cow, the goat, the chickens provided them with all they needed. The son said, "If thieves knew about this, your lives wouldn't be safe."

"There are no thieves here."

"What will happen to the money?"

"You take it."

Slowly, Berl and Berlcha grew accustomed to their son and his American Yiddish. Berlcha could hear him better now. She even recognized his voice. He was saying, "Perhaps we should build a large synagogue."

"The synagogue is big enough," Berl replied.

"Perhaps a home for old people."

"No one sleeps in the street."

The next day after the Sabbath meal was eaten, a Gentile from Zakroczym brought a paper—it was the cable. Berl and Berlcha lay down for a nap. They soon began to snore. The goat, too, dozed off. The son put on his cloak and his hat and went for a walk. He strode with his long legs across the marketplace. He stretched out a hand and touched a roof. He wanted to smoke a cigar, but he remembered it was forbidden on the Sabbath. He had a desire to talk to someone, but it seemed that the whole of Lentshin was asleep. He entered the synagogue. An old man was sitting there, reciting psalms. Samuel asked, "Are you praying?"

"What else is there to do when one gets old?"

"Do you make a living?"

The old man did not understand the meaning of these words. He smiled, showing his empty gums, and then he said, "If God gives health, one keeps on living."

Samuel returned home. Dusk had fallen. Berl went to the synagogue for the evening prayers and the son remained with his mother. The room was filled with shadows.

Berlcha began to recite in a solemn singsong, "God of Abraham, Isaac, and Jacob, defend the poor people of Israel and Thy name. The Holy Sabbath is departing; the welcome week is coming to us. Let it be one of health, wealth, and good deeds."

"Mother, you don't need to pray for wealth," Samuel said. "You are wealthy already."

Berlcha did not hear—or pretended not to. Her face had turned into a cluster of shadows.

In the twilight Samuel put his hand into his jacket pocket and touched his passport, his checkbook, his letters of credit. He had come here with big plans. He had a valise filled with presents for his parents. He wanted to bestow gifts on the village. He brought not only his own money but funds from the Lentshin Society in New York, which had organized a ball for the benefit of the village. But this village in the hinterland needed nothing. From the synagogue one could hear hoarse chanting. The cricket, silent all day, started again its chirping. Berlcha began to sway and utter holy rhymes inherited from mothers and grandmothers:

> *Thy holy sheep*
> *In mercy keep,*
> *In Torah and good deeds;*
> *Provide for all their needs,*
> *Shoes, clothes, and bread*
> *And the Messiah's tread.*

Translated from the Yiddish by the Author and Dorothea Straus

Rabindranath Tagore
(1861–1941)

Rabindranath Tagore was born into a wealthy, upper-caste Hindu family in Calcutta. One of the major influences in his life was his family and in particular his father, who was a writer, scholar, and mystic. "Most members of my family," Tagore said, "had some gift—some were artists, some poets, some musicians—and the whole atmosphere of our home was permeated with the spirit of creation."

Tagore began writing poetry when he was eight; he dictated his final poem just hours before his death. In between, he published more than sixty volumes of poetry. His first collection of poems, *Evening Songs* (1882), established Tagore's reputation in India, but it was not until 1912, when Tagore traveled to England and the United States, that he established his worldwide reputation. On this trip, he met Ezra Pound, W. B. Yeats, George Bernard Shaw, and other Western artists. The same year, *Gitanjali*, a small volume of poetry bearing a preface by W. B. Yeats, was published in English translation. This work was hailed by critics as a great literary event. Tagore won the Nobel Prize in literature for this collection in 1913. He was the first non-Western writer to receive the award.

Tagore also wrote about two hundred short stories, many of which have been translated into English. About short stories, Tagore wrote: "If I do nothing but write short stories I am happy, and I make a few readers happy. The main cause of happiness is that the people about whom I write become my companions. They are with me when I am confined to my room in the rains. On a sunny day they move about me on the banks of the Padma."

Kabuliwallah
Rabindranath Tagore

The title character in this story, Rahamat, a poor Muslim fruit seller, is called a Kabuliwallah—a man from Kabul, the capital of Afghanistan, northwest of India. The narrator and his family, on the other hand, are upper-caste Hindu Indians. According to the caste system, the hereditary class system of Hinduism developed in India centuries ago, a lower-caste Hindu could not eat, sit, or socialize in any way with an upper-caste Hindu. At the time of the story, caste rules were strictly enforced, and a poor Muslim would have little chance of social contact with upper-caste Hindus.

My five-year-old daughter Mini can't stop talking for a minute. It only took her a year to learn to speak, after coming into the world, and ever since she has not wasted a minute of her waking hours by keeping silent. Her mother often scolds her and makes her shut up, but I can't do that. When Mini is quiet, it is so unnatural that I cannot bear it. So she's rather keen on chatting to me.

One morning, as I was starting the seventeenth chapter of my novel, Mini came up to me and said, "Father, Ramdoyal the gatekeeper calls a crow a *kauyā* instead of a *kāk*. He doesn't know anything, does he!"

Before I had a chance to enlighten her about the multiplicity of languages in the world, she brought up another subject. "Guess what, Father, Bhola says it rains when an elephant in the sky squirts water through its trunk. What nonsense he talks! On and on, all day."

Without waiting for my opinion on this matter either, she suddenly asked, "Father, what relation is Mother to you?"

"Good question," I said to myself, but to Mini I said, "Run off and play with Bhola. I've got work to do."

But she then sat down near my feet beside my writing-table, and, slapping her knees, began to recite *"āgdum bāgdum"* at top speed. Meanwhile, in my seventeenth chapter, Pratap Singh was leaping under cover of night from his high prison-window into the river below, with Kanchanmala in his arms.

My study looks out on to the road. Mini suddenly abandoned the *"āgdum bāgdum"* game, ran over to the window and shouted, "Kabuliwallah, Kabuliwallah!"

Dressed in dirty baggy clothes, pugree on his head, bag hanging from his shoulder, and with three or four boxes of grapes in his hands, a tall Kabuliwallah was ambling along the road. It was hard to say exactly what thoughts the sight of him had put into my beloved daughter's mind, but she began to shout and shriek at him. That swinging bag spells trouble, I thought: my seventeenth chapter won't get finished today. But just as the Kabuliwallah, attracted by Mini's yells, looked towards us with a smile and started to approach our house, Mini gasped and ran into the inner rooms, disappearing from view. She had a blind conviction that if one looked inside that swinging bag one would find three or four live children like her.

Meanwhile the Kabuliwallah came up to the window and smilingly salaamed. I decided that although the plight of Pratap Singh and Kanchanmala was extremely critical, it would be churlish not to invite the fellow inside and buy something from him.

I bought something. Then I chatted to him for a bit. We talked about Abdur Rahman's efforts to preserve the integrity of Afghanistan against the Russians and the British. When he got up to leave, he asked, "Babu, where did your little girl go?"

To dispel her groundless fears, I called Mini to come out. She clung to me and looked suspiciously at the Kabuliwallah and his bag. The Kabuliwallah took some raisins and apricots out and offered them to her, but she would not take them, and clung to my knees with doubled suspicion. Thus passed her first meeting with the Kabuliwallah.

A few days later when for some reason I was on my way out of the house one morning, I saw my daughter sitting on a bench in front of the door, nattering unrestrainedly; and the Kabuliwallah was sitting at her feet listening—grinning broadly, and from time to time making comments in his hybrid sort of Bengali. In all her five years of life, Mini had never found so patient a listener, apart from her father. I also saw that the fold of her little sari was crammed with raisins and nuts. I said to the Kabuliwallah, "Why have you given all these? Don't give her any more." I then took a half-rupee out of my pocket and gave it to him. He unhesitatingly took the coin and put it in his bag.

When I returned home, I found that this half-rupee had caused a full-scale row. Mini's mother was holding up a round shining object and saying crossly to Mini, "Where did you get this half-rupee from?"

"The Kabuliwallah gave it to me," said Mini.

"Why did you take it from the Kabuliwallah?" said her mother.

"I didn't ask for it," said Mini tearfully. "He gave it to me himself."

I rescued Mini from her mother's wrath, and took her outside. I learnt that this was not just the second time that Mini and the Kabuliwallah had met: he had been coming nearly every day and, by bribing her eager little heart with pistachio-nuts, had quite won her over. I found that they now had certain fixed jokes and routines: for example as soon as Mini saw Rahamat, she giggled and asked, "Kabuliwallah, O Kabuliwallah, what have you got in your bag?" Rahamat would laugh back and say—giving the word a peculiar nasal twang—"An *elephant*." The notion of an elephant in his bag was the source of immense hilarity; it might not be a very subtle joke, but they both seemed to find it very funny, and it gave me pleasure to see, on an autumn morning, a young child and a grown man laughing so heartily.

They had a couple of other jokes. Rahamat would say to Mini, "Little one, don't ever go off to your *śvaśur-bāri*." Most Bengali girls grow up hearing frequent references to their *śvaśur-bāri*, but my wife and I are rather progressive people and we don't keep talking to our young daughter about her future marriage. She therefore couldn't clearly understand what Rahamat meant; yet to remain silent and give no reply was wholly against her nature, so she would turn the idea round and say, "Are *you* going to your *śvaśur-bāri*?" Shaking his huge fist at an imaginary father-in-law Rahamat said, "I'll settle him!" Mini laughed merrily as she imagined the fate awaiting this unknown creature called a *śvaśur*.

It was perfect autumn weather. In ancient times, kings used to set out on their world-conquests in autumn. I have never been away from Calcutta; precisely because of that, my mind roves all over the world. I seem to be condemned to my house, but I constantly yearn for the world outside. If I hear the name of a foreign land, at once my heart races towards it; and if I see a foreigner, at once an image of a cottage on some far bank or wooded mountainside forms in my mind, and I think of the free and pleasant life I would lead there. At the same time, I am such a rooted sort of individual that whenever I have to leave my familiar spot I practically collapse. So a morning spent sitting at my table in my little study, chatting with this Kabuliwallah, was quite enough wandering for me. High, scorched, blood-coloured, forbidding mountains on either side of a narrow desert path; laden camels passing; turbaned merchants and wayfarers, some on camels, some walking, some with spears in their hands, some with old-fashioned flintlock guns: my friend would talk of his native land in his booming, broken Bengali, and a mental picture of it would pass before my eyes.

Mini's mother is very easily alarmed. The slightest noise in the street makes her think that all the world's drunkards are charging straight at our house. She cannot dispel from her mind—despite her experience of life (which isn't great)—the apprehension that the world is overrun with thieves, bandits, drunkards, snakes, tigers, malaria, caterpillars, cockroaches and white-skinned marauders. She was not too happy about Rahamat the Kabuliwallah. She repeatedly told me to keep a close eye on him. If I tried to laugh off her suspicions, she would launch into a succession of questions: "So do people's children never go missing? And is there no slavery in Afghanistan? Is it completely impossible for a huge Afghan to kidnap a little child?" I had to admit that it was not impossible, but I found it hard to believe. People are suggestible to varying degrees; this was why my wife remained so edgy. But I still saw nothing wrong in letting Rahamat come to our house.

Every year, about the middle of the month of Māgh, Rahamat went home. He was always very busy before he left, collecting money owed to him. He had to go from house to house; but he still made time to visit Mini. To see them together, one might well suppose that they were plotting something. If he couldn't come in the morning he would come in the evening; to see his lanky figure in a corner of the darkened house, with his baggy pyjamas hanging loosely around him, was indeed a little frightening. But my heart would light up as Mini ran to meet him, smiling and calling, "O Kabuliwallah, Kabuliwallah," and the usual innocent jokes passed between the two friends, unequal in age though they were.

One morning I was sitting in my little study correcting proof-sheets. The last days of winter had been very cold, shiveringly so. The morning sun was shining through the window on my feet below my table, and this touch of warmth was very pleasant. It must have been about eight o'clock—early morning walkers, swathed in scarves, had mostly finished their dawn stroll and had returned to their homes. It was then that there was a sudden commotion in the street.

I looked out and saw our Rahamat in handcuffs, being marched along by two policemen, and behind him a crowd of curious boys. Rahamat's clothes were blood-stained, and one of the policemen was holding a blood-soaked knife. I went outside and stopped him, asking what was up. I heard partly from him and partly from Rahamat himself that a neighbour of ours had owed Rahamat something for a Rampuri chadar; he had tried to lie his way out of the debt, and in the ensuing brawl Rahamat had stabbed him.

Rahamat was mouthing various unrepeatable curses against the lying debtor, when Mini ran out of the house calling, "Kabuliwallah, O Kabuliwallah." For a moment Rahamat's face lit up with pleasure. He had no bag over his shoulder today, so they couldn't have their usual discussion about it. Mini came straight out with her "Are *you* going to your *śvaśur-bāri*?"

"Yes, I'm going there now," said Rahamat with a smile. But when he saw that his reply had failed to amuse Mini, he brandished his handcuffed fists and said, "I would have killed my *śvaśur*, but how can I with these on?"

Rahamat was convicted of assault, and sent to prison for several years. He virtually faded from our minds. Living at home, carrying on day by day with our routine tasks, we gave no thought to how a free-spirited mountain-dweller was passing his years behind prison-walls. As for the fickle Mini, even her father would have to admit that her behaviour was not very praiseworthy. She swiftly forgot her old friend. At first Nabi the groom replaced him in her affections; later, as she grew up, girls rather than little boys became her favourite companions. She even stopped coming to her father's study. And I, in a sense, dropped her.

Several years went by. It was autumn again. Mini's marriage had been decided, and the wedding was fixed for the *pūjā*-holiday. Our pride and joy would soon, like Durga going to Mount Kailas, darken her parents' house by moving to her husband's.

It was a most beautiful morning. Sunlight, washed clean by monsoon rains, seemed to shine with the purity of smelted gold. Its radiance lent an extraordinary grace to Calcutta's back-streets, with their squalid, tumbledown, cheek-by-jowl dwellings. The *sānāi* started to play in our house when night was scarcely over. Its wailing vibrations seemed to rise from deep within my rib cage. Its sad Bhairavī *rāga* joined forces with the autumn sunshine, in spreading through the world the grief of my imminent separation. Today my Mini would be married.

From dawn on there was uproar, endless coming and going. A canopy was being erected in the yard of the house, by binding bamboo-poles together; chandeliers tinkled as they were hung in the rooms and verandahs; there was constant loud talk.

I was sitting in my study doing accounts, when Rahamat suddenly appeared and salaamed before me. At first I didn't recognize him. He had no bag; he had lost his long hair; his former vigour had gone. But when he smiled, I recognized him.

"How are you, Rahamat?" I said. "When did you come?"

"I was let out of prison yesterday evening," he replied.

His words startled me. I had never confronted a would-be murderer before; I shrank back at the sight of him. I began to feel that on this auspicious morning it would be better to have the man out of the way. "We've got something on in our house today," I said. "I'm rather busy. Please go now."

He was ready to go at once, but just as he reached the door he hesitated a little and said, "Can't I see your little girl for a moment?"

It seemed he thought that Mini was still just as she was when he had known her: that she would come running as before, calling "Kabuliwallah, O Kabuliwallah!"; that their old merry banter would resume. He had even brought (remembering their old friendship) a box of grapes and a few nuts and raisins wrapped in paper—extracted, no doubt, from some Afghan friend of his, having no bag of his own now.

"There's something on in the house today," I said. "You can't see anyone."

He looked rather crestfallen. He stood silently for a moment longer, casting a solemn glance at me; then, saying "Babu salaam," he walked towards the door. I felt a sudden pang. I thought of calling him back, but then I saw that he himself was returning.

"I brought this box of grapes and these nuts and raisins for the little one," he said. "Please give them to her." Taking them from him, I was about to pay him for them when he suddenly clasped my arm and said, "Please, don't give me any money— I shall always be grateful, Babu. Just as you have a daughter, so do I have one, in my own country. It is with her in mind that I came with a few raisins for your daughter: I didn't come to trade with you."

Then he put a hand inside his big loose shirt and took out from somewhere close to his heart a crumpled piece of paper. Unfolding it very carefully, he spread it out on my table. There was a small handprint on the paper: not a photograph, not a painting—the hand had been rubbed with some soot and pressed down on to the paper. Every year Rahamat carried this memento of his daughter in his breast-pocket when he came to sell raisins in Calcutta's streets: as if the touch of that soft, small, childish hand brought solace to his huge, homesick breast. My eyes swam at the sight of it. I forgot then that he was an Afghan raisin-seller and I was a Bengali Babu. I understood then that he was as I am, that he was a father just as I am a father. The handprint of his little mountain-dwelling Parvati reminded me of my own Mini.

At once I sent for her from the inner part of the house. Objections came back: I refused to listen to them. Mini, dressed as a bride—sandal-paste pattern on her brow, red silk sari— came timidly into the room and stood close by me.

The Kabuliwallah was confused at first when he saw her: he couldn't bring himself to utter his old greeting. But at last he smiled and said, "Little one, are you going to your *śvaśur-bāri*?"

Mini now knew the meaning of *śvaśur-bāri*; she couldn't reply as before—she blushed at Rahamat's question and looked away. I recalled the day when Mini and the Kabuliwallah had first met. My heart ached.

Mini left the room, and Rahamat, sighing deeply, sat down

on the floor. He suddenly understood clearly that his own daughter would have grown up too since he last saw her, and with her too he would have to become re-acquainted: he would not find her exactly as she was before. Who knew what had happened to her these eight years? In the cool autumn morning sunshine the *sānāi* went on playing, and Rahamat sat in a Calcutta lane and pictured to himself the barren mountains of Afghanistan.

I took out a banknote and gave it to him. "Rahamat," I said, "go back to your homeland and your daughter; by your blessed reunion, Mini will be blessed."

By giving him this money, I had to trim certain items from the wedding-festivities. I wasn't able to afford the electric illuminations I had planned, nor did the trumpet-and-drum band come. The womenfolk were very displeased at this; but for me, the ceremony was lit by a kinder, more gracious light.

Translated from the Bengali by William Radice

Isabel Allende
(1942–   )

Born in Lima, Peru, Isabel Allende was the daughter of a Chilean diplomat serving in Peru and the niece of Salvador Allende, who later became president of Chile. Allende spent many of her early years in Europe, the Middle East, and other parts of the world. At fifteen, she returned to Chile to finish high school. As a young writer, she contributed a column to a feminist magazine, edited a children's magazine, hosted a television program, produced plays, and began writing short stories.

President Salvador Allende was overthrown and died violently (in what was later claimed to be a suicide) in a 1973 military coup, an event that changed his niece's outlook on the world. "I think I have divided my life [into] before that day and after that day," she said. "In that moment, I realized that everything was possible—that violence was a dimension that was always around you."

Allende remained in Chile for over a year after the coup, working with church groups to provide aid and support for people suffering from persecution by the new regime. In time, this regime threatened her life, and she was forced to flee to Venezuela with other members of her family. Although she was an experienced journalist, she was unable to find work there and didn't write at all for several years. In 1988, she married an American and moved to the United States. Recently, the political conditions in Chile have improved, and Allende returns frequently for visits. "That's so important for me," she says. "All my roots are there. I have felt [like] a foreigner everywhere in the world since I left my country."

While living in Venezuela, Allende learned that her grandfather, who was nearly one hundred years old, was dying. Recalling that he believed that people didn't die until they were forgotten, she wrote a long letter containing her memories of family and country. "I wanted to prove to him that I had forgotten nothing, that his spirit was going to live with us forever," Allende said. She never sent the letter, but it became the basis for *The House of the Spirits* (1985), her first novel. She explained, "When you lose everything, everything that is dear to you . . . memory becomes more important."

The Stories of Eva Luna (1991), from which "And of Clay Are We Created" was taken, is her fourth book and her first collection of short stories.

Allende has always worked to advance human rights and prevent injustice. However, she does not see herself as a part of an organized political movement: "I'm a very chaotic person. I think I'm an anarchist! I can never accept the rules and I'm always defying all forms of authority. Everything that's organized, I'm always against." Yet she considers it her duty to speak out for those who cannot speak for themselves. "All of us who write and are fortunate enough to be published," she insists, "ought to assume the responsibility of serving the cause of freedom and justice."

And of Clay Are We Created
Isabel Allende

*"And of Clay Are We Created" was inspired by the erup-
tion of the Nevada del Ruiz volcano in Colombia on
November 13, 1985. Allende sat riveted to the television,
watching news coverage of the eruption, which sent
rivers of mud flowing down upon villages and killing
over twenty thousand people. The coverage focused in
particular on one small child who was caught in the mud
and on a reporter who tried to help her. Allende created
this story from that event and incorporated it into a book
of short stories,* The Stories of Eva Luna. *Rolf Carlé, the
reporter in the story, was one of the men in Eva Luna's
life.*

They discovered the girl's head protruding from the mudpit, eyes wide open, calling soundlessly. She had a First
Communion name, Azucena Lily. In that vast cemetery
where the odor of death was already attracting vultures from
far away, and where the weeping of orphans and wails of the
injured filled the air, the little girl obstinately clinging to life
became the symbol of the tragedy. The television cameras
transmitted so often the unbearable image of the head bud-
ding like a black squash from the clay that there was no one
who did not recognize her and know her name. And every
time we saw her on the screen, right behind her was Rolf
Carlé, who had gone there on assignment, never suspecting

that he would find a fragment of his past, lost thirty years before.

First a subterranean sob rocked the cotton fields, curling them like waves of foam. Geologists had set up their seismographs weeks before and knew that the mountain had awakened again. For some time they had predicted that the heat of the eruption could detach the eternal ice from the slopes of the volcano, but no one heeded their warnings; they sounded like the tales of frightened old women. The towns in the valley went about their daily life, deaf to the moaning of the earth, until that fateful Wednesday night in November when a prolonged roar announced the end of the world, and walls of snow broke loose, rolling in an avalanche of clay, stones, and water that descended on the villages and buried them beneath unfathomable meters of telluric vomit. As soon as the survivors emerged from the paralysis of that first awful terror, they could see that houses, plazas, churches, white cotton plantations, dark coffee forests, cattle pastures—all had disappeared. Much later, after soldiers and volunteers had arrived to rescue the living and try to assess the magnitude of the cataclysm, it was calculated that beneath the mud lay more than twenty thousand human beings and an indefinite number of animals putrefying in a viscous soup. Forests and rivers had also been swept away, and there was nothing to be seen but an immense desert of mire.

When the station called before dawn, Rolf Carlé and I were together. I crawled out of bed, dazed with sleep, and went to prepare coffee while he hurriedly dressed. He stuffed his gear in the green canvas backpack he always carried, and we said goodbye, as we had so many times before. I had no presentiments. I sat in the kitchen, sipping my coffee and planning the long hours without him, sure that he would be back the next day.

He was one of the first to reach the scene, because while other reporters were fighting their way to the edges of that morass in jeeps, bicycles, or on foot, each getting there however he could, Rolf Carlé had the advantage of the television helicopter, which flew him over the avalanche. We watched on our screens the footage captured by his assistant's camera, in which he was up to his knees in muck, a microphone in his hand, in the midst of a bedlam of lost children, wounded survivors, corpses, and devastation. The story came to us in his calm voice. For years he had been a familiar figure in newscasts, reporting live at the scene of battles and catastrophes with awesome tenacity. Nothing could stop him, and I was always amazed at his equanimity in the face of danger and suffering, it seemed as if nothing could shake his fortitude or deter his curiosity. Fear seemed never to touch him, although he had confessed to me that he was not a courageous man, far from it. I believe that the lens of the camera had a strange effect on him; it was as if it transported him to a different time from which he could watch events without actually participating in them. When I knew him better, I came to realize that this fictive distance seemed to protect him from his own emotions.

Rolf Carlé was in on the story of Azucena from the beginning. He filmed the volunteers who discovered her, and the first persons who tried to reach her, his camera zoomed in on the girl, her dark face, her large desolate eyes, the plastered-down tangle of her hair. The mud was like quicksand around her, and anyone attempting to reach her was in danger of sinking. They threw a rope to her that she made no effort to grasp until they shouted to her to catch it; then she pulled a hand from the mire and tried to move, but immediately sank a little deeper. Rolf threw down his knapsack and the rest of his equipment and waded into the quagmire, commenting for his assistant's microphone that it was cold and that one could begin to smell the stench of corpses.

"What's your name?" he asked the girl, and she told him her flower name. "Don't move, Azucena," Rolf Carlé directed, and kept talking to her, without a thought for what he was saying, just to distract her, while slowly he worked his way forward in mud up to his waist. The air around him seemed as murky as the mud.

It was impossible to reach her from the approach he was attempting, so he retreated and circled around where there seemed to be firmer footing. When finally he was close enough, he took the rope and tied it beneath her arms, so they could pull her out. He smiled at her with that smile that crinkles his eyes and makes him look like a little boy; he told her that everything was fine, that he was here with her now, that soon they would have her out. He signaled the others to pull, but as soon as the cord tensed, the girl screamed. They tried again, and her shoulders and arms appeared, but they could move her no farther; she was trapped. Someone suggested that her legs might be caught in the collapsed walls of her house, but she said it was not just rubble, that she was also held by the bodies of her brothers and sisters clinging to her legs.

"Don't worry, we'll get you out of here," Rolf promised. Despite the quality of the transmission, I could hear his voice break, and I loved him more than ever. Azucena looked at him, but said nothing.

During those first hours Rolf Carlé exhausted all the resources of his ingenuity to rescue her. He struggled with poles and ropes, but every tug was an intolerable torture for the imprisoned girl. It occurred to him to use one of the poles as a lever but got no result and had to abandon the idea. He talked a couple of soldiers into working with him for a while, but they had to leave because so many other victims were calling for help. The girl could not move, she barely could breathe, but she did not seem desperate, as if an ancestral resignation allowed her to accept her fate. The reporter, on the other hand, was determined to snatch her from death. Someone brought him a tire, which he placed beneath her arms like a life buoy, and then laid a plank near the hole to hold his weight and allow him to stay closer to her. As it was impossible to remove the rubble blindly, he tried once or twice to dive toward her feet, but emerged frustrated, covered with mud, and spitting gravel. He concluded that he would have to have a pump to drain the water, and radioed a request for one, but received in return a message that there was no available transport and it could not be sent until the next morning.

"We can't wait that long!" Rolf Carlé shouted, but in the

pandemonium no one stopped to commiserate. Many more hours would go by before he accepted that time had stagnated and reality had been irreparably distorted.

A military doctor came to examine the girl, and observed that her heart was functioning well and that if she did not get too cold she could survive the night.

"Hang on, Azucena, we'll have the pump tomorrow," Rolf Carlé tried to console her.

"Don't leave me alone," she begged.

"No, of course I won't leave you."

Someone brought him coffee, and he helped the girl drink it, sip by sip. The warm liquid revived her and she began telling him about her small life, about her family and her school, about how things were in that little bit of world before the volcano had erupted. She was thirteen, and she had never been outside her village. Rolf Carlé, buoyed by a premature optimism, was convinced that everything would end well: the pump would arrive, they would drain the water, move the rubble, and Azucena would be transported by helicopter to a hospital where she would recover rapidly and where he could visit her and bring her gifts. He thought, She's already too old for dolls, and I don't know what would please her; maybe a dress. I don't know much about women, he concluded, amused, reflecting that although he had known many women in his lifetime, none had taught him these details. To pass the hours he began to tell Azucena about his travels and adventures as a newshound, and when he exhausted his memory, he called upon imagination, inventing things he thought might entertain her. From time to time she dozed, but he kept talking in the darkness, to assure her that he was still there and to overcome the menace of uncertainty.

That was a long night.

Many miles away, I watched Rolf Carlé and the girl on a television screen. I could not bear the wait at home, so I went to National Television, where I often spent entire nights with Rolf editing programs. There, I was near his world, and I could at least get a feeling of what he lived through during those three decisive days. I called all the important people in the city, senators, commanders of the armed forces, the North American ambassador, and the president of National Petroleum, begging them for a pump to remove the silt, but obtained only vague promises. I began to ask for urgent help on radio and television, to see if there wasn't *someone* who could help us. Between calls I would run to the newsroom to monitor the satellite transmissions that periodically brought new details of the catastrophe. While reporters selected scenes with most impact for the news report, I searched for footage that featured Azucena's mudpit. The screen reduced the disaster to a single plane and accentuated the tremendous distance that separated me from Rolf Carlé; nonetheless, I was there with him. The child's every suffering hurt me as it did him; I felt his frustration, his impotence. Faced with the impossibility of communicating with him, the fantastic idea came to me that if I tried, I could reach him by force of mind and in that way give him encouragement. I concentrated until I was dizzy—a frenzied and futile activity. At times I would be overcome with compassion and burst out crying; at other times, I was so drained I felt as if I were staring through a telescope at the light of a star dead for a million years.

I watched that hell on the first morning broadcast, cadavers of people and animals awash in the current of new rivers formed overnight from the melted snow. Above the mud rose the tops of trees and the bell towers of a church where several people had taken refuge and were patiently awaiting rescue teams. Hundreds of soldiers and volunteers from the Civil Defense were clawing through rubble searching for survivors, while long rows of ragged specters awaited their turn for a cup of hot broth. Radio networks announced that their phones were jammed with calls from families offering shelter to orphaned children. Drinking water was in scarce supply, along with gasoline and food. Doctors, resigned to amputating arms and legs without anesthesia, pled that at least they be sent serum and painkillers and antibiotics; most of the roads, however, were impassable, and worse were the bureaucratic obstacles that stood in the way. To top it all, the clay contaminated by decomposing bodies threatened the living with an outbreak of epidemics.

Azucena was shivering inside the tire that held her above the surface. Immobility and tension had greatly weakened her, but she was conscious and could still be heard when a microphone was held out to her. Her tone was humble, as if apologizing for all the fuss. Rolf Carlé had a growth of beard, and dark circles beneath his eyes; he looked near exhaustion. Even from that enormous distance I could sense the quality of his weariness, so different from the fatigue of other adventures. He had completely forgotten the camera; he could not look at the girl through a lens any longer. The pictures we were receiving were not his assistant's but those of other reporters who had appropriated Azucena, bestowing on her the pathetic responsibility of embodying the horror of what had happened in that place. With the first light Rolf tried again to dislodge the obstacles that held the girl in her tomb, but he had only his hands to work with; he did not dare use a tool for fear of injuring her. He fed Azucena a cup of the cornmeal mush and bananas the Army was distributing, but she immediately vomited it up. A doctor stated that she had a fever, but added that there was little he could do: antibiotics were being reserved for cases of gangrene. A priest also passed by and blessed her, hanging a medal of the Virgin around her neck. By evening a gentle, persistent drizzle began to fall.

"The sky is weeping," Azucena murmured, and she, too, began to cry.

"Don't be afraid," Rolf begged. "You have to keep your strength up and be calm. Everything will be fine. I'm with you, and I'll get you out somehow."

Reporters returned to photograph Azucena and ask her the same questions, which she no longer tried to answer. In the meanwhile, more television and movie teams arrived with spools of cable, tapes, film, videos, precision lenses, recorders, sound consoles, lights, reflecting screens, auxiliary motors, cartons of supplies, electricians, sound technicians, and cameramen: Azucena's face was beamed to millions of screens around the world. And all the while Rolf Carlé kept pleading for a pump. The improved technical facilities bore results, and National Television began receiving sharper pictures and clearer sound; the distance seemed suddenly compressed, and I had the horrible sensation that Azucena and Rolf were by my side, separated from me by impenetrable glass. I was able to follow events hour by hour; I knew everything my love did to wrest the girl from her prison and help her endure her suffering; I overheard fragments of what they said to one another and could guess the rest; I was present when she taught Rolf to pray, and when he distracted her with the stories I had told him in a thousand and one nights beneath the white mosquito netting of our bed.

When darkness came on the second day, Rolf tried to sing Azucena to sleep with old Austrian folk songs he had learned from his mother, but she was far beyond sleep. They spent most of the night talking, each in a stupor of exhaustion and hunger, and shaking with cold. That night, imperceptibly, the unyielding floodgates that had contained Rolf Carlé's past for so many years began to open, and the torrent of all that had lain hidden in the deepest and most secret layers of memory poured out, leveling before it the obstacles that had blocked his consciousness for so long. He could not tell it all to Azucena; she perhaps did not know there was a world beyond the sea or time previous to her own; she was not capable of imagining Europe in the years of the war. So he could not tell her of defeat, nor of the afternoon the Russians had led them to the concentration camp to bury prisoners dead from starvation. Why should he describe to her how the naked bodies piled like a mountain of firewood resembled fragile china? How could he tell this dying child about ovens and gallows? Nor did he mention the night that he had seen his mother naked, shod in stiletto-heeled red boots, sobbing with humiliation. There was much he did not tell, but in those hours he relived for the first time all the things his mind had tried to erase. Azucena had surrendered her fear to him and so, without wishing it, had obliged Rolf to confront his own. There, beside that hellhole of mud, it was impossible for Rolf to flee from himself any longer, and the visceral terror he had lived as a boy suddenly invaded him. He reverted to the years when he was the age of Azucena, and younger, and, like her, found himself trapped in a pit without escape, buried in life, his head barely above ground; he saw before his eyes the boots and legs of his father, who had removed his belt and was whipping it in the air with the never-forgotten hiss of a viper coiled to strike. Sorrow flooded through him, intact and precise, as if it had lain always in his mind, waiting. He was once again in the armoire where his father locked him to punish him for imagined misbehavior, there where for eternal hours he had crouched with his eyes closed, not to see the darkness, with his hands over his ears, to shut out the beating of his heart, trembling, huddled like a cornered animal. Wandering in the mist of his memories he found his sister Katharina, a sweet, retarded child who spent her life hiding, with the hope that her father would forget the disgrace of her having been born. With Katharina, Rolf crawled beneath the dining room table, and with her hid there under the long white tablecloth, two children forever embraced, alert to footsteps and voices. Katharina's scent melded with his own sweat, with aromas of cooking, garlic, soup, freshly baked bread, and the unexpected odor of putrescent clay. His sister's hand in his, her frightened breathing, her silk hair against his cheek, the candid gaze of her eyes. Katharina . . . Katharina materialized before him, floating on the air like a flag, clothed in the white tablecloth, now a winding sheet, and at last he could weep for her death and for the guilt of having abandoned her. He understood then that all his exploits as a reporter, the feats that had won him such recognition and fame, were merely an attempt to keep his most ancient fears at bay, a stratagem for taking refuge behind a lens to test whether reality was more tolerable from that perspective. He took excessive risks as an exercise of courage, training by day to conquer the monsters that tormented him by night. But he had come face to face with the moment of truth; he could not continue to escape his past. He *was* Azucena; he was buried in the clayey mud; his terror was not the distant emotion of an almost forgotten childhood, it was a claw sunk in his throat. In the flush of his tears he saw his mother, dressed in black and clutching her imitation-crocodile pocketbook to her bosom, just as he had last seen her on the dock when she had come to put him on the boat to South America. She had not come to dry his tears, but to tell him to pick up a shovel: the war was over and now they must bury the dead.

"Don't cry. I don't hurt anymore. I'm fine," Azucena said when dawn came.

"I'm not crying for you," Rolf Carlé smiled. "I'm crying for myself. I hurt all over."

The third day in the valley of the cataclysm began with a pale light filtering through storm clouds. The President of the Republic visited the area in his tailored safari jacket to confirm that this was the worst catastrophe of the century, the country was in mourning; sister nations had offered aid; he had ordered a state of siege; the Armed Forces would be merciless, anyone caught stealing or committing other offenses would be shot on sight. He added that it was impossible to remove all the corpses or count the thousands who had disappeared; the entire valley would be declared holy ground, and bishops would come to celebrate a solemn mass for the souls of the victims. He went to the Army field tents to offer relief in the form of vague promises to crowds of the rescued, then to the improvised hospital to offer a word of encouragement to doctors and nurses worn down from so many hours of tribulations. Then he asked to be taken to see Azucena, the little girl the whole world had seen. He waved to her with a limp statesman's hand, and microphones recorded his emotional voice and paternal tone as he told her that her courage had served as an example to the nation. Rolf Carlé interrupted to ask for a pump, and the President assured him that he personally would attend to the matter. I caught a glimpse of Rolf for a few seconds kneeling beside the mudpit. On the evening news broadcast, he was still in the same position; and I, glued to the screen like a fortuneteller to her crystal ball, could tell that something fundamental had changed in him. I knew somehow that during the night his defenses had crumbled and he had given in to grief; finally he was vulnerable. The girl had touched a part of him that he himself had no access to, a part he had never shared with me. Rolf had wanted to console her, but it was Azucena who had given him consolation.

I recognized the precise moment at which Rolf gave up the fight and surrendered to the torture of watching the girl die. I was with them, three days and two nights, spying on them from the other side of life. I was there when she told him that in all her thirteen years no boy had ever loved her and that it was a pity to leave this world without knowing love. Rolf assured her that he loved her more than he could ever love anyone, more than he loved his mother, more than his sister, more than all the women who had slept in his arms, more than he loved me, his life companion, who would have given anything to be trapped in that well in her place, who would have exchanged her life for Azucena's, and I watched as he leaned down to kiss her poor forehead, consumed by a sweet, sad emotion he could not name. I felt how in that instant both were saved from despair, how they were freed from the clay, how they rose above the vultures and helicopters, how together they flew above the vast swamp of corruption and laments. How, finally, they were able to accept death. Rolf Carlé prayed in silence that she would die quickly, because such pain cannot be borne.

By then I had obtained a pump and was in touch with a general who had agreed to ship it the next morning on a military cargo plane. But on the night of that third day, beneath the unblinking focus of quartz lamps and the lens of a hundred cameras, Azucena gave up, her eyes locked with those of the friend who had sustained her to the end. Rolf Carlé removed the life buoy, closed her eyelids, held her to his chest for a few moments, and then let her go. She sank slowly, a flower in the mud.

You are back with me, but you are not the same man. I often accompany you to the station and we watch the videos of Azucena again; you study them intently, looking for something you could have done to save her, something you did not think of in time. Or maybe you study them to see yourself as if in a mirror, naked. Your cameras lie forgotten in a closet; you do not write or sing; you sit long hours before the window, staring at the mountains. Beside you, I wait for you to complete the voyage into yourself, for the old wounds to heal. I know that when you return from your nightmares, we shall again walk hand in hand, as before.

Translated from the Spanish by Margaret Sayers Peden

VISIONS
OF THE
FUTURE

Shinichi Hoshi
(1926–1997)

Shinichi Hoshi is well known in Japan for his quirky imagination and intriguing science fiction stories, many of which end with a surprising twist. After completing one thousand and one stories, Hoshi decided that he had accomplished what he had set out to do long ago. Like the famous storyteller Scheherazade in *The Arabian Nights* (originally entitled *The Thousand and One Nights*), Hoshi said, "One thousand and one stories are enough."

He—y, Come On Ou—t!
Shinichi Hoshi

The typhoon had passed and the sky was a gorgeous blue. Even a certain village not far from the city had suffered damage. A little distance from the village and near the mountains, a small shrine had been swept away by a landslide.

"I wonder how long that shrine's been here."

"Well, in any case, it must have been here since an awfully long time ago."

"We've got to rebuild it right away."

While the villagers exchanged views, several more of their number came over.

"It sure was wrecked."

"I think it used to be right here."

"No, looks like it was a little more over there."

Just then one of them raised his voice. "Hey what in the world is this hole?"

Where they had all gathered there was a hole about a meter in diameter. They peered in, but it was so dark nothing could be seen. However, it gave one the feeling that it was so deep it went clear through to the center of the earth.

There was even one person who said, "I wonder if it's a fox's hole."

"Hey—y, come on ou—t!" shouted a young man into the hole. There was no echo from the bottom. Next he picked up a pebble and was about to throw it in.

"You might bring down a curse on us. Lay off," warned an old man, but the younger one energetically threw the pebble in. As before, however, there was no answering response from the bottom. The villagers cut down some trees, tied them with rope and made a fence which they put around the hole. Then they repaired to the village.

"What do you suppose we ought to do?"

"Shouldn't we build the shrine up just as it was over the hole?"

A day passed with no agreement. The news traveled fast, and a car from the newspaper company rushed over. In no time a scientist came out, and with an all-knowing expression on his face he went over to the hole. Next, a bunch of gawking curiosity seekers showed up; one could also pick out here and there men of shifty glances who appeared to be concessionaires. Concerned that someone might fall into the hole, a policeman from the local substation kept a careful watch.

One newspaper reporter tied a weight to the end of a long cord and lowered it into the hole. A long way down it went. The cord ran out, however, and he tried to pull it out, but it would not come back up. Two or three people helped out, but when they all pulled too hard, the cord parted at the edge of the hole. Another reporter, a camera in hand, who had been watching all of this, quietly untied a stout rope that had been wound around his waist.

The scientist contacted people at his laboratory and had them bring out a high-powered bull horn, with which he was going to check out the echo from the hole's bottom. He tried switching through various sounds, but there was no echo. The scientist was puzzled, but he could not very well give up with everyone watching him so intently. He put the bull horn right up to the hole, turned it to its highest volume, and let it sound continuously for a long time. It was a noise that would have carried several dozen kilometers above ground. But the hole just calmly swallowed up the sound.

In his own mind the scientist was at a loss, but with a look of apparent composure he cut off the sound and, in a manner suggesting that the whole thing had a perfectly plausible explanation, said simply, "Fill it in."

Safer to get rid of something one didn't understand.

The onlookers, disappointed that this was all that was going to happen, prepared to disperse. Just then one of the concessionaires, having broken through the throng and come forward, made a proposal.

"Let me have that hole. I'll fill it in for you."

"We'd be grateful to you for filling it in," replied the mayor of the village, "but we can't very well give you the hole. We have to build a shrine there."

"If it's a shrine you want, I'll build you a fine one later. Shall I make it with an attached meeting hall?"

Before the mayor could answer, the people of the village all shouted out.

"Really? Well, in that case, we ought to have it closer to the village."

"It's just an old hole. We'll give it to you!"

So it was settled. And the mayor, of course, had no objection.

The concessionaire was true to his promise. It was small, but closer to the village he did build for them a shrine with an attached meeting hall.

About the time the autumn festival was held at the new shrine, the hole-filling company established by the concessionaire hung out its small shingle at a shack near the hole.

The concessionaire had his cohorts mount a loud campaign in the city. "We've got a fabulously deep hole! Scientists say it's at least five thousand meters deep! Perfect for the disposal of such things as waste from nuclear reactors."

Government authorities granted permission. Nuclear power plants fought for contracts. The people of the village were a bit worried about this, but they consented when it was explained that there would be absolutely no above-ground contamination for several thousand years and that they would share in the profits. Into the bargain, very shortly a magnificent road was built from the city to the village.

Trucks rolled in over the road, transporting lead boxes. Above the hole the lids were opened, and the wastes from nuclear reactors tumbled away into the hole.

From the Foreign Ministry and the Defense Agency boxes of

unnecessary classified documents were brought for disposal. Officials who came to supervise the disposal held discussions on golf. The lesser functionaries, as they threw in the papers, chatted about pinball.

The hole showed no signs of filling up. It was awfully deep, thought some; or else it might be very spacious at the bottom. Little by little the hole-filling company expanded its business.

Bodies of animals used in contagious disease experiments at the universities were brought out, and to these were added the unclaimed corpses of vagrants. Better than dumping all of its garbage in the ocean, went the thinking in the city, and plans were made for a long pipe to carry it to the hole.

The hole gave peace of mind to the dwellers of the city. They concentrated solely on producing one thing after another. Everyone disliked thinking about the eventual consequences. People wanted only to work for production companies and sales corporations; they had no interest in becoming junk dealers. But, it was thought, these problems too would gradually be resolved by the hole.

Young girls whose betrothals had been arranged discarded old diaries in the hole. There were also those who were inaugurating new love affairs and threw into the hole old photographs of themselves taken with former sweethearts. The police felt comforted as they used the hole to get rid of accumulations of expertly done counterfeit bills. Criminals breathed easier after throwing material evidence into the hole.

Whatever one wished to discard, the hole accepted it all. The hole cleansed the city of its filth; the sea and sky seemed to have become a bit clearer than before.

Aiming at the heavens, new buildings went on being constructed one after the other.

One day, atop the high steel frame of a new building under construction, a workman was taking a break. Above his head he heard a voice shout:

"He—y, come on ou—t!"

But, in the sky to which he lifted his gaze there was nothing at all. A clear blue sky merely spread over all. He thought it must be his imagination. Then, as he resumed his former position, from the direction where the voice had come, a small pebble skimmed by him and fell on past.

The man, however, was gazing in idle reverie at the city's skyline growing ever more beautiful, and he failed to notice.

Translated from the Japanese by Stanleigh Jones

Dino Buzzati
(1906–1972)

Dino Buzzati—a true "Renaissance man"—was a journalist, painter, novelist, short-story writer, playwright, and cartoonist.

Buzzati was born into a wealthy family near Belluno in northern Italy. The family split their time between the magnificent Dolomite Mountains of their hometown and the city of Milan, where Buzzati's father was a professor of law. Although Buzzati followed in his father's footsteps by earning a law degree, he had been writing short stories and poetry since childhood. His first job was as a journalist for one of Italy's top newspapers, *Il Corriere della Sera*. Buzzati became one of the newspaper's star writers and editors.

Soon, he was publishing short stories and novels. His most famous novel, *Il deserto dei Tartari* (*The Tartar Steppe*), was published in Italy in 1940 and appeared in English twelve years later. Drago, the main character of this ironic, nihilistic tale, is stationed at a remote outpost to wait for the Tartar invasion. He waits . . . and waits . . . and waits. By the time the invaders finally storm in, Drago is an old man living at a country inn.

In his "spare" time, Buzzati wrote plays, composed music, and painted. His play *A Clinical Case* toured Europe in the 1950s in a production arranged by the famous French writer Albert Camus. *Poema a fumetti* (*A Poem in the Form of a Cartoon*), Buzzati's comic-strip version of the Greek legend of Orpheus and Eurydice, set in modern Italy, is a creative mixture of art and words.

All of Buzzati's work—whatever the genre—shares a preoccupation with people in uncertain, often absurd or terrifying circumstances. His characters make their way in an irrational universe; in this regard, his writing resembles that of certain other twentieth-century writers—Franz Kafka, Jean-Paul Sartre, and Samuel Beckett.

A Siberian Shepherd's Report of the Atom Bomb

Dino Buzzati

During the years of the cold war (1945–1991), the Soviet Union tested its nuclear weapons on the cold, empty plains of Siberia. Imagine how the isolated shepherds who lived there reacted to the sudden flash of light, the cloud-like mass on the horizon, the thunderous sound, and the hot wind.

A mong us shepherds of the tribe there is a very old legend that says when Noah gathered all the animals of creation in his ark, the animals from the mountains and from the valleys made a truce among themselves and with man, recognizing Noah as their master for the time they were to remain in the ark—all, that is, except Moma, the huge tigress that snarled when Noah approached her and was the only animal Noah feared. That was why the tigress found no room in the ark and why the flood caught her in her cave. But she was extremely strong. She remained afloat by sheer strength, swimming for forty days and forty nights and more until the waters subsided, the trees rose out of the sea and the earth reappeared. The tigress Moma was then so tired she fell asleep. She is still asleep in the depths of the great forests of Amga, Ghoi, Tepotorgo, and Urakancha.

The legend also says that when the great tigress wakes up, all the other animals will flee from the forest, for man there will be a good hunting season, and Moma will reign in the great forests until the god Beyal descends from the sky to devour her.

Who among us believes this legend? Since our solitude is so great, many stories are told around campfires and all of us are accustomed to believing and not believing. Rare and most uncertain is the news that comes to us from distant lands, for our wandering life is entrusted to the will of heaven. What, for example, do we shepherds of the steppe know of the measureless realm that stretches toward the setting sun? Old laws forbid us to go beyond the boundary line, and even if we were to cross it, we should have to travel endless distances through great dangers before reaching the nearest inhabited regions. It is beyond the boundary line that lie the forests of Amga, Ghoi, Tepotorgo, and Urakancha, where the tigress Moma fell asleep at the end of the flood.

Sometimes troops of armed horsemen gallop by along the boundary line. Once in a while they stop, look toward us, make measurements, and drive red poles with strange signs into the ground. After a few days the wind of the steppe uproots the poles and carries them God knows where. Sometimes even airplanes, those strange flying machines, fly over us. Nothing else happens.

But what is the use telling all this if not to explain our uneasiness? Recently strange and dreadful things have happened. No serious harm has come to us, but we feel fearful forebodings.

We noticed the first unusual happening last spring. The soldiers galloped by more frequently and they drove heavier poles, which the wind would not be able to uproot, into the ground. The poles are still there.

In the middle of June, two large snakes were killed near our camp. Creatures like these had never been seen before. The following day hundreds were seen. They did not bother us or our flocks—they were all moving toward the East. They were of different kinds and of every size. This strange happening astonished us.

Then we noticed that the snakes were not alone. Rats, moles, skunks, worms, and numberless kinds of insects began to cross the plain, all moving in the same direction. They were strangely mixed together, but they showed no hostility toward each other, even though they belonged to species that are ordinarily enemies.

We saw even rabbits, wild goats, and quite a number of small, four-footed creatures of whose very existence we had not known. Some of them were really very beautiful, with fur that is highly prized. Then came the birds. They, too, were fleeing toward the East, abandoning their homeland. But what were they running away from? What danger hung over them? Instinct does not easily deceive animals. Even we men were uneasy. Yet what good reason did we have to abandon the region which this year was so good for pasture? No matter how much we wondered, we could not imagine a plausible explanation for this great emigration. An earthquake? A plague? What disease could strike so many different species at the same time, the beetle as well as the marmot, the serpent as well as the wildcat? A fire? No smoke could be seen on the horizon nor did the wind smell of smoke. Someone among us jokingly mentioned the old legend of Moma the tigress. I did not like that joke at all.

Finally, it seemed that the whole forest on the other side of the boundary was empty. The last to come through were the wood pigeons and swarming columns of ants that continued for miles and miles. Some stragglers followed, a few at a time. Then the flow stopped completely. The echo of our guns ceased (these had been days of triumph for the hunters), and a sepulchral silence settled over the Siberian steppe. At night, we would foolishly strain our ears. Could it be that we expected the roar of Moma the tigress?

One day this great uneasiness even took hold of our flocks. It was clear that the goats, sheep, and rams were becoming excited, that they, too, were trying to escape to the East. We had to chase some of our fleeing livestock for a long time on horseback. It was necessary to build heavy enclosures.

Many of us were afraid. For no good reason, many wanted to move camp to the East. There were bitter arguments. We finally agreed to take the advice of the elders. They met and decided—we would depart with the next dawn.

It was a hot July evening. The sun had just set and the refreshing breath of night was descending when the dogs suddenly began to bark. Just after sunset, from the direction of the forest and at a great distance, an extraordinary light was seen. It seemed as if the sun had turned back, as if its burning face had become swollen on the rim of the horizon. The mass wavered a few moments, then burst, shooting forth a whirl of frightful flames—red, white, violet, green, yellow. The sun had blown up!

How long did it last? Instinctively, I thought it was the end of the world. But it was not. When it was dark again, I raised my dazzled eyes to the zenith. No, the stars were still there.

Then the thunder came. And with the thunder—so frightful a noise was never heard—came the wind, a hot, suffocating wind that took our breath away and razed everything to the ground. I thought I would not be able to stand it, but the wind, too, passed on.

When we recovered our senses, we again kindled the fires the burning wind had blown out, and set forth in search of our livestock, which were fleeing crazily in every direction because the enclosure had been broken to pieces. At that moment, the necessity of the chase prevailed over every other fear. But suddenly we stopped and stood motionless—even the goats, the sheep, the old people. We were all paralyzed together.

Above the bellowing and bleating, above our excited shouts, another voice was heard. No, it was not so powerful as the thunder of a little while before. Yet in a way it was even worse. Once, twice, three times, mournful and cold, it filled the night and froze our hearts. It was the roar of the tigress.

The fires, the fires! Leaving the flock to its fate, we rushed to gather twigs and weeds to increase the number of our fires. Soon there was an almost unbroken chain of flames to protect us. At last the great tigress Moma had awakened and was coming toward us.

At that very moment a long, deep roar rose on the other side of the fires. In the darkness we could see something move. Suddenly it appeared, illuminated by the red shadows. It was she, Moma. She was not an ordinary tiger. She was a monster of gigantic proportions.

Not one of us fired. We saw that the huge beast hardly moved any longer—she was about to die. Her eyes had turned to shapeless lumps of black pulp. Her hide was scorched. On her right side was an open gash as deep as a cave, from which blood flowed.

Moma the tigress, right in front of our eyes, hunched her back to the height of two horses one standing on top of the other and let out a hellish shriek. I felt that I was done for. I fired my rifle without even aiming. The others did the same.

Her huge body fell with a crash. Was she dead? We continued to fire shot after shot, senselessly. The tigress no longer moved.

These are the strange facts referred to at the beginning of this report. The legendary tigress really existed—and even though we immediately burned her carcass because of its horrible stench, the immense skeleton has remained right there on the spot and anyone can come and measure it. But who awakened her? Who took away her life and her promised reign? What was the terrifying explosion that night? The sun had nothing to do with it—in a few hours it was born again at just the right time and in its usual place. What had happened? Could some infernal power have taken over the forests? And if its flames devoured mighty Moma, could it not capriciously reduce us to ashes too? How then can we live calmly? No one sleeps at night and in the morning we wake up tired.

Translated from the Italian by John Fisher

C. P. Cavafy
(1863–1933)

C. P. Cavafy (the pen name of Konstantinos Petrou Kavafis) was the great poet of Alexandria, Egypt. In fact, the city became the central metaphor of his poetry. Despite his legendary status as the poet of the city, however, Cavafy attracted almost no official recognition for his work, and what little notice he did receive came very late in his life.

Like many other great poets, Cavafy was ahead of his time. He shunned the worn-out language, imagery, and tone of nineteenth-century Romanticism in favor of the rhythms and colloquial language of everyday speech. Furthermore, he worked into his poetry dramatic elements that had not been used in Greek verse since Hellenistic times (the three centuries following the death of Alexander the Great in 323 B.C.).

Relatively unknown outside Alexandria during his life, Cavafy is now considered the most important twentieth-century poet writing in Greek. His poems are admired for their brilliant descriptions of history, precise use of language, and astute political commentary.

Waiting for the Barbarians
C. P. Cavafy

"Waiting for the Barbarians" is set in ancient Rome toward the end of the empire, when an emperor ruled with the help of a group of senators. A consul was one of two leaders who held the highest administrative position, and a praetor was a person who supervised law courts and made sure that the laws were obeyed. Why are these rulers very eager to throw themselves into the hands of barbarians who are rumored to be ready to overrun the region? The poem is written as a series of questions and answers.

What are we waiting for all crowded in the forum?
     The Barbarians are to arrive today.
Within the Senate-house why is there such inaction?
The Senators making no laws what are they sitting there for?
5   Because the Barbarians arrive today.
     What laws now should the Senators be making?
     When the Barbarians come they'll make the laws.

Why did our Emperor get up so early in the morning?
And at the greatest city gate why is he sitting there now,
10 Upon his throne, officially, why is he wearing his crown?
     Because the Barbarians arrive today.
     The Emperor is waiting to receive
     Their Leader. And in fact he has prepared
     To give him an address. On it he has
15 Written him down all sorts of names and titles.

Why have our two Consuls gone out, both of them, and the
    Praetors

Today with their red togas on, with their embroidered togas?
Why are they wearing bracelets, and all those amethysts too,
And all those rings on their fingers with splendid flashing
    emeralds?
Why should they be carrying today their precious walking-
20   sticks,
With silver knobs and golden tops so wonderfully carved?
    Because the Barbarians will arrive today;
    Things of this sort dazzle the Barbarians.

And why are the fine orators not come here as usual
25 To get their speeches off, to say what they have to say?
    Because the Barbarians will be here today;
      And they are bored with eloquence and speech-
      making.

Why should this uneasiness begin all of a sudden,
And confusion? How serious people's faces have become.
30 Why are all the streets and squares emptying so quickly,
And everybody turning home again so full of thought?
    Because night has fallen and the Barbarians have
      not come.
    And some people have arrived from the frontier;
    They said there are no Barbarians any more.

    And now what will become of us without
35   Barbarians?—
Those people were some sort of a solution.

Translated from the Greek by John Mavrogordato

Derek Walcott
(1930–   )

"To change your language," Derek Walcott believes, "you must change your life." For his mastery of language in both poetry and prose, Derek Walcott is regarded as the finest Caribbean poet writing in English and one of the leading English-language poets of the twentieth century. For his achievements, Derek Walcott was awarded the 1992 Nobel Prize in literature.

Walcott was born on St. Lucia, a Caribbean island noted for its lush green valleys, vast banana plantations, and sleeping volcano. Although St. Lucia was a British colony when Walcott was a child and its official language was English, most people spoke a *patois*, a mixture of French, English, and Caribbean dialect. Walcott learned English as a second language and quickly mastered its subtleties.

Despite his deep roots in Caribbean culture, Walcott, who was of mixed African and European descent, felt he did not quite fit in. Perhaps this is why today he often writes about loneliness and isolation.

Walcott started writing seriously when he was in his early teens and published his first poem when he was just fourteen years old. His first book of poetry, *Twenty-five Poems*, appeared four years later, in 1948. Since no professional publisher was willing to underwrite the project, Walcott's mother, a teacher, paid for publication, although she could ill afford the expense. Walcott paid her back by peddling copies of the book himself. At twenty, Walcott had his first play, *Henry Christophe* (1950), produced. That same year, he left St. Lucia on a scholarship to the University of the West Indies in Jamaica.

Walcott's Nobel Prize was won in large part because of his Greek-style epic poem called *Omeros* (1990). The characters in *Omeros* are ordinary Caribbean women and fishermen who have names like Helen, Achille, and Hector—the names of characters in Homer's great epics, the *Iliad* and the *Odyssey*. (*Omeros* is the Greek word for Homer.) Walcott doesn't think it is unusual that he set his narrative poem within the framework of these ancient epics. He says that in St. Lucia he grew up surrounded by the sea, just as Homer was surrounded by the Aegean, and that in *Omeros* he gathered together stories of the Caribbean "tribe," just as Homer tied together old stories from the Aegean world. To Walcott, his epic poem is a long thankyou to the island people he came from.

Walcott has spent a good deal of time in the United States, where he has taught creative writing at some of America's top colleges. He maintains his strong roots in the Caribbean and has a permanent home in Trinidad.

The Season of Phantasmal Peace
Derek Walcott

Then all the nations of birds lifted together
the huge net of the shadows of this earth
in multitudinous dialects, twittering tongues,
stitching and crossing it. They lifted up
5   the shadows of long pines down trackless slopes,
the shadows of glass-faced towers down evening streets,
the shadow of a frail plant on a city sill—
the net rising soundless as night, the birds' cries soundless,
    until
there was no longer dusk, or season, decline, or weather,
10 only this passage of phantasmal light
that not the narrowest shadow dared to sever.

And men could not see, looking up, what the wild geese drew,
what the ospreys trailed behind them in silvery ropes
that flashed in the icy sunlight; they could not hear
15 battalions of starlings waging peaceful cries,
bearing the net higher, covering this world
like the vines of an orchard, or a mother drawing
the trembling gauze over the trembling eyes
of a child fluttering to sleep;
                     it was the light
20 that you will see at evening on the side of a hill
in yellow October, and no one hearing knew
what change had brought into the raven's cawing,
the killdeer's screech, the ember-circling chough
such an immense, soundless, and high concern
25 for the fields and cities where the birds belong,
except it was their seasonal passing, Love,

made seasonless, or, from the high privilege of their birth,
something brighter than pity for the wingless ones
below them who shared dark holes in windows and in
    houses,
30   and higher they lifted the net with soundless voices
above all change, betrayals of falling suns,
and this season lasted one moment, like the pause
between dusk and darkness, between fury and peace,
but, for such as our earth is now, it lasted long.

Václav Havel
(1936–   )

"Foreigners are sometimes amazed at the suffering that we are willing to undergo here, and at the same time they are amazed at the things we are still able to laugh at," says Václav Havel, speaking of his people and his country. Havel, playwright and president of the first non-Communist government to rule the Czech people since the 1940s, understands this suffering first-hand. His childhood, however, suggested that his life would take a much more comfortable turn.

Havel was born before World War II into a wealthy and accomplished family that owned a vast country estate and a luxury apartment in Prague. As an adult, living under a Communist government, Havel realized that he felt embarrassed by his upper-class childhood. "I felt alone, inferior, lost, ridiculed," he explained. "It was as though I subconsciously felt, or feared, that everyone had—rightly—entered some kind of silent mutual agreement that my privileges were undeserved." This feeling would come to permeate Havel's plays.

When Václav was twelve years old, Czechoslovakia became a Soviet-style state. During the purges that followed, the Communists confiscated the family's belongings. Havel's father retained enough power, however, to keep his family in Prague, in two tiny rooms within their old apartment.

Václav had his education interrupted when he was fifteen years old. As part of the Communists' plan to destroy the privileged classes, he was apprenticed to a carpenter. The Havels used their remaining political connections to transfer him to a job as a laboratory assistant. For five years, Havel worked eight hours a day in the laboratory and traveled across town to spend four hours in night school. In this way, he managed to complete high school.

He also started writing—a pastime that could be dangerous at that time. Under the Communists, a writer could be thrown into prison for trying to publish something not approved by the government. When he was eighteen years old, Havel graduated from high school and applied to many universities to study art history and philosophy. Rejected because he wasn't a member of the Communist Party, Havel entered the Czech University of Technology, which accepted everyone. Two years later, he again tried to study the humanities, was again rejected, and was promptly drafted.

After completing his military service, Havel became a stagehand at the ABC Theater. When not moving props, Havel wrote plays. In 1960, taking advantage of a temporary relaxation of government controls on culture, Havel joined the Theater on the Balustrade, one of the small, influential experimental theaters in Prague. Although still a stagehand, Havel now had a chance to get his plays produced.

For eight years, he devoted himself to theater and established himself as an international playwright. Today, he is considered the foremost contemporary dramatist of the Czech Republic. His plays are powerful condemnations of mechanized bureaucracy and its effect on the individual.

In 1968, government controls tightened as democratization began to spread during what was called the Prague Spring. Then Soviet tanks thundered into Czechoslovakia in August 1968, and most of the hard-won reforms were repealed. Although Havel was forbidden to work in the theater and his plays were banned, he refused to defect to the West. Instead, he resisted the Communist regime so publicly and forcefully that he was arrested and imprisoned three times. He spent nearly five years in prison.

In the 1980s, large-scale demonstrations and the democratic reforms that were sweeping through Eastern Europe resulted in the resignation of the Communist ruling party. In 1989, after this "Velvet Revolution," the Czech people elected Havel president of Czechoslovakia, a position he held until 1992, when the republic of Slovakia seceded from the federation with the Czechs. In 1993, Havel was elected by Parliament as the first president of the Czech Republic.

The New Measure of Man
Václav Havel
PHILADELPHIA, JULY 4, 1994

Havel delivered "The New Measure of Man" as his acceptance speech for the Philadelphia Liberty Medal. The medal was awarded to him on July 4, 1994, in front of Independence Hall in Philadelphia, where America's Declaration of Independence was adopted in 1776. The version of the speech used here was published in Havel's book The Art of the Impossible.

I take this occasion—in front of this historic building, where you have paid me the high honor of awarding me the Philadelphia Liberty Medal—as an invitation to set my own sights equally high. I would like, therefore, to turn my thoughts today to the state of the world and the prospects that lie before it. I have also decided to do something that personally I find just as demanding: I will attempt to address you in English. I hope you will understand me.

There are thinkers who claim that, if the modern age began with the discovery of America, it also ended in America. This is said to have occurred in the year 1969, when America sent the first men to walk on the moon. From this historic moment, they say, a new age in the life of humanity can be dated.

I think there are good reasons for suggesting that the modern age has ended. Today, many things indicate that we are going through a transitional period, when it seems that something is on the way out and something else is being painfully born. It is as if something were crumbling, decaying, and exhausting itself, while something else, still indistinct, were arising from the rubble.

Periods of history when values undergo a fundamental shift are certainly not unprecedented. This happened in the Hellenistic period, when from the ruins of the classical world the Middle Ages were gradually born. It happened during the Renaissance, which opened the way to the modern era. The distinguishing features of such transitional periods are a mixing and blending of cultures, and a plurality or parallelism of intellectual and spiritual worlds. These are periods when all consistent value systems collapse, when cultures distant in time and space are discovered or rediscovered. These are periods when there is a tendency to quote, to imitate, and to amplify, rather than to state with authority or to integrate. New meaning is gradually born from the encounter, or the intersection, of many different elements.

Today, this state of mind or of the human world is called postmodernism. For me, a symbol of that state is a Bedouin mounted on a camel and clad in traditional robes under which he is wearing jeans, with a transistor radio in his hands and an ad for Coca-Cola on the camel's back. I am not ridiculing this, nor am I shedding an intellectual tear over the commercial expansion of the West which destroys alien cultures. I see it, rather, as a typical expression of this multicultural era, a signal that an amalgamation of cultures is taking place. I see it as proof that something is happening, something is being born, that we are in a phase when one age is succeeding another, when everything is possible. Yes, everything is possible, because our civilization does not have its own unified style, its own spirit, its own aesthetic.

This is related to the crisis, or to the transformation, of science as the basis of the modern conception of the world.

The dizzying development of this science, with its unconditional faith in objective reality and its complete dependency on general and rationally knowable laws, led to the birth of modern technological civilization—the first civilization in the history of the human race to span the entire globe and firmly bind together all human societies, submitting them to a common global destiny. It was this science that enabled man, for the first time, to see Earth from space with his own eyes, that is, to see it as another star in the sky.

At the same time, however, the relationship to the world that modern science fostered and shaped now appears to have exhausted its potential. It is increasingly clear that, strangely, the relationship is missing something. It fails to connect with the most intrinsic nature of reality, and with natural human experience. It is now more of a source of disintegration and doubt than a source of integration and meaning. It produces what amounts to a state of schizophrenia, completely alienating man as an observer from himself as a being. Classical modern science described only the surface of things, a single dimension of reality. And the more dogmatically science treated it as the only dimension, as the very essence of reality, the more misleading it became. Today, for instance, we may know immeasurably more about the universe than our ancestors did, yet it increasingly seems that they knew something more essential about it than we do, something that escapes us. The same thing is true of nature and of ourselves. The more thoroughly all our organs and their functions, their internal structures, and the biochemical reactions that take place within them are described, the more we seem to fail to grasp the spirit, purpose, and meaning of the system that they create together and that we experience as our unique "self."

And thus today we find ourselves in a paradoxical situation. We enjoy the achievements of modern civilization that have made our physical existence on this earth easier in so many important ways. Yet we do not know exactly what to do with ourselves, where to turn. The world of our experiences seems chaotic, disconnected, confusing. There appear to be no integrating forces, no unified meaning, no true inner understanding of phenomena in our experience of the world. Experts can explain anything in the objective world to us, yet we understand our own lives less and less. In short, we live in the postmodern world, where everything is possible and almost nothing is certain.

This state of affairs has its social and political consequences. The single planetary civilization to which we all belong confronts us with global challenges. We stand helpless before them, because our civilization has essentially globalized only the surface of our lives. But our inner selves continue to have a life of their own. And the fewer answers the era of rational knowledge provides to the basic questions of human Being, the more deeply it would seem that people—behind its back, as it were—cling to the ancient certainties of their tribe. For this reason, individual cultures, increasingly lumped together by contemporary civilization, are realizing with new urgency their own inner autonomy and the inner differences of others. Cultural conflicts are increasing and are understandably more dangerous today than at any other time in history. The end of the era of rationalism has been catastrophic. Armed with the same supermodern weapons, often from the same suppliers, and followed by television cameras, the members of various tribal cults are at war with one another. By day, we work with statistics; in the evening, we consult astrologers and frighten ourselves with thrillers about vampires. The abyss between the rational and the spiritual, the external and the internal, the objective and the subjective, the technical and the moral, the universal and the unique, grows constantly deeper.

Politicians are rightly worried by the problem of finding the key to the survival of a civilization that is global and at the same time clearly multicultural; of how generally respected mechanisms of peaceful coexistence can be set up, and on what set of principles they are to be established.

These questions have been highlighted with particular urgency by the two most important political events in the second half of the twentieth century: the collapse of colonial hegemony and the fall of communism. The artificial world order of the past decades has collapsed, but a new, more just order has not yet emerged. The central political task of the final years of this century, then, is the creation of a new model of coexistence among the various cultures, peoples, races, and religious spheres within a single interconnected civilization. This task is all the more urgent because other threats to contemporary humanity, brought about by the one-dimensional development of civilization, are growing more serious all the time.

Many believe this task can be accomplished through technical means; that is, they believe it can be accomplished through the invention of new organizational, political, and diplomatic instruments. Yes, it is clearly necessary to invent organizational structures appropriate to the present multicultural age. But such efforts are doomed to failure if they do not grow out of something deeper, out of generally held values.

This, too, is well known. And in searching for the most natural source of a new world order, we usually look to the traditional foundation of modern justice: to a set of values that—among other things—were first declared in this building and that are a great achievement of the modern age. I am referring to respect for the unique human being and for his or her liberties and inalienable rights, and the principle that all power derives from the people. I am, in short, referring to the fundamental ideas of modern democracy.

What I am about to say may sound provocative, but I feel more and more strongly that not even these ideas are enough, that we must go further and deeper. The point is that the solution they offer is still, as it were, modern, derived from the climate of the Enlightenment and from a view of man and his relation to the world that has been characteristic of the Euro-American sphere for the last two centuries. Today, however, we are in a different place and facing a different situation, one to which classically modern solutions in themselves do not give a satisfactory response. After all, the very principle of inalienable human rights, conferred on man by the Creator, grew out of the typically modern notion that man—as a being capable of knowing nature and the world—was the pinnacle of creation and lord of the world. This modern anthropocentrism meant that He who allegedly endowed men with his inalienable rights inevitably began to disappear from the world. He was so far beyond the grasp of modern science that He was gradually pushed into a sphere of privacy of sorts, if not directly into a sphere of private fancy—that is, into a place where public obligations no longer apply. The existence of an authority higher than man himself simply began to get in the way of human aspirations.

The idea of human rights and freedoms must be an integral part of any meaningful world order. Yet I think it must be anchored in a different place, and in a different way, from what has been the case so far. If it is to be more than just a slogan mocked by half the world, it cannot be expressed in the language of a departing era, and it must not be mere froth floating on the subsiding waters of faith in a purely scientific relationship to the world.

Paradoxically, inspiration for the renewal of this lost integrity can once again be found in science. In a science that is new— let us say postmodern; a science producing ideas that in a certain sense allow it to transcend its own limits. I will give two examples.

The first is the Anthropic Cosmological Principle. Its authors and adherents have pointed out that, from the countless possible courses of its evolution, the universe took the only one that enabled life to emerge. This is not yet proof that the aim of the universe has always been that it should one day see itself through our eyes. But how else can this matter be explained?

I think the Anthropic Cosmological Principle brings us to an idea perhaps as old as humanity itself; that we are not at all just an accidental anomaly, the microscopic caprice of a tiny particle whirling in the endless depths of the universe. Instead, we are mysteriously connected to the entire universe; we are mirrored in it, just as the entire evolution of the universe is mirrored in us. Until recently it might have seemed that we were an unhappy bit of mildew on a heavenly body whirling in space among many that have no mildew on them at all. This was something that classical science could explain. Yet, the moment it begins to appear that we are deeply connected to the entire universe, science has reached the limits of its powers. Because it is founded on the search for universal laws, it cannot deal with singularity—that is, with uniqueness. The universe is a unique event and a unique story, and so far we are the unique point of that story. But unique events and stories are the domain of poetry, not science. With the formulation of the Anthropic Cosmological Principle, science finds itself on the border between formula and story, between science and myth. In that, however, science has paradoxically returned, in a roundabout way, to man, and offers him—in new clothing—his lost integrity. It does so by anchoring him once more in the cosmos.

The second example is the Gaia Hypothesis. This theory brings together proof that the dense network of mutual interactions between the organic and inorganic portions of the earth's surface form a single system, a kind of megaorganism, the living planet Gaia—named after an ancient goddess who is recognizable as an archetype of the Earth Mother in perhaps all religions. According to the Gaia Hypothesis, we are parts of a greater whole. Our destiny is not dependent merely on what we do for ourselves but also on what we do for Gaia as a whole. If we endanger her, she will dispense with us in the interests of a higher value—that is, life itself.

What makes the Anthropic Principle and the Gaia Hypothesis so inspiring? One simple thing: both remind us, in modern language, of what we have long suspected, of what we have long projected into our forgotten myths, and of what perhaps has always lain dormant within us as archetypes—that is, the awareness of being anchored in the earth and the universe, the awareness that we are not here alone or for ourselves alone, but are an integral part of a higher, mysterious entity against whom it is not advisable to blaspheme. This forgotten awareness is encoded in all religions. All cultures anticipate it in various forms. It is one of the things that form the basis of man's understanding of himself, of his place in the world, and ultimately of the world as such.

A modern philosopher once said: "Only a God can save us now."

Yes, the only real hope for people today is probably a renewal of our certainty that we are rooted in the earth and, at the same time, in the cosmos. This awareness endows us with the capacity for self-transcendence. Politicians at international forums may reiterate a thousand times that the basis of the new world order must be universal respect for human rights, but it will mean nothing as long as this imperative does not derive from respect for the miracle of Being, the miracle of the universe, the miracle of nature, the miracle of our own existence. Only someone who submits to the authority of the universal order and of creation, who values the right to be a part of it and a participant in it, can genuinely value himself and his neighbors, and thus honor their rights as well.

It logically follows that, in today's multicultural world, the truly reliable path to coexistence, to peaceful coexistence and creative cooperation, must start from what is at the root of all cultures and what lies infinitely deeper in human hearts and minds than political opinions, convictions, antipathies, or sympathies. It must be rooted in self-transcendence: transcendence as a hand reaching out to those close to us, to foreigners, to the human community, to all living creatures, to nature, to the universe; transcendence is a deeply and joyously experienced need to be in harmony even with what we ourselves are not, with what we do not understand, with what seems distant from us in time and space, but with which we are nevertheless mysteriously linked because, together with us, all this constitutes a single world; transcendence as the only real alternative to extinction.

The Declaration of Independence, adopted 218 years ago in this building, states that the Creator gave man the right to liberty. It seems that man can realize that liberty only if he does not forget the One who endowed him with it.

Translated from the Czech by Paul Wilson

Acknowledgments

For permission to reprint copyrighted material, grateful acknowledgment is made to the following sources:

Barricade Books: "He—y, Come On Ou—t!" by Shinichi Hoshi, translated by Stanleigh Jones, from *The Best Japanese Science-Fiction Stories,* edited by John L. Apostolou and Martin H. Greenberg. Copyright © 1978 by Shinichi Hoshi.

Susan Bergholz Literary Services, New York: Quotes by Julia Alvarez from interview. Copyright © 1992 by Julia Alvarez and Catherine Wiley. First published in *The Bloomsbury Review,* vol. 12, no. 2, March 1992, pp. 9–10. "Audition" from *The Other Side / El Otro Lado* by Julia Alvarez. Copyright © 1995 by Julia Alvarez. Published by Dutton, a division of Penguin USA. All rights reserved.

Creative Arts Book Company: "Momotaro: Boy of the Peach" from *The Dancing Kettle and Other Japanese Folk Tales,* retold by Yoshiko Uchida. Copyright © 1986 by Yoshiko Uchida.

Edwidge Danticat and the Watkins/Loomis Agency: "The Book of the Dead" by Edwidge Danticat. Copyright © 1999 by Edwidge Danticat. Originally published in *The New Yorker,* June 1999.

Doubleday, a division of Random House, Inc.: "Civil Peace" from *Girls at War and Other Stories* by Chinua Achebe. Copyright © 1972, 1973 by Chinua Achebe. From *An Introduction to Haiku,* translated by Harold G. Henderson. Copyright © 1958 by Harold G. Henderson.

Farrar, Straus & Giroux, LLC: "Landscapes" from *Legacies: Selected Poems* by Heberto Padilla, translated by Alastair Reid and Andrew Hurley. Translation copyright © 1982 by Alastair Reid and Andrew Hurley. "Love" from *Extravagaria* by Pablo Neruda, translated by Alastair Reid. Translation copyright © 1974 by Alastair Reid. "The Son from America" from *A Crown of Feathers and Other Stories* by Isaac Bashevis Singer. Copyright © 1973 by Isaac Bashevis Singer. "The Season of Phantasmal Peace" from *Collected Poems: 1948–1984* by Derek Walcott. Copyright © 1986 by Derek Walcott.

Samuel A. French, Inc.: *A Marriage Proposal* by Anton Chekhov, translated by Hilmar Baukhage and Barrett H. Clark. Copyright 1914 and renewed 1942 by Barrett H. Clark.

David Higham Associates: "The Return of Oisin" from *The High Deeds of Finn Mac Cool* by Rosemary Sutcliff. Copyright © 1967 by Rosemary Sutcliff.

Houghton Mifflin Co.: "The Great Flood" from *Greek Myths* by Olivia E. Coolidge. Copyright © 1949 and renewed © 1977 by Olivia E. Coolidge. All rights reserved.

John Johnson (Author's Agent) Ltd.: "The Prisoner Who Wore Glasses" from *Tales of Tenderness and Power* by Bessie Head. Copyright © 1989 by The Estate of Bessie Head. "Kabuliwallah" from *Rabindranath Tagore: Selected Short Stories,* translated by William Radice. Copyright © 1991, 1994 by William Radice.

Alfred A. Knopf, Inc.: "The Philadelphia Liberty Medal" (retitled "The New Measure of Man") from *The Art of the Impossible: Politics as Morality in Practice* by Václav Havel, translated by Paul Wilson. Copyright © 1994, 1997 by Václav Havel and Paul Wilson.

Little, Brown and Company, Inc.: "The Quest of the Golden Fleece" from *Mythology* by Edith Hamilton. Copyright 1942 by Edith Hamilton; copyright renewed © 1969 by Dorian Fielding Reid and Doris Fielding Reid. From *Long Walk to Freedom* by Nelson Mandela. Copyright © 1994 by Nelson Rolihlahla Mandela.

Arnoldo Mondadori Editore: "A Siberian Shepherd's Report of the Atom Bomb" from *Literary Review,* vol. 3, no. 1, Autumn 1959.

W. W. Norton & Company, Inc.: From *The History of That Ingenious Gentleman Don Quijote de La Mancha* by Miguel de Cervantes Saavedra, translated by Burton Raffel. Translation copyright © 1995 by Burton Raffel.

Penguin Books Ltd.: "The Piece of String" by Guy de Maupassant from *Maupassant: Selected Short Stories,* translated by Roger Colet (Penguin Classics, 1971). Copyright © 1971 by Guy de Maupassant.

Prentice-Hall, Inc., Upper Saddle River, NJ: "The Fall of Troy" from *The Aeneid of Virgil: A Verse Translation* by Rolfe Humphries. Copyright © 1987 by Prentice-Hall, Inc.

Russell & Volkening as agents for Nadine Gordimer: "The Train from Rhodesia" from *The Soft Voice of the Serpent and Other Stories* by Nadine Gordimer. Copyright © 1950 and renewed © 1978 by Nadine Gordimer.

Scribner, a division of Simon & Schuster: "And of Clay Are We Created" from *The Stories of Eva Luna* by Isabel Allende, translated by Margaret Sayers Peden. Copyright © 1989 by Isabel Allende; English translation copyright © 1991 by Macmillan Publishing Company.

Simon & Schuster: "A Sunrise on the Veld" from *African Stories* by Doris Lessing. Copyright © 1951, 1953, 1954, 1957, 1958, 1962, 1963, 1964, 1965, 1972, 1981 by Doris Lessing.

Sources Cited

Quote by Nadine Gordimer from interview with Beth Austin from *The Chicago Tribune,* October 4, 1991.

From "A Visit with Nadine Gordimer" by Edmund Morris from *The New York Times Book Review,* June 7, 1981.

From 1997 speech "Artful Words" by Nadine Gordimer from http://www.indexoncensorship.org/issue397/.

Quotes by Bessie Head from an interview by Betty McGinnis Fradkin in *World Literature Written in English,* vol. 18, no. 1. Published in 1979. Published by the National Institute of Education, Division of Literature and Drama, 1979.

Quote by Doris Lessing from *Counterpoint* by Roy Newquist. Published by Rand McNally, NY, 1964.